Rick Steves®

SNAPSHOT

Madrid & Toledo

CONTENTS

▶ **INTRODUCTION**. v

▶ **MADRID** 1

   Orientation. 3

   Map: Madrid. 4

   Map: Greater Madrid .7

   Map: Central Madrid. 10

   Map: Madrid Metro 14

   Tours 15

   Walks. 19

   Map: Puerta del Sol to
Royal Palace Loop 21

   Map: Gran Vía Walk .33

   Sights. 34

   Map: Royal Palace. 36

   Map: Madrid's Museum Neighborhood. . . .47

   Map: Prado Museum Overview 48

   Shopping 74

   Nightlife. 76

   Sleeping 79

   Map: Madrid Center Hotels 80

   Eating. 86

   Map: Madrid Center Restaurants. 88

   Connections 98

▶ **NORTHWEST OF MADRID**. **105**

   Map: Northwest of Madrid 106

▶ **MONASTERIO DE SAN LORENZO
DE EL ESCORIAL** 107

   Map: El Escorial Town 108

   Map: El Escorial—Ground Floor. 110

▶ **VALLEY OF THE FALLEN**. 115

▶ **SEGOVIA**. 118

   Orientation. 119

   Walk. 120

   Map: Segovia 123

Sleeping 128
Eating. 129
Connections 131
▸ **ÁVILA** 133
Orientation. 133
Sights 134
Map: Ávila. 136
Sleeping 138
Eating. 139
Connections 140
▸ **TOLEDO** **141**
Orientation. 142
Map: Toledo Overview. 143
Map: Central Toledo. 146
Sights. 150
Map: Toledo's Cathedral 152
Shopping 169
Sleeping 170
Map: Toledo Hotels. 172
Eating. 176
Map: Toledo Restaurants 178
Connections 181
▸ **LA MANCHA** 182
▸ **PRACTICALITIES** **185**
Money 185
Staying Connected. 186
Making Hotel Reservations 187
Eating 188
Transportation 188
Helpful Hints 189
Resources from Rick Steves 190
Additional Resources 191
How Was Your Trip?. 191
Spanish Survival Phrases 193
▸ **INDEX** **195**

INTRODUCTION

This Snapshot guide, excerpted from my guidebook *Rick Steves Spain,* introduces you to majestic Madrid. Spain's capital is home to some of Europe's top art treasures (the Prado Museum's collection, plus Picasso's *Guernica* in the Reina Sofía) and a lively selection of characteristic tapas bars, where you can assemble a memorable feast of Spanish specialties. Explore the city's cozy-feeling historic core, tour its lavish Royal Palace, and beat the heat on a rowboat at the lush and inviting Retiro Park.

This book also covers several side-trips from Madrid. Toledo, the hill-capping onetime capital of Spain, features one of the country's most magnificent cathedrals, a medieval vibe, and top paintings by favorite son El Greco. Northwest of Madrid, you'll find Spain's grandest palace at the Inquisition-era El Escorial, a jarring jolt of the 20th century at Franco's Valley of the Fallen, and a pair of charming towns: Segovia, with its towering Roman aqueduct, and Ávila, encircled by a medieval wall.

To help you have the best trip possible, I've included the following topics in this book:

• **Planning Your Time,** with advice on how to make the most of your limited time

• **Orientation,** including tourist information (abbreviated as TI), tips on public transportation, local tour options, and helpful hints

• **Sights** with ratings:

    ▲▲▲—Don't miss

    ▲▲—Try hard to see

    ▲—Worthwhile if you can make it

    No rating—Worth knowing about

• **Sleeping** and **Eating,** with good-value recommendations in every price range

• **Connections,** with tips on trains, buses, and driving

Practicalities, near the end of this book, has information on money, phoning, hotel reservations, transportation, and more, plus Spanish survival phrases.

To travel smartly, read this little book in its entirety before you go. It's my hope that this guide will make your trip more meaningful and rewarding. Traveling like a temporary local, you'll get the absolute most out of every mile, minute, and dollar.

Buen viaje!

MADRID

Today's Madrid is upbeat and vibrant. You'll feel it. Even the living-statue street performers have a twinkle in their eyes.

Madrid is the hub of Spain. This modern capital—Europe's second-highest, at more than 2,000 feet—has a population of 3.3 million, with about 6 million living in greater Madrid.

Like its people, the city is relatively young. In medieval times, it was just another village, wedged between the powerful kingdoms of Castile and Aragon. When newlyweds Ferdinand and Isabel united those kingdoms (in 1469), Madrid—sitting at the center of Spain—became the focal point of a budding nation. By 1561, Spain ruled the world's most powerful empire, and King Philip II moved his capital from tiny Toledo to spacious Madrid. Successive kings transformed the city into a European capital. By 1900, Madrid had 500,000 people, concentrated within a small area. In the mid-20th century, the city exploded with migrants from the countryside, creating today's modern sprawl. Fortunately for tourists, there's still an intact, easy-to-navigate historic core.

Madrid is working hard to make itself more livable. Massive urban-improvement projects such as pedestrianized streets, parks, commuter lines, and Metro stations are popping up everywhere. The investment is making once-shady neighborhoods safe and turning ramshackle zones into trendy ones. These days the broken concrete and traffic chaos of the not-so-distant past are gone. Even with austerity measures related to Spain's ongoing economic crisis, funding for the upkeep of this great city center has been maintained. Madrid feels orderly and welcoming.

Tourists are the real winners. Dive headlong into the grandeur and intimate charm of Madrid. Feel the vibe in Puerta del Sol, the pulsing heart of modern Madrid and of Spain itself. The lavish Royal Palace, with its gilded rooms and frescoed ceilings, rivals Versailles. The Prado has Europe's top collection of paintings, and nearby hangs Picasso's chilling masterpiece, *Guernica*. Retiro Park invites you to take a shady siesta and hopscotch through a mosaic of lovers, families, skateboarders, pets walking their masters, and expert bench-sitters. Save time for Madrid's elegant shops and people-friendly pedestrian zones. On Sundays, cheer for the bull at a bullfight or bargain like mad at a megasize flea market. Swelter through the hot, hot summers or bundle up for the cold, dry winters. Save some energy for after dark, when Madrileños pack the streets for an evening paseo that can continue past midnight. Lively Madrid has enough street-singing, bar-hopping, and people-watching vitality to give any visitor a boost of youth.

PLANNING YOUR TIME

Madrid is worth two days and three nights on even the fastest trip. Divide your time among the city's top three attractions: the Royal Palace (worth a half-day), the Prado Museum (also worth a half-day), and the contemporary bar-hopping scene.

While the Prado and palace are open daily, the Reina Sofía (with Picasso's *Guernica*) is closed on Tuesday, and other sights are closed on Monday, including the Monasterio de San Lorenzo de El Escorial, outside of Madrid. If you're here on a Sunday, consider going to the flea market (year-round) and/or a bullfight (some Sun in March-mid-Oct; generally daily during San Isidro festival in May-early June).

For good day-trip possibilities from Madrid, see the next two chapters (Northwest of Madrid and Toledo).

Day 1

Morning: Take a brisk 20-minute good-morning-Madrid walk from Puerta del Sol to the Prado (taking the pedestrianized Calle de las Huertas). Spend the rest of the morning at the Prado.

Afternoon: Enjoy an afternoon siesta in Retiro Park. Then tackle modern art at the Reina Sofía. Ride bus #27 from this area out through Madrid's modern section to Puerta de Europa for a dose of the nontouristy, no-nonsense big city.

Evening: End your day with a progressive tapas dinner at a series of characteristic bars.

Day 2

Morning: Follow my self-guided walk, which loops to and from Puerta del Sol, with a tour through the Royal Palace in the middle.

Afternoon: Your afternoon is free for other sights, shopping, or a side-trip to the palace at El Escorial. Be out at the magic hour—before sunset—when beautifully lit people fill Madrid.
Evening: Take in a flamenco or zarzuela performance.

Orientation to Madrid

Puerta del Sol marks the center of Madrid. No major sight is more than a 20-minute walk or a €7 taxi ride from this central square. Get out your map and frame off Madrid's historic core: To the west of Puerta del Sol is the Royal Palace. To the east, you'll find the Prado Museum, along with the Reina Sofía museum. North of Puerta del Sol is Gran Vía, a broad east-west boulevard bubbling with shops and cinemas. Between Gran Vía and Puerta del Sol is a lively pedestrian shopping zone. And southwest of Puerta del Sol is Plaza Mayor, the center of a 17th-century, slow-down-and-smell-the-cobbles district.

This entire historic core around Puerta del Sol—Gran Vía, Plaza Mayor, the Prado, and the Royal Palace—is easily covered on foot. A wonderful chain of pedestrian streets crosses the city east to west, from the Prado to Plaza Mayor (along Calle de las Huertas) and from Puerta del Sol to the Royal Palace (on Calle del Arenal). Stretching north from Gran Vía, Calle de Fuencarral is a trendy shopping and strolling pedestrian street.

TOURIST INFORMATION

Madrid is home to two types of tourist information offices: city TIs run by the Madrid City Council, and regional TIs run by the privately owned Turismo Madrid. Both are helpful, but you'll get more biased information from Turismo Madrid.

City-run TIs share a website (www.esmadrid.com), a central phone number (tel. 914-544-410), and hours (daily 9:30-20:30); exceptions are noted in the listings below. The best and most central city TI is on **Plaza Mayor.** They offer several guided walks in English each day (described later, under "Tours in Madrid"). They can also help direct travelers to the nearby foreign tourist assistance office (SATE; see "Helpful Hints" for details).

Madrid's other city-run TIs are at **Plaza de Colón** (in the underground passage accessed from Paseo de la Castellana and Calle de Goya), **Palacio de Cibeles** (inside, up the stairs and to the right, Tue-Sun 10:00-20:00, closed Mon), **Plaza de Cibeles** (at Paseo del Prado), and **Paseo del Arte** (on Plaza Sánchez Bustillo, near the Reina Sofía museum). During the busy summer months, the city council deploys high-tech mobile TIs to major sites around town. Travelers will find city TIs at the **airport** (Terminals 2 and 4, daily 9:00-20:00).

MADRID

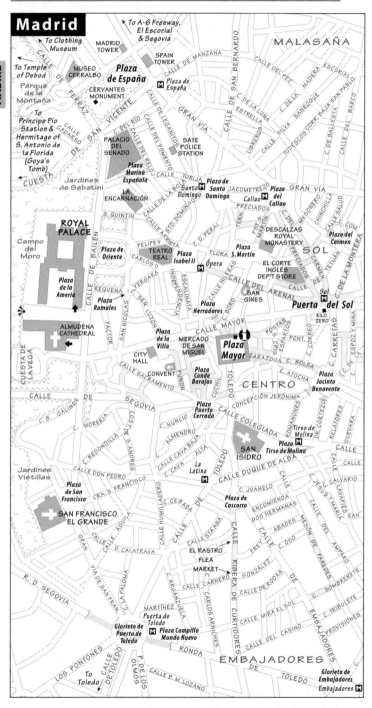

Madrid

To Clothing Museum

To Temple of Debod

Parque de la Montaña

To Príncipe Pío Station & Hermitage of S. Antonio de la Florida (Goya's Tomb)

To A-6 Freeway, El Escorial & Segovia

MADRID TOWER

Plaza de España

SPAIN TOWER

CERVANTES MONUMENT

MUSEO CERRALBO

MALASAÑA

Plaza de España

SATE POLICE STATION

Jardines de Sabatini

PALACIO DEL SENADO

Plaza Marina Española

LA ENCARNACIÓN

Plaza de Santo Domingo

Santo Domingo

Plaza del Callao

Callao

GRAN VÍA

ROYAL PALACE

Campo del Moro

Plaza de Oriente

FELIPE V

TEATRO REAL

Plaza Isabel II

Ópera

Plaza S. Martín

DESCALZAS ROYAL MONASTERY

Plaza del Carmen

SOL

Plaza de la América

Plaza Ramales

ALMUDENA CATHEDRAL

Plaza de la Villa

MERCADO DE SAN MIGUEL

CITY HALL

CONVENT

EL CORTE INGLÉS DEP'T STORE

SAN GINES

Puerta del Sol

Sol

KILO. ZERO

Plaza Herradores

CALLE MAYOR

Plaza Mayor

Plaza Conde Barajas

CENTRO

Plaza Jacinto Benavente

Jardines Vistillas

Plaza Puerta Cerrada

Plaza de San Francisco

SAN FRANCISCO EL GRANDE

La Latina

SAN ISIDRO

Plaza Tirso de Molina

Tirso de Molina

Plaza de Cascorro

Plaza de la América

EL RASTRO FLEA MARKET

EMBAJADORES

Puerta de Toledo

Plaza Campillo Mundo Nuevo

To Toledo

Glorieta de Puerta de Toledo

RONDA

Glorieta de Embajadores

Embajadores

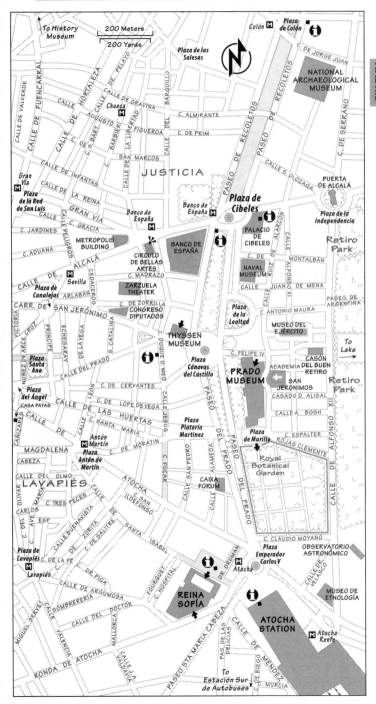

To History Museum

200 Meters
200 Yards

N

Colón

Plaza de Colón

Plaza de las Salesas

C. DE JORGE JUAN

NATIONAL ARCHAEOLOGICAL MUSEUM

CALLE DE VALVERDE

CALLE DE FUENCARRAL

CALLE DE HORTALEZA

CALLE DE PELAYO

CALLE DE GRAVINA

Chueca

C. DE BART.

CALLE DE LA LIBERTAD

BARBIERI

AUGUSTO

FIGUEROA

C. DEL BARQUILLO

C. ALMIRANTE

C. DE PRIM

SAN MARCOS

PASEO DE RECOLETOS

PASEO DE RECOLETOS

CALLE DE SERRANO

CALLE DE INFANTAS

JUSTICIA

CALLE S. OLOZAGA

PUERTA DE ALCALÁ

Gran Vía

Gran Vía

Plaza de la Red de San Luis

CALLE DE LA REINA

GRAN VÍA

Banco de España

Banco de España

Plaza de Cibeles

Plaza de la Independencia

C. JARDINES

C. ADUANA

CALLE GRACIA

C. PELIGROS

METROPOLIS BUILDING

CALLE DE ALCALÁ

CEDACEROS

CÍRCULO DE BELLAS ARTES

BANCO DE ESPAÑA

PALACIO DE CIBELES

Retiro Park

C. DE ALFONSO XI

CALLE RUIZ DE ALARCÓN

MONTALBÁN

Sevilla

Plaza de Canalejas

C. MADRAZO

ZARZUELA THEATER

C. DE

NAVAL MUSEUM

CARR. DE SAN JERÓNIMO

ARLABÁN

C. DE ZORRILLA

CONGRESO DIPUTADOS

JUAN DE MENA

PASEO DE ARGENTINA

VICTORIA

PRÍNCIPE

ECHEGARAY

CALLE DE LA VEGA

S. CATALINA

C. DE LA CRUZ

THYSSEN MUSEUM

C. ANTONIO MAURA

Plaza de la Lealtad

MUSEO DEL EJÉRCITO

To Lake

Plaza Santa Ana

CALLE DEL PRADO

C. DE CERVANTES

C. DE LEÓN

C. DE LOPE DE VEGA

Plaza Cánovas del Castillo

C. FELIPE IV

CASÓN DEL BUEN RETIRO

PRADO MUSEUM

ACADEMIA

SAN JERÓNIMOS

Retiro Park

Plaza del Ángel

CASA PATAS

CALLE DE LAS HUERTAS

C. SANTA MARÍA

CASADO D. ALISAL

CALLE A. BOSH

CALLE DE ALFONSO XII

CAÑIZARES

CALLE DE

MAGDALENA

Antón Martín

Plaza Platería Martínez

C. ESPALTER

Plaza de Murillo

ROJAS CLEMENTE

CABEZA

Plaza Antón de Martín

C. DE MORATÍN

C. FÚCAR

PASEO DEL PRADO

Royal Botanical Garden

CALLE DEL OLMO

LAVAPIÉS

C. DEL OLIVAR

CALLE MARÍA

ATOCHA

SAN ILDEFONSO

C. SAN PEDRO

CAIXA FORUM

PASEO DEL PRADO

C. TRES PECES

C. AVE MARÍA

CALLE BUENAVISTA

DE

C. DE ZURITA

C. DE SALITRE

SANTA ISABEL

C. CLAUDIO MOYANO

CARLOS

ESP

OBSERVATORIO ASTRONÓMICO

Plaza de Lavapiés

C. DE LA FE

DR. PIGA

FOURQUET

Plaza Emperador Carlos V

Atocha

CALLE DR. VELASCO

Lavapiés

CALLE DE ARGUMOSA

C. HOSPITAL

DR. DRUMAN

REINA SOFÍA

MUSEO DE ETNOLOGÍA

MIGUEL SERVET

C. SOMBRERERÍA

CALLE DEL DOCTOR

MALLORCA

CALLE STA. MARÍA CABEZA

VALENCIA

ATOCHA STATION

Atocha Renfe

RONDA DE ATOCHA

CALLE JA VALDAIA

PAS. DE LAS DELICIAS

CALLE DE MÉNDEZ

C. DE RIEGO

C. MURCIA

To Estación Sur de Autobuses

MADRID

Regional Turismo Madrid TIs share a website (www. turismomadrid.es) and are located near the **Prado Museum** (Duque de Medinaceli, across from Palace Hotel, Mon-Sat 8:00-15:00, Sun 9:00-14:00), **Chamartín train station** (near track 20, Mon-Sat 8:00-20:00, Sun 9:00-14:00), and **Atocha train station** (AVE arrivals side, Mon-Sat 8:00-20:00, Sun 9:00-20:00). There are also regional TIs at the **airport** (Terminals 1 and 4, Mon-Sat 9:00-20:00, Sun 9:00-14:00).

At most TIs, you can get the *Es Madrid* English-language monthly, which lists events around town. TIs occasionally distribute the *Guía del Ocio* (described later) for free; just ask. Pick up and use the free, well-designed *Public Transport* map, which includes detailed transportation routes throughout the city center.

Sightseeing Pass: Very energetic travelers can save a little money and some valuable sightseeing time by buying the **Madrid Card.** It covers more than 50 sights (including the Royal Palace, Prado, Thyssen-Bornemisza, and Reina Sofía) and lets you skip lines—a definite plus in high season, especially at the palace and the Prado. Additionally, the pass covers the Bernabéu Stadium tour, all the Essential Madrid tours, and it's good for a 10 percent discount at El Corte Inglés. The three-day card is the best bargain (€67; other options include €47/24 hours and €60/48 hours, online discounts available, www.madridcard.com). You can pay extra to add the hop-on, hop-off bus tour (saves a maximum of €2) or public transport (only worthwhile if you ride multiple times a day).

Entertainment Guides: For arts and culture listings, the TI's printed material is not very good. Pick up the Spanish-language weekly entertainment guide *Guía del Ocio* (€1, sold at newsstands, sometimes free at TI or hotels) or visit www.guiadelocio.com. It lists daily live music *("Conciertos")*, museums (under *"Arte"*—with the latest times, prices, and special exhibits), restaurants (an exhaustive listing), TV schedules, and movies ("V.O." means original version, *"V.O. en inglés sub"* means a movie is played in English with Spanish subtitles rather than dubbed).

Helpful Website: While not officially part of the TI, www. madridman.com is run with passion by American Scott Martin and offers tips on sightseeing, hotels, restaurants, and more.

ARRIVAL IN MADRID

For more information on arriving at or departing from Madrid's airport, train stations, and bus stations, see "Madrid Connections," at the end of this chapter.

By Train: Madrid's two train stations, Chamartín and Atocha, are both on Metro lines with easy access to downtown Madrid.

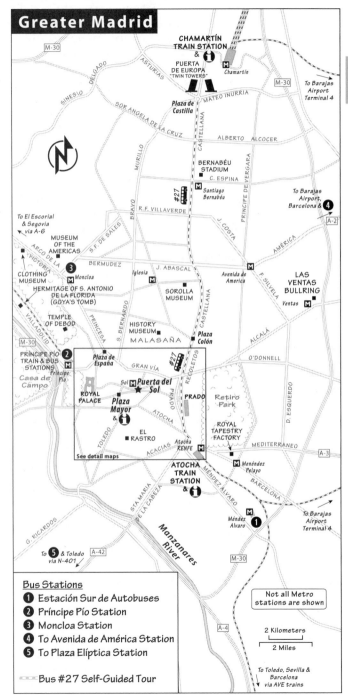

Greater Madrid

CHAMARTÍN
TRAIN STATION
&
PUERTA
DE EUROPA
"TWIN TOWERS"

M-30

ASTURIAS

SINESIO DELGADO

Chamartín

M-30

To Barajas
Airport
Terminal 4

Plaza de
Castilla

MATEO INURRIA

SOR ANGELA DE LA CRUZ

ALBERTO ALCOCER

MURILLO

CASTELLANA

BERNABÉU
STADIUM

C. ESPINA

PRINCIPE DE VERGARA

#27

Santiago
Bernabéu

To Barajas
Airport,
Barcelona & 4

A-2

BRAVO

R.F. VILLAVERDE

J. COSTA

AMÉRICA

ARCO DE LA VICTORIA

S.F. DE SALES

To El Escorial
& Segovia
via A-6

MUSEUM
OF THE
AMERICAS

BERMUDEZ

J. ABASCAL

Avenida de
América

F. SILVELA

LAS
VENTAS
BULLRING

3

Moncloa

Iglesia

SOROLLA
MUSEUM

Ventas

CLOTHING
MUSEUM

HERMITAGE OF S. ANTONIO
DE LA FLORIDA
(GOYA'S TOMB)

VALLADOLID

TEMPLE
OF DEBOD

PRINCESA

S. BERNARDO

HISTORY
MUSEUM

MALASAÑA

CASTELLANA

Plaza
Colón

ALCALÁ

M-30

PRÍNCIPE PÍO
TRAIN & BUS
STATIONS

2

Plaza de
España

GRAN VÍA

#27

REQUETOS

O'DONNELL

Príncipe
Pío

Casa de
Campo

Sol

Puerta del
Sol

ROYAL
PALACE

Plaza
Mayor
&

PRADO

PRADO

Retiro
Park

D. ESQUERDO

ATOCHA

TOLEDO

EL
RASTRO

ACACIAS

Atocha
RENFE

ROYAL
TAPESTRY
FACTORY

MEDITERRANEO

A-3

See detail maps

ATOCHA
TRAIN
STATION
&

MÉNDEZ ALVARO

Menéndez
Pelayo

BARCELONA

STA MARIA DE LA CABEZA

G. RICARDOS

A-42

To 5 & Toledo
via N-401

Manzanares
River

Méndez
Alvaro

1

To Barajas
Airport
Terminal 4

M-30

A-4

Bus Stations

1 Estación Sur de Autobuses
2 Príncipe Pío Station
3 Moncloa Station
4 To Avenida de América Station
5 To Plaza Elíptica Station

- - - Bus #27 Self-Guided Tour

Not all Metro
stations are shown

2 Kilometers

2 Miles

To Toledo, Sevilla &
Barcelona
via AVE trains

Chamartín handles most international trains and the AVE (AH-vay) train to and from Segovia. Atocha generally covers southern Spain, as well as the AVE trains to and from Barcelona, Córdoba, Sevilla, and Toledo.

Traveling Between Chamartín and Atocha Stations: You can take the Metro (line 1, 30-40 minutes, €1.50), but the *cercanías* trains are faster (6/hour, 13 minutes, Atocha-Sol-Chamartín lines C3 and C4 are the most convenient, €1.65, free with rail pass or any regular train ticket to Madrid—show it at ticket window in the middle of the turnstiles, depart from Atocha's track 6 and generally Chamartín's track 1, 3, 8, or 9—but check the *Salidas Inmediatas* board to be sure).

By Bus: Madrid has several bus stations, each one handy to a Metro station: Príncipe Pío (Metro: Príncipe Pío); Estación Sur de Autobuses (for Ávila, Salamanca, and Granada; Metro: Méndez Álvaro); Plaza Elíptica (for Toledo, Metro: Plaza Elíptica); Moncloa (for El Escorial and Segovia; Metro: Moncloa); and Avenida de América (for Pamplona and Burgos, Metro: Avenida de América). If you take a taxi from the station to your hotel, you'll pay a €3 supplement.

By Plane: Both international and domestic flights arrive at Madrid's Barajas Airport. Options for getting into town include public bus, *cercanías* train, Metro, taxi, and minibus shuttle.

HELPFUL HINTS

Theft Alert: Be wary of pickpockets—anywhere, anytime. Areas of particular risk are Puerta del Sol (the central square), El Rastro (the flea market), Gran Vía (the paseo zone: Plaza del Callao to Plaza de España), the Ópera Metro station (or anywhere on the Metro), bus #27, the airport, and any crowded street. Be alert to the people around you: Someone wearing a heavy jacket in the summer is likely a pickpocket. Teenagers may dress like Americans and work the areas around the three big art museums; being under 18, they can't be charged in any meaningful way by the police. Assume any fight or commotion is a scam to distract people about to become victims of a pickpocket. Wear your money belt. For help if you get ripped off, see the next listing.

Tourist Emergency Aid: SATE is an assistance service for tourists who might need, for any reason, to visit a police station or lodge a complaint. Help ranges from canceling stolen credit cards to assistance in reporting a crime (central police station, daily 9:00-24:00, near Plaza de Santo Domingo at Calle Leganitos 19). They can help you get to the police station and will even act as an interpreter if you have trouble communicating

Daily Reminder

Sunday: The National Archaeological Museum, Sorolla Museum, Descalzas Royal Monastery, and Clothing Museum close earlier than usual today (15:00), as does the Bullfighting Museum (13:00). The Prado Museum and Centro de Arte Reina Sofía also close a bit earlier than normal, at 19:00. The flea market at El Rastro runs until 15:00. Midday, Retiro Park erupts into a carnival-like atmosphere. Bullfights take place on some Sundays (March through mid-Oct). The Royal Tapestry Factory and some flamenco places are closed today.

Monday: These sights are closed today: Naval Museum, Palacio de Cibeles, Descalzas Royal Monastery, Museum of the Americas, National Archaeological Museum, Madrid History Museum, Clothing Museum, Hermitage of San Antonio de la Florida, Temple of Debod, and Monasterio de San Lorenzo de El Escorial (next chapter). The Thyssen-Bornemisza Museum has shorter hours today (12:00-16:00).

Tuesday: The Reina Sofía is closed today.

Wednesday: All major sights are open.

Thursday: All major sights are open. The Museum of the Americas is open later than usual today (until 19:00).

Friday: All major sights are open.

Saturday: The Royal Tapestry Factory and Bullfighting Museum are closed today. Midday, enjoy the scene at Retiro Park.

Late-Hours Sightseeing: Sights with evening hours (20:30 or later) include the Reina Sofía (Mon and Wed-Sat until 21:00), the Thyssen-Bornemisza Museum (exhibits only, Sat until 21:00 in summer), and the Clothing Museum (Thu until 22:30 in July-Aug).

Free Sightseeing: The Prado is free every evening from 18:00 (17:00 on Sun), the Reina Sofía has free evening hours Mon and Wed-Sat from 19:00 (15:00 on Sun), and the Thyssen-Bornemisza is free on Mondays. The Museum of the Americas is free on Sundays, and the following are free all day Sunday and on Saturday afternoons: National Archaeological Museum and the Sorolla Museum (Sat from 14:00), as well as the Clothing Museum (from 14:30). These sights are always free: Palacio de Cibeles, Hermitage of San Antonio de la Florida, Bullfighting Museum, Madrid History Museum, and Temple of Debod.

MADRID

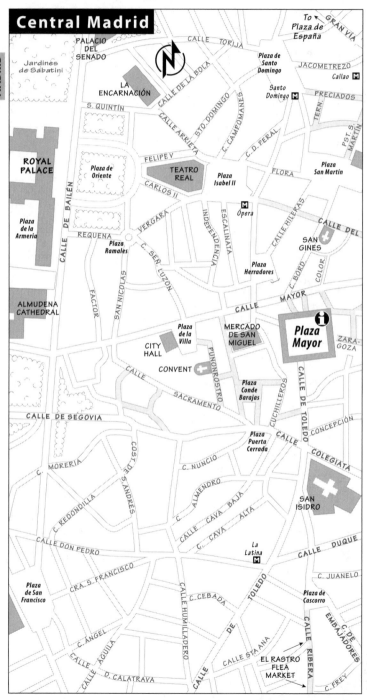

Central Madrid

To Plaza de España
GRAN VÍA

CALLE TORIJA

PALACIO DEL SENADO

Jardines de Sabatini

JACOMETREZO

Plaza de Santo Domingo

Callao M

LA ENCARNACIÓN

CALLE DE LA BOLA

Santo Domingo M

PRECIADOS

S. QUINTÍN

CALLE ARRIETA

STO. DOMINGO

C. CAMPOMANES

C. D. PERAL

PST. S. MARTÍN

ROYAL PALACE

FELIPE V

Plaza de Oriente

TEATRO REAL

Plaza Isabel II

FLORA

Plaza San Martín

CALLE DE BAILÉN

CARLOS II

VERGARA

C. SEN. LUZON

Plaza de la Armería

REQUENA

Plaza Ramales

INDEPENDENCIA

ESCALINATA

Ópera M

CALLE HILERAS

CALLE DEL

SAN GINES

ALMUDENA CATHEDRAL

FACTOR

SAN NICOLAS

Plaza Herradores

CALLE   MAYOR

C. BORD.

COLOR.

Plaza de la Villa

CITY HALL

CONVENT

PUÑONROSTRO

MERCADO DE SAN MIGUEL

Plaza Mayor i

ZARA-GOZA

CALLE

SACRAMENTO

Plaza Conde Barajas

CUCHILLEROS

CALLE DE TOLEDO

CALLE DE SEGOVIA

CONCEPCIÓN

C. MORERÍA

COSTA DE S. ANDRÉS

Plaza Puerta Cerrada

C. NUNCIO

CALLE

COLEGIATA

C. REDONDILLA

C. ALMENDRO

SAN ISIDRO

CALLE DON PEDRO

CALLE CAVA BAJA

C. CAVA ALTA

La Latina M

CALLE   DUQUE

Plaza de San Francisco

CRA. S. FRANCISCO

C. JUANELO

Plaza de Cascorro

C. ANGEL

C. CEBADA

CALLE HUMILLADERO

TOLEDO

DE

CALLE STA. ANA

CALLE RIBERA

C. DE EMBAJADORES

CALLE   AGULA

CALLE   D. CALATRAVA

EL RASTRO FLEA MARKET

C. FREY

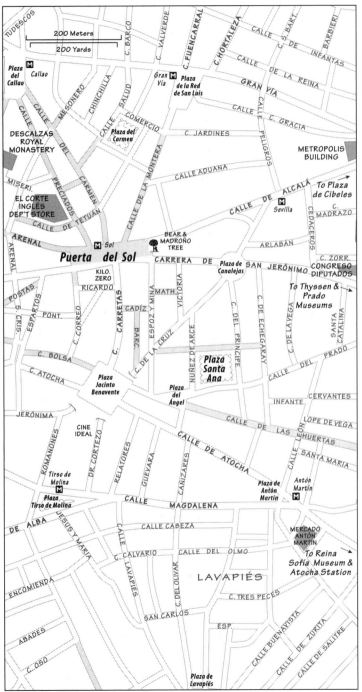

with the police. Or you can call in your report to the SATE line (24-hour tel. 902-102-112, English spoken once you get connected to a person), then go to the police station (where they'll likely speak only Spanish) to sign your statement.

You may see a police station in the Sol Metro station; this office handles only Metro theft.

Prostitution: Diverse by European standards, Madrid is spilling over with immigrants from South America, North Africa, and Eastern Europe. Many young women come here, fall on hard times, and end up on the streets. While it's illegal to make money from someone else selling sex (i.e., pimping), prostitutes over 18 can solicit legally (€30, FYI). Calle de la Montera (leading from Puerta del Sol to Plaza Red de San Luis) is lined with what looks like a bunch of high-school girls skipping out of school for a cigarette break. Again, don't stray north of Gran Vía around Calle de la Luna and Plaza Santa María Soledad—while the streets may look inviting, this area is a meat-eating flower.

One-Stop Shopping: The dominant department store is **El Corte Inglés,** which takes up several huge buildings in the commercial pedestrian zone just off Puerta del Sol (Mon-Sat 10:00-22:00, Sun 11:00-21:00, navigate with the help of the info desk near the door of the main building—the tallest building with the biggest sign, a block off Puerta del Sol, Preciados 3, tel. 913-798-000). They give out good, free Madrid maps. In the main building, you'll find two handy travel agencies (see listing later), a post office, souvenirs, a modern cafeteria (seventh floor), and a supermarket with a fancy "Club del Gourmet" section (with edible souvenirs) in the basement. Across the street is its Librería branch— a huge bookstore with English-language guidebooks. The second building fronting Puerta del Sol contains six floors of music, computers, home electronics, and SIM cards for mobile phones (passport required, second floor), with a box office on the top floor selling tickets to whatever's on in town. Locals figure you'll find anything you need at El Corte Inglés. Salespeople wear flag pins indicating which languages they can speak. If doing any serious shopping here, look into their discounts (10 percent for tourists) and VAT refund policy (21 percent but with a minimum purchase requirement).

Internet Access: Plaza Mayor has free Wi-Fi, and more public spaces may offer it soon. You can get online on all Madrid buses and trains—look for *Wi-Fi gratis* signs. Most hotels offer Wi-Fi and a guest computer in the lobby. Any *locutorio* call center should have a few computers and is generally the cheapest Internet option in the neighborhood. Near the Puerta del Sol, **Workcenter** has plenty of terminals and is a productive place to kill time if you're waiting for the tapas-crawl action to heat up (Mon-Fri 8:00-21:00, Sat-Sun 10:00-14:30 & 17:00-20:30, Calle Sevilla 4, tel. 913-601-395).

Bookstores: For books in English, try **FNAC Callao** (Calle Preciados 28, tel. 902-100-632), **Casa del Libro** (English on ground floor, Gran Vía 29, tel. 902-026-402), and **El Corte Inglés** (guidebooks and some fiction, in its Librería branch kitty-corner from main store, fronting Puerta del Sol—see "One-Stop Shopping," earlier).

Laundry: Ask your hotelier if they have laundry service. Or do it yourself at **Colada Express** (€5/load to wash, €3/load to dry, free Wi-Fi, daily 9:00-22:00, Calle Campomanes 8, tel. 657-876-464). **Higiensec** offers self-service laundry (€7/load to wash, a few euros more to dry) as well as drop-off laundry service and dry cleaning (Mon-Sat 9:00-21:00, closed Sun, between Calle del Arenal and Calle Mayor at Plaza Herradores 8, tel. 915-428-492).

Travel Agencies: The grand department store **El Corte Inglés** has two travel agencies (air and rail tickets, but not reservations for rail-pass holders, €2 fee, on first and seventh floors, for hours and contact info see "One-Stop Shopping," earlier). They also have a travel agency in the Atocha train station. These are fast and easy places to buy AVE and other train tickets.

Updates to This Book: For updates to this book, check www.ricksteves.com/update.

GETTING AROUND MADRID

If you want to use Madrid's excellent public transit, pick up the fine *Public Transport* map/flier (free, available at TIs or at Metro info booths in most stations—near the entrance turnstiles). The

metropolitan Madrid transit website (www.ctm-madrid.es) covers all public transportation options (Metro, bus, and suburban rail).

By Metro: The city's broad streets can be hot and exhausting. A subway trip of even a stop or two saves time and energy. Madrid's Metro is simple, speedy, and cheap. It costs €1.50 for a ride within zone A, which covers most of the city, but not trains out to the airport. The 10-ride, €12.20 Metrobus ticket can be shared by several travelers and works on both the Metro and buses. Buy tickets in the Metro (from easy-to-use machines or ticket booths), at newspaper stands, or at Estanco tobacco

MADRID

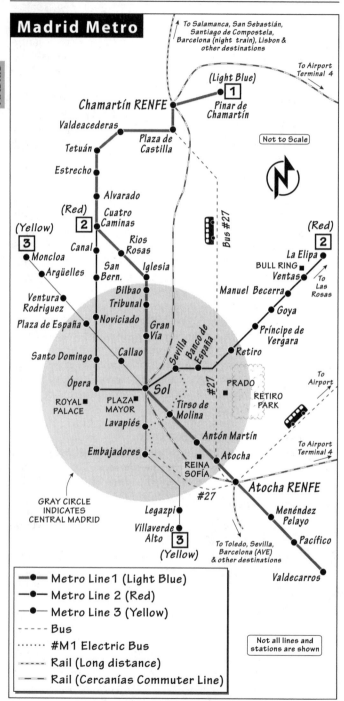

Madrid Metro

To Salamanca, San Sebastián,
Santiago de Compostela,
Barcelona (night train), Lisbon &
other destinations

To Airport
Terminal 4

(Light Blue)
1

Chamartín RENFE
Pinar de
Chamartín

Valdeacederas

Tetuán
Plaza de
Castilla

Estrecho

Not to Scale

Alvarado

(Red)
2
Cuatro
Caminas

(Yellow)
3
Moncloa
Canal
Ríos
Rosas

Argüelles
San
Bern.
Iglesia

(Red)
2
La Elipa
BULL RING
Ventas

Ventura
Rodríguez
Bilbao
Tribunal

Plaza de España
Noviciado
Gran
Vía

Manuel Becerra

To
Las
Rosas

Santo Domingo
Callao

Goya

Príncipe de
Vergara

Ópera
Sevilla
Banco de España
Retiro

To
Airport

ROYAL
PALACE
PLAZA
MAYOR
Sol

PRADO

RETIRO
PARK

Tirso de
Molina

#27

Lavapiés

Antón Martín

To Airport
Terminal 4

Embajadores
Atocha

REINA
SOFÍA

Atocha RENFE

GRAY CIRCLE
INDICATES
CENTRAL MADRID

#27
Menéndez
Pelayo

Legazpi

Pacífico

Villaverde
Alto
3
(Yellow)

To Toledo, Sevilla,
Barcelona (AVE)
& other destinations

Valdecarros

Bus #27

●━●	Metro Line 1 (Light Blue)
━●	Metro Line 2 (Red)
─●	Metro Line 3 (Yellow)
- - -	Bus
......	#M1 Electric Bus
╌╌╌	Rail (Long distance)
─·─	Rail (Cercanías Commuter Line)

Not all lines and
stations are shown

shops. Insert your ticket in the turnstile, then retrieve it and pass through. The Metro runs 6:00-1:30 in the morning. At all times, be alert to thieves, who thrive in crowded stations.

Study your Metro map—the simplified map on the opposite page can get you started. The lines are color-coded and numbered; use end-of-the-line station names to choose your direction of travel. Once in the Metro station, signs direct you to the train line and direction (e.g., Linea 1, *Valdecarros*). To transfer, follow signs in the station leading to connecting lines. Once you reach your final stop, look for the green *salida* signs pointing to the exits. Use the helpful neighborhood maps to choose the right *salida* and save yourself lots of walking. Metro info: www.metromadrid.es.

By Bus: City buses, though not as easy as the Metro, can be useful (€1.50 tickets sold on bus, €12.20 for a 10-ride Metrobus ticket, bus maps at TI or info booth on Puerta del Sol, poster-size maps usually posted at bus stops, buses run 6:00-24:00, much less frequent *Buho* buses run all night). Bus info: www.emtmadrid.es.

By Taxi: Madrid's 15,000 taxis are reasonably priced and easy to hail. A green light on the roof indicates that a taxi is available. Foursomes travel as cheaply by taxi as by Metro. For example, a ride from the Royal Palace to the Prado costs about €6. After the drop charge (about €3, higher on weekends and late at night), the per-kilometer rate depends on the time: *Tarifa 1* (€1.05/kilometer) is charged Mon-Fri 6:00-21:00; *Tarifa 2* (€1.20/kilometer) is valid after 21:00 and on Saturdays, Sundays, and holidays. If your cabbie uses anything other than *Tarifa 1* on weekdays (shown as an isolated "1" on the meter), you're being cheated. Rates can be higher if you go outside Madrid. There is a flat rate of €30 between the city center and any *one* of the airport terminals. Other legitimate charges include the €3 supplement for leaving any train or bus station, €20 per hour for waiting, and a few extra euros if you call to have the taxi come to you. Make sure the meter is turned on as soon as you get into the cab so the driver can't tack anything onto the official rate. If the driver starts adding up "extras," look for the sticker detailing all legitimate surcharges (which should be on the passenger window).

Tours in Madrid

ON FOOT
Food and Walking Tours
Essential Madrid's interesting tours in English depart from the Plaza Mayor TI (€17, 20 percent discount for booking three different tours, 2 hours). Check their booklet or website for specifics and departure times, which change frequently (www.esmadrid.com). Groups can be very small, so you almost feel like you have a private

Madrid at a Glance

▲▲▲**Royal Palace** Spain's sumptuous, lavishly furnished national palace. **Hours:** Daily April-Sept 10:00-20:00, Oct-March 10:00-18:00. See page 34.

▲▲▲**Prado Museum** One of the world's great museums, loaded with masterpieces by Diego Velázquez, Francisco de Goya, El Greco, Hieronymus Bosch, Albrecht Dürer, and more. **Hours:** Mon-Sat 10:00-20:00, Sun 10:00-19:00. See page 45.

▲▲▲**Centro de Arte Reina Sofía** Modern-art museum featuring Picasso's epic masterpiece *Guernica*. **Hours:** Mon and Wed-Sat 10:00-21:00, Sun 10:00-19:00, closed Tue. See page 60.

▲▲▲**Paseo** Evening stroll among the Madrileños. **Hours:** Sundown until the wee hours. See page 76.

▲▲**Puerta del Sol** Madrid's lively central square. **Hours:** Always bustling. See page 19.

▲▲**Thyssen-Bornemisza Museum** A great complement to the Prado, with lesser-known yet still impressive works and an especially good Impressionist collection. **Hours:** Mon 12:00-16:00, Tue-Sun 10:00-19:00, Sat until 21:00 in summer (exhibits only). See page 59.

▲▲**National Archaeological Museum** Traces the history of Iberia through artifacts. **Hours:** Tue-Sat 9:30-20:00, Sun 9:30-15:00, closed Mon. See page 68.

▲▲**Bullfight** Spain's controversial pastime. **Hours:** Scattered Sundays and holidays March-mid-Oct, plus almost daily in May-early June. See page 73.

▲▲**Flamenco** Captivating music and dance performances, at various venues throughout the city. **Hours:** Shows every night, some places closed on Sun. See page 77.

guide. Buy your ticket at the TI, by phone at 902-221-424, or online at www.entradas.com (search for "Essential Madrid"). Tours can fill up in high season, so booking at least a few hours in advance is a good idea. (Bike tours are also available, but you are responsible for renting your own bike. Ask the TI for details.)

Letango Tours offers private tours, packages, and stays all over Spain with a focus on families and groups. It's run by Carlos Galvin, a Spaniard who led tours for my groups for more than a decade, and his wife Jennifer, who's from Seattle. Their kid-friendly

▲**Plaza Mayor** Historic cobbled square. **Hours:** Always open. See page 23.

▲**Retiro Park** Festive green escape from the city, with rental rowboats and great people-watching. **Hours:** Closes at dusk. See page 66.

▲**Royal Botanical Garden** A relaxing museum of plants, with specimens from around the world. **Hours:** Daily 10:00-21:00, shorter hours off-season. See page 66.

▲**Naval Museum** Seafaring history of a country famous for its Armada. **Hours:** Tue-Sun 10:00-19:00, until 15:00 in Aug, closed Mon. See page 67.

▲**Museum of the Americas** Pre-Columbian and colonial artifacts from the New World. **Hours:** Tue-Sat 9:30-15:00, Thu until 19:00, Sun 10:00-15:00, closed Mon. See page 68.

▲**Clothing Museum** A clothes look at the 18th to 21st century. **Hours:** Tue-Sat 9:30-19:00, Thu until 22:30 in July-Aug, Sun 10:00-15:00, closed Mon. See page 69.

▲**Hermitage of San Antonio de la Florida** Church with Goya's tomb, plus frescoes by the artist. **Hours:** Tue-Sun 9:30-20:00, closed Mon. See page 69.

▲**El Rastro** Europe's biggest flea market, filled with bargains and pickpockets. **Hours:** Sun 9:00-15:00, best before 11:00. See page 74.

▲**Zarzuela** Madrid's delightful light opera. **Hours:** Evenings. See page 76.

"Madrid Discoveries" tour, mixing a market walk and history with a culinary-and-tapas introduction, gets you close to the Madrileños and their culture (€250/group, up to 5 people, kids go free, 3-plus hours). Carlos and Jennifer also lead walking and driving tours, including to Barcelona, whitewashed villages, wine country, Jewish sights, and more (mobile 655-818-740 and 661-752-458, www.letango.com, tours@letango.com).

At **Madrid Tours & Tastings,** Nygil Murrell's passions for Spanish history, food, and wine are superbly brought together in his old-town walking tours (€15/person), tapas tours, including a vegetarian option (from €75/person), and wine tastings (from €65/person). Tapas and wine tours are limited to six people; private tours are also available. Nygil's blog is loaded with insightful and beautifully photographed stories of Madrid life from an American expat's perspective (mobile 620-883-900, www.madridtandt.com, nmurrell@madridtandt.com).

Hernán Amaya Satt and his expert team at **Madrid Museum Tours** organize more than 40 itineraries, including nine different Prado tours, a gossip-filled "secrets of Madrid" walk, and activities around the city and beyond (€165/3 hours, mobile 680-450-231, www.madridmuseumtours.com, info@madridmuseumtours.com). Ask about discounts.

Local Guides
Frederico, Cristina, and their team are licensed guides who lead city walks through Madrid. They specialize in family tours of Madrid and excel at engaging kids and teens in museums (prices per group: €155/2 hours, €195/4 hours, €235/6 hours) and to nearby towns (with public or private transit, tel. 913-102-974, mobile 649-936-222, www.spainfred.com, info@spainfred.com).

Stephen Drake-Jones, a British expat, leads walks of historic old Madrid almost daily (11:00 and 20:00, or private tour by appointment). A historian with a passion for the Duke of Wellington (the general who stopped Napoleon), Stephen founded Madrid's Wellington Society and has been its chairman for over 30 years. For €65, you become a member and get a 3.5-hour tour with three stops for drinks and tapas (€10 more for fine wines).

On his themed tours, eccentric Stephen sorts out Madrid's Habsburg and Bourbon history, plus the Spanish Civil War and Hemingway's Madrid. He likes wine, a lot—if that's a problem, skip the tour (for details on his other tours, see www.wellsoc.org; mobile 609-143-203, chairman@wellsoc.org).

Other good licensed local guides include: **Inés Muñiz Martin** (guiding since 1997 and a third-generation Madrileña, €120-180/2-5 hours, 25 percent more on weekends and holidays, mobile 629-147-370, www.immguidedtours.com, info@immguidedtours.com), and **Susana Jarabo** (with a master's in art history, €200/4 hours; extra rental charge to tour by bike, scooter, or Segway; mobile 667-027-722, susanjarabo@yahoo.es).

ON WHEELS
Hop-On, Hop-Off Bus
Madrid City Tour makes two different hop-on, hop-off circuits through the city: historic and modern. Buy a ticket from the driver

(€21/1 day, €25/2 days), and you can hop from sight to sight and route to route as you like, listening to a recorded English commentary along the way. Each route has about 15 stops and takes about 1.5 hours, with buses departing every 10 or 20 minutes. The two routes intersect at the south side of Puerta del Sol and in front of Starbucks across from the Prado (daily March-Oct 9:30-22:00, Nov-Feb 10:00-18:00, tel. 917-791-888, www.madridcitytour.es).

Big-Bus City Sightseeing Tours
Juliá Travel leads bus tours departing from Plaza de España 7 (office open Mon-Fri 8:00-19:00, Sat-Sun 8:00-15:00, tel. 915-599-605). Their city offerings include a 2.5-hour Madrid tour with a live guide in two or three languages (€27, one stop for a drink at Hard Rock Café, one shopping stop, no museum visits, daily at 9:00 and 15:00, no reservation required—just show up 15 minutes before departure). See their website for other tours and services (www.juliatravel.com).

Self-Guided Tours by Bus or Minibus
A ride on public **bus #27** from the museum neighborhood up Paseo del Prado and Paseo de la Castellana to the Puerta de Europa and back gives visitors a glimpse of the modern side of Madrid, while a ride on electric **minibus #M1** takes you through the characteristic, gritty old center.

Madrid Walks

Two self-guided walks provide a look at two different sides of Madrid. For a taste of old Madrid, start with my "Puerta del Sol to Royal Palace Loop," which winds through the historic center. My "Gran Vía Walk" lets you glimpse a more modern side of Spain's capital.

PUERTA DEL SOL TO ROYAL PALACE LOOP
Madrid's historic center is pedestrian-friendly and filled with spacious squares, a trendy market, bulls' heads in a bar, and a cookie-dispensing convent. Allow about two hours for this self-guided, mile-long triangular walk. You'll start and finish on Madrid's central square, Puerta del Sol (Metro: Sol).

• *Head to the middle of the square, by the equestrian statue of King Charles III, and survey the scene.*

❶ Puerta del Sol
The bustling Puerta del Sol, rated ▲▲, is Madrid's—and Spain's—center. It's a hub for

To Plaza de España & Madrid Tower

ROYAL PALACE ❾

Campo Del Moro

Plaza de la Amería

ROYAL PALACE ENTRANCE

MAIN ENTRANCE

ALMUDENA CATHEDRAL ❽

SIDE ENTRANCE

CUESTA DE LA VEGA

100 Meters
100 Yards

S. QUINTÍN

CALLE DE BAILÉN

PHILIP IV STATUE
Plaza de Oriente ❿

CAFÉ DE ORIENTE

REQUENA

Plaza Ramales

FACTOR

SAN NICOLAS

C. SER LUZON

VERGARA

LA ENCARNACIÓN

CALLE ARRIETA

STO. DOMINGO

FELIPE V

ROYAL THEATER

Plaza Isabel II ⓫

CARLOS II

C. D. PERAL

Ópera

ESCALINATA

INDEPENDENCIA

Plaza Herradores

ASSASSINATION ATTEMPT MEMORIAL ❼

CALLE

Plaza de la Villa

TOWN HALL ❻

CONVENT ❺

CALLE SACRAMENTO

SAN MIGUEL MARKET ❹

PUÑONROSTRO

Plaza Conde Barajas

❶ Puerta del Sol
❷ Calle de Postas
❸ Plaza Mayor
❹ Mercado de San Miguel
❺ Church & Convent of Corpus Christi
❻ Town Hall

the Metro, *cercanías* (local) trains, revelers, protestors, and pick-pockets. In recent years it has undergone a facelift to become a mostly pedestrianized, wide-open space...without a bench or spot of shade in sight. Nearly traffic-free, it's a popular site for political demonstrations. Don't be surprised if you come across a large, peaceful protest here.

The equestrian statue in the middle of the square honors **King Charles III** (1716-1788) whose enlightened urban policies earned him the affectionate nickname "the best mayor of Madrid." He decorated the city squares with beautiful fountains, got those meddlesome Jesuits out of city government, established the public school system, mandated underground sewers, opened his private Retiro Park to the general public, built the Prado, made the Royal Palace the wonder of Europe, and generally cleaned up Madrid. (For more on Charles, see page 39.)

Head to the slightly uphill end of the square and find the **statue of a bear** pawing a tree—a symbol of Madrid since medieval times. Bears used to live in the royal hunting grounds outside the city. And the *madroño* trees produce a berry that makes the tradi-

Puerta del Sol to Royal Palace Loop

- ❼ Assassination Attempt Memorial
- ❽ Almudena Cathedral
- ❾ Royal Palace
- ❿ Plaza de Oriente
- ⓫ Plaza de Isabel II
- ⓬ Calle del Arenal

tional *madroño* liqueur. Near the statue, locate the Metro entrance and the glass-fish entrance to the *cercanías* trains.

Charles III faces a red-and-white building with a bell tower. This was Madrid's first post office, founded by Charles III in the 1760s. Today it's the **county governor's office** (Residencia de la Comunidad de Madrid), home to the president who governs greater Madrid. The building is notorious for having once been dictator Francisco Franco's police headquarters. An amazing number of those detained and interrogated by the Franco police tried to "escape" by jumping out its windows to their deaths. Notice the hats of the civil guardsmen at the entry. It's said the hats have square backs, cleverly designed so that the men can lean against the wall while enjoying a cigarette. On the opposite side of the square look up to see the famous Tío Pepe sign. A neon advertisement for this sherry wine was on display in Puerta del Sol from the 1950s until 2011, when it disappeared, much to the dismay of locals. It returned in 2014 to light the rooftops again.

Appreciate the **harmonious architecture** of the buildings that circle the square—yellow-cream, four stories, balconies of iron, shuttered windows, and balustrades along the rooflines (with TV antennas on top).

Crowds fill the square on New Year's Eve as the rest of Spain watches the Times Square-style action on TV. The bell atop the governor's office chimes 12 times, while Madrileños eat one grape for each ring to bring good luck through each of the next 12 months.

• *Cross the square, walking to the governor's office.*

Look at the curb directly in front of the entrance to the governor's office. The marker is **"kilometer zero,"** the symbolic center of Spain (with its six main highways indicated). Standing on the zero marker with your back to the governor's office, get oriented visually: At twelve o'clock (straight ahead), notice how the pedestrian commercial zone (with the huge El Corte Inglés department store) is thriving. At two o'clock starts the seedier Calle de la Montera, a street with shady characters and prostitutes that leads to the trendy, pedestrianized Calle de Fuencarral. At three o'clock is the biggest Apple store in Europe; the Prado is about a mile farther to your right. At ten o'clock, you'll see the pedestrianized Calle del Arenal Street (which leads to the Royal Palace) dumping into this square... just where you will end this walk.

On either side of the entrance to the governor's office are **two plaques** tied to important dates, expressing thanks from the regional government to its citizens for assisting in times of dire need. To the left of the entry, a plaque on the wall honors those who helped during the terrorist bombings of March 11, 2004 (we have our 9/11—Spain commemorates its 3/11). A similar plaque on the right marks the spot where the war against Napoleon started in 1808. When Napoleon invaded Spain and tried to appoint his brother (rather than the Spanish heir) as king of Spain, an angry crowd gathered outside this building. The French soldiers attacked and simply massacred the mob. Painter Francisco de Goya, who worked just up the street, observed the event and captured the tragedy in his paintings *Second of May, 1808* and *Third of May, 1808*, now in the Prado.

On the corner of Puerta del Sol and Calle Mayor (downhill end of Puerta del Sol, across from McDonald's) is the busy *confitería* **La Mallorquina**, *"fundada en 1.894"* (daily 9:00-21:00, closed mid-July-Aug). Go inside for a tempting peek at racks with goodies hot out of the oven. Enjoy observing the churning energy at the bar lined with Madrileños popping in for a fast coffee and a sweet treat. The shop is famous for its cream-filled *Napolitana* pastry (€1.20). Or sample Madrid's answer to doughnuts, *rosquillas* (*tontas* means "silly"—plain, and *listas* means "all dressed up and ready to go"—with icing, about €1 each). The room upstairs is more genteel, with nice views of the square. Buy a pastry. (Or buy two, one to give to a beggar outside.)

MADRID

From inside the shop, look back toward the entrance and notice the tile above the door with the 18th-century view of Puerta del Sol. Compare this with today's view out the door. This was before the square was widened, when a church stood at its top end.

Puerta del Sol ("Gate of the Sun") is named for a long-gone gate with the rising sun carved onto it, which once stood at the eastern edge of the old city. From here, we begin our walk through the historic town that dates back to medieval times.

• *Head west on busy Calle Mayor, just past McDonald's, and veer left up the pedestrian alley called...*

❷ Calle de Postas

The street sign shows the post coach heading for that famous first post office. Medieval street signs posted on the lower corners of buildings included pictures so the illiterate (and monolingual tourists) could "read" them. Fifty yards up the street on the left, at Calle San Cristóbal, is Pans & Company, a popular Catalan sandwich chain offering lots of healthy choices. While Spaniards consider American fast food unhealthy—both culturally and physically—they love it. McDonald's and Burger King are thriving in Spain.

• *Continue up Calle de Postas, and take a slight right on Calle de la Sal through the arcade, where you emerge into...*

❸ Plaza Mayor

This square, worth ▲, is a vast, cobbled, traffic-free chunk of 17th-century Spain. In medieval times, this was the city's main square.

The equestrian statue (wearing a ruffled collar) honors Philip III, who (in 1619) transformed the medieval marketplace into a Baroque plaza. The square is 140 yards long and 102 yards wide, enclosed by three-story buildings with symmetrical windows, balconies, slate  roofs, and steepled towers. Each side of the square is uniform, as if a grand palace were turned inside-out. This distinct "look," pioneered by architect Juan de Herrera (who finished El Escorial), is found all over Madrid.

This site served as the city's 17th-century open-air theater. Upon this stage, much Spanish history has been played out: bullfights, fires, royal pageantry, and events of the gruesome Inquisition. Worn-down reliefs on the seatbacks under the lampposts tell the story. During the Inquisition, many were tried here—suspected heretics, Protestants, Jews, tour guides without a local license, and Muslims whose "conversion" to Christianity was dubious. The guilty were paraded around the square before their executions, wearing billboards listing their many sins (bleachers were built for bigger audiences, while the wealthy rented balconies). The heretics were burned, and later, criminals were slowly strangled as they held a crucifix, hearing the reassuring words of a priest as the life was squeezed out of them with a garrote.

The square's buildings are mainly private apartments. Want one? Costs run from €400,000 for a tiny attic studio to €2 million and up for a 2,500-square-foot flat. The square is painted a demo-

cratic shade of burgundy—the result of a citywide vote. Since the end of decades of dictatorship in 1975, there's been a passion for voting here. Three different colors were painted as samples on the walls of this square, and the city voted for its favorite.

A stamp-and-coin market bustles at Plaza Mayor on Sundays (10:00-14:00). The Casa Yustas shop at #30 (in the northeast corner) has been making hats here since 1894.

The building to Philip's left, on the north side beneath the twin towers, was once home to the baker's guild and now houses the TI. It's wonderfully air-conditioned and offers daily walking tours. Consider reserving a spot now (for details, see "Tours in Madrid," earlier).

Day or night, Plaza Mayor is a colorful place to enjoy an affordable cup of coffee or overpriced food. Throughout Spain, lesser *plazas mayores* provide peaceful pools in the whitewater river of Spanish life.

For some interesting, if gruesome, bullfighting lore, drop by **La Torre del Oro Bar Andalú.** This bar is a good place to finish off your Plaza Mayor visit (north side of the square at #26, a few doors to the left of the TI). The bar has *Andalú* (Andalusian) ambience and an entertaining staff. Warning: They may push expensive tapas on tourists. The price list posted outside the door makes your costs perfectly clear: "*barra*" indicates the price at the bar; "*terraza*" is the price at an outdoor table. Step inside, stand at the bar, and order a drink—a *caña* (small draft beer) shouldn't cost more than €2. At the outdoor tables, only larger size *cañas dobles* are available (for €4.50).

The interior is a temple to bullfighting, festooned with gory decor. Notice the breathtaking action captured in the many photographs. Look under the stuffed head of Barbero the bull. At eye level you'll see a *puntilla,* the knife used to put poor Barbero out of his misery at the arena. The plaque explains: weight, birth date, owner, date of death, which matador killed him, and the location. Just to the left of Barbero, there's a photo of longtime dictator Franco with the famous bullfighter Manuel Benítez Pérez—better known as El Cordobés, the Elvis of bullfighters and a working-class hero. At the top of the stairs to the WC, find the photo of El Cordobés and Robert Kennedy—looking like brothers. To the left of them (and elsewhere in the bar) is a shot of Che Guevara enjoying a bullfight.

At the end of the bar, in a glass case, is the "suit of lights" the great El Cordobés wore in an ill-fated 1967 fight, in which the bull gored him. El Cordobés survived; the bull didn't. Find the photo of Franco with El Cordobés at the far end, to the left of Segador the bull. Near the Kennedy photo is a shot of El Cordobés' illegitimate son being gored. Disowned by El Cordobés senior, yet still using his dad's famous name after a court battle, the junior El Cordobés is one of this generation's top fighters.

Back in the case with the "suit of lights," notice the photo of a matador (not El Cordobés) horrifyingly hooked by a bull's horn. For a series of photos showing this episode (and the same matador healed afterward), look to the left of Barbero back by the door.

Consider taking a break at one of Torre del Oro's sidewalk tables (or at any café/bar terrace facing Madrid's grandest square). Cafetería Margerit (nearby) occupies the sunniest corner of the square and is a good place to enjoy a coffee with the view. The scene is easily worth the extra euro you'll pay for the drink.

• *Leave Plaza Mayor on Calle de Ciudad Rodrigo (at the northwest corner of the square), passing a series of solid turn-of-the-20th-century storefronts and sandwich joints, such as Casa Rúa, famous for their cheap* bocadillos de calamares—*fried squid rings on a roll. Emerging from the arcade, turn left and head downhill toward the covered market hall.*

❹ Mercado de San Miguel

To wash down those *calamares* in a more refined setting, pop into the Mercado de San Miguel (daily 10:00-24:00). This historic iron-and-glass structure from 1916 stands on the site of an even earlier marketplace. Renovated in the 21st century, it now hosts some 30 high-end vendors of fresh produce, gourmet foods, wines by the glass, tapas, and full meals. Locals and tourists alike pause here for its food, natural-light ambience, and social scene.

Alongside the market, look down the street called Cava de San Miguel. If you like singing and sangria, come back after 22:00 and visit one of the *mesones* that line the street. These cave-like bars, stretching far back from the street, get packed with Madrileños out on dates who—emboldened by sangria and the setting—are prone to suddenly breaking out in song. It's a lowbrow, electric-keyboard, karaoke-type ambience, best on Friday and Saturday nights. The odd shape of these bars isn't a contrivance for the sake of atmosphere—Plaza Mayor was built on a slope, and these underground vaults are part of a structural system that braces the leveled plaza.

• *After you walk through the market and exit, continue west a few steps, then turn left, heading downhill on Calle del Conde de Miranda. At the first corner, turn right and cross the small plaza to the brick church in the far corner.*

❺ Church and Convent of Corpus Christi

The proud coats of arms over the main entry announce the rich family that built this Hieronymite church and convent in 1607. In 17th-century Spain, the most prestigious thing a noble family could do was build and maintain a convent. To harvest all the goodwill created in your community, you'd want your family's insignia right there for all to see. (You can see the donating couple, like a 17th-century Bill and Melinda, kneeling before the communion wafer in the central panel over the entrance.) Inside is a quiet oasis with a Last Supper altarpiece.

Now for a unique shopping experience. A half-block to the right from the church entrance is its associated convent—it's the big brown door on the left, at Calle del Codo 3 (Mon-Sat 9:30-13:00 & 16:00-18:30, closed Sun). The sign reads: *Venta de Dulces* (Sweets for Sale). To buy goodies from the cloistered nuns, buzz the *monjas* button, then wait patiently for the sister to respond over the intercom. Say *"dulces"* (DOOL-thays), and she'll let you in. When the lock buzzes, push open the door and follow the sign to the *torno*, the lazy Susan that lets the sisters sell their baked goods without being seen. Scan the menu, announce your choice to the sequestered sister (she may tell you she has only one or two of the options available), place your money on the *torno*, and your goodies (and change) will appear. *Galletas* (shortbread cookies) are the least expensive item (a *medio*-kilo costs about €9). Or try the *pastas de almendra* (almond cookies).

• *Continue uphill on Calle del Codo (where those in need of bits of armor shopped—see the street sign) and turn left, heading toward the Plaza de la Villa (pictured here). Before entering the square, notice an **old door** to the left of the **Real Sociedad Económica** sign, made of wood lined with metal. This is considered the oldest door in town on Madrid's oldest building—inhabited since 1480. It's set in a Moorish keyhole*

arch. Look up at what was a prison tower. Now continue into the square called Plaza de la Villa, dominated by Madrid's...

❻ Town Hall

The impressive structure features Madrid's distinctive architectural style—symmetrical square towers, topped with steeples and a slate roof. The building still functions as Madrid's ceremonial Town Hall, though the city council and hands-on duties have moved elsewhere. Over the doorway, the three coats of arms sport many symbols of Madrid's rulers: Habsburg crowns, castles of Castile, and (the shield on the left) the city symbol—the berry-eating bear. This square was the ruling center of medieval Madrid, a tiny remnant of the 14th-century town. Even before then, when Madrid was an Arab-Moorish community, this was the only square in town.

Imagine how Philip II took this city by surprise in 1651 when he decided to move the capital of Europe's largest empire (even bigger than ancient Rome at the time) from Toledo to humble Madrid. To better administer their empire, the Habsburgs went on a building spree. But because their empire was drained of its riches by prolonged religious wars, they built Madrid with cheap brick instead of elegant granite.

The statue in the garden is of Philip II's admiral, Don Alvaro de Bazán—mastermind of the Christian victory over the Turkish Ottomans at the naval battle of Lepanto in 1571. This pivotal battle, fought off the coast of Greece, slowed the Ottoman threat to Christian Europe. However, mere months after Bazán's death in 1588, his "invincible" Spanish Armada was destroyed by England...and Spain's empire began its slow fade.

• *From here, walk along busy Calle Mayor, which leads downhill toward the Royal Palace. A few blocks down Calle Mayor, on a tiny square, you'll find the...*

❼ Assassination Attempt Memorial

This statue memorializes a 1906 assassination attempt. The target was Spain's King Alfonso XIII and his bride, Victoria Eugenie, as they paraded by on their wedding day. While the crowd was throwing flowers, an anarchist (what terrorists used to be called) threw a bouquet lashed to a bomb from a balcony at #84 (across the street). He missed the royal newlyweds, but killed 23 people. Gory photos of the event hang inside the recommended Casa Ciriaco restaurant, which now occupies #84 (photos to the right of the entrance). The king and queen went on to live to a ripe old age, producing many great-grandchildren, including the current king, Felipe VI.

• *Continue down Calle Mayor one more block to a busy street, Calle de Bailén. Take in the big, domed...*

❽ Almudena Cathedral
(Catedral de Nuestra Señora de la Almudena)

Madrid's massive, gray-and-white cathedral (110 yards long and 80 yards high) opened in 1993, 100 years after workers started building it. This is the side entrance for tourists (€1 donation requested). The main entrance (selling €6 museum-and-cupola tickets) is a block north, facing the Royal Palace. If you go inside, you'll see a refreshingly modern and colorful ceiling, a glittering 5,000-pipe organ, and a grand 15th-century painted altarpiece—striking in the otherwise Neo-Gothic interior. The highlight is the 12th-century coffin (empty, painted leather on wood, in a chapel behind the altar) of Madrid's patron saint, Isidro. A humble farmer, the exceptionally devout Isidro was said to have been helped by angels who did the plowing for him while he prayed. Forty years after he died, this coffin was opened, and his body was found to have been miraculously preserved. This convinced the pope to canonize Isidro as the patron saint of Madrid and of farmers, with May 15 as his feast day.

Turn right on Calle de Bailén to reach the main entrance. The doors feature reliefs of the cathedral's 1993 consecration, including one with Pope John Paul II and former king and queen Juan Carlos I and his wife Sofía.

• *From the cathedral's front steps, face the imposing...*

❾ Royal Palace

Since the ninth century, this spot has been Madrid's center of power: from Moorish castle to Christian fortress to Renaissance palace to the current structure, built in the 18th century. With its expansive courtyard surrounded by imposing Baroque architecture, it represents the wealth of Spain before its decline. Its 2,800 rooms, totaling nearly 1.5 million square feet, make it Europe's largest palace.

• *You could visit the palace now, using my self-guided tour. Or, to follow the rest of this walk back to Puerta del Sol, continue one long block north up Calle de Bailén (walking alongside the palace) to where the street opens up into...*

❿ Plaza de Oriente

As its name suggests, this square faces east. The grand yet people-friendly plaza is typical of today's Europe, where energetic governments are converting car-congested wastelands into public spaces like this. A recent mayor of Madrid earned the nickname "The Mole" for all the digging he did. Where's the traffic? Under your feet.

Notice the quiet. You're surrounded by more than three million people, yet you can hear the birds, bells, and fountain. The park is decorated with statues of Visigothic kings who ruled from the third to seventh century. Romans allowed them to administer their province of Hispania on the condition that they'd provide food and weapons to the empire. The Visigoths inherited real power after Rome fell, but lost it to invading Moors in 711. The fine bronze equestrian statue of Philip IV (honoring the king who built the Royal Palace) was a striking technical feat in its day, as the horse stood up on its hind legs (possible only with the help of Galileo's clever calculations and by using the tail for more support). The king faces Madrid's opera house, the 1,700-seat **Royal Theater** (Teatro Real), rebuilt in 1997. To your left, in the distance, the once-impressive **Madrid Tower** skyscraper (460 feet tall, built of concrete in 1957) marks Plaza de España.

• *Walk along the Royal Theater, on the right side, to the...*

⓫ Plaza de Isabel II

This square is marked by a statue of Isabel II, who ruled Spain in the 19th century. Although she's immortalized here, Isabel had a rocky reign, marked by uprisings and political intrigue. A revolution in 1868 forced her to abdicate, and she lived out her life in exile.

Evidence of Moorish walls turn up in this neighborhood and elsewhere in Madrid. Check out the tactile model in this square: The position of the old Moorish fortress and walls is outlined, with the modern city faintly depicted underneath. Feel it. Notice also the grooved sidewalk you're standing on—designed for the white canes of people who can't see.

• *From here, follow Calle del Arenal, walking gradually uphill. You're heading straight to Puerta del Sol.*

⓬ Calle del Arenal

As depicted on the tiled street signs, this was the "street of sand"—where sand was stockpiled during construction. Each cross street is named for a medieval craft that, historically, was plied along that lane (for example, "Calle de Bordadores" means "Street of the Embroiderers"). Wander slowly uphill. As you stroll, imagine this street as a traffic inferno—which it was until the city pedestrianized it a decade ago. Notice also how orderly the side streets are. Where a mess of cars once lodged chaotically on the sidewalks, smart bollards *(bolardos)* now keep vehicles off the walkways. The fancier facades (such as the former International Hotel at #19) are in the "eclectic" style (Spanish for Historicism—meaning a new interest in old styles) of the late 19th century.

The brick **St. Ginés Church** (on the right) means temptation to most locals. It marks the turn to the best *chocolatería* in town.

Spain's Royal Families:
From Habsburg to Bourbon

Spain as we know it was born when four long-established medieval kingdoms were joined by the 1469 marriage of Isabel, ruler of Castile and León, and Ferdinand, ruler of Aragon and Navarre. The so-called "Catholic Monarchs" (Reyes Católicos) wasted no time in driving the Islamic Moors out of Spain (the Reconquista). By 1492, Isabel and Ferdinand conquered a fifth kingdom, Granada, establishing more or less the same borders that Spain has today.

This was an age when "foreign policy" was conducted, in part, by marrying royal children into other royal families. Among the dynastic marriages of their children, Isabel and Ferdinand arranged for their third child, Juana "the Mad," to marry the crown prince of Austria, Philip "the Fair." This was a huge coup for the Spanish royal family. A member of the Habsburg dynasty, Philip was heir to the Holy Roman Empire, which then encompassed much of today's Austria, Czech Republic, Hungary, Transylvania, the Low Countries, southern Italy, and more. And when Juana's brothers died, making her ruler of the kingdoms of Spain, it paved the way for her son, Charles, to inherit the kingdoms of his four grandparents—creating a vast realm and famously making him the most powerful man in Europe. He ruled as Charles I (king of Spain, from 1516) and Charles V (Holy Roman emperor, from 1519).

He was followed by Philip II, Philip III, Philip IV, and finally Charles II. Over this period, Spain rested on its Golden Age laurels, eventually squandering much of its wealth and losing some of its holdings. Arguably the most inbred of an already very inbred dynasty (his parents were uncle and niece), Charles II was weak, sickly, and unable to have children, ending the 200-year Habsburg dynasty in Spain with his death in 1700.

Charles II willed the Spanish crown to the Bourbons of France, and his grandnephew Philip of Anjou, whose granddaddy was the "Sun King" Louis XIV of France, took the throne. But the rest of Europe feared allowing the already powerful Louis XIV

From the uphill corner of the church, look to the end of the lane where—like a high-calorie red-light zone—a neon sign spells out *Chocolatería San Ginés*...every local's favorite place for hot chocolate and *churros* (always open). Also notice the charming bookshop clinging like a barnacle to the wall of the church. It's been selling books on this spot since 1650.

Next door is the **Joy Eslava disco,** a former theater famous for operettas in the Gilbert-and-Sullivan days and now a popular club. In Spain, when you're 18 you can do it all (buy tobacco, drink, drive, serve in the military). This place is an alcohol-free disco for the younger kids until midnight, when it becomes a thriving adult to add Spain (and its vast New World holdings) to his empire. Austria, the Germanic States, Holland, and England backed a different choice (Archduke Charles of Austria). So began the War of Spanish Succession (1700-1714), involving all of Europe. The French eventually prevailed, but with the signing of the Treaty of Utrecht (1713), Philip had to give up any claim to the throne of France. This let him keep the Spanish crown but ensured that his heirs—the future Spanish Bourbon dynasty—couldn't become too powerful by merging with the French Bourbons.

In 1714, the French-speaking Philip became the first king of the Bourbon dynasty in Spain (with the name Philip V). He breathed much-needed new life into the monarchy, which had grown ineffectual and corrupt under the inbred Habsburgs. When the old wooden Habsburg royal palace burned on Christmas Eve of 1734, Philip (who was born at Versailles) built a new and spectacular late-Baroque-style palace as a bold symbol of his new dynasty. This is the palace that wows visitors to Madrid today. Construction was finished in 1764, and Philip V's son Charles III was the palace's first occupant. Charles III's decorations are what you'll see if you visit the palace's interior.

The Bourbon palace remained the home of Spain's kings from 1764 until 1931, when democratic elections led to the Second Spanish Republic and forced King Alfonso XIII into exile. After Francisco Franco took power in 1939, he sidelined the royals by making himself ruler-for-life. But later he handpicked as his successor Alfonso XIII's grandson, the Bourbon Prince Juan Carlos, whom Franco believed would continue his hardline policies. When Franco died in 1975, Juan Carlos surprised everyone by voluntarily turning the real power back over to Spain's parliament. Today Spain is a constitutional monarchy with a figurehead Bourbon king, Felipe VI, son of Juan Carlos I, who abdicated the throne in 2014.

space, with the theater floor and balconies all teeming with clubbers. Their slogan: "Go big or go home."

Next, at #11, **Soccer Shop** carries team regalia, postcards of today's stars, official mouth guards, and so on for soccer fans. Many Europeans come to Madrid primarily to see its 80,000-seat Bernabéu soccer stadium. The Starbucks on the next corner (opposite) is popular with young locals for its inviting ambience and American-style muffins, even though the coffee is too tame for many Spaniards.

Kitty-corner from there (at #7) is **Ferpal,** an old-school deli with an inviting bar and easy takeout options. Wallpapered with ham hocks, it's famous for selling the finest Spanish cheeses, hams, and other tasty treats. Spanish saffron is half what you'd pay for

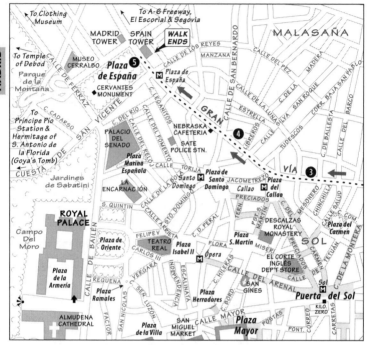

it back in the US. While they sell quality sandwiches, cheap and ready-made, it's fun to buy some bread and—after a little tasting—choose a ham or cheese for a memorable picnic or snack. If you're lucky, you may get to taste a tiny bit of Spain's best ham (Ibérico de Bellota). Close your eyes and let the taste fly you to a land of very happy acorn-fed pigs.

Across the street, in a little mall (at #8), a lovable mouse cherished by Spanish children is celebrated with a six-inch-tall bronze statue in the lobby. Upstairs is the fanciful **Casita Museo de Ratón Pérez** (€3, daily 11:00-14:00 & 17:00-20:00, Spanish only) with a fun window display. A steady stream of adoring children and their parents pour through here to learn about the wondrous mouse who is Spain's tooth fairy.

On the other side of the street (#3, opposite Burger King) is **Pronovias,** a famous Spanish wedding-dress shop that attracts brides-to-be from across Europe. Computer terminals inside let young women virtual-shop for the dress of their dreams.

• *You're just a few steps from where you started this walk, at Puerta del Sol. Back in the square, you're met by a statue popularly known as* La Mariblanca. *This mythological Spanish Venus—with Madrid's coat of arms at her feet—stands tall amid all the modernity, as if protecting the people of this great city.*

To History Museum

200 Meters
200 Yards

Gran Vía Walk

❶ Circulo de Bellas Artes
❷ 1910s Gran Vía (Banco de España to Gran Vía Metro)
❸ 1920s Gran Vía (Gran Vía to Callao Metro)
❹ 1930s Gran Vía (Callao to Plaza de España Metro)
❺ Plaza de España

MADRID

Plaza de las Salesas

CALLE DE VALVERDE
CALLE DE FUENCARRAL
CALLE DE PELAYO
CALLE DE HORTALEZA
CALLE DE GRAVINA
BARQUILLO
CALLE
DE
AUGUSTO
FIGUEROA
C. DE S. BARTOLOMÉ
C. DE LA LIBERTAD
Chueca Ⓜ
C. ALMIRANTE
C. DE PRIM
SAN MARCOS
CALLE DE INFANTAS
JUSTICIA
CALLE DE OLOZAGA
PUERTA DE ALCALÁ

Gran Vía Ⓜ
❷
MC D
Plaza de la Red de San Luis
GRAN VÍA
C. DE LA REINA
C. GRACIA
CALLE PELIGROS
Banco de España
Banco de España Ⓜ
WALK BEGINS
Plaza de Cibeles
Ⓜ
Plaza de la Independencia

C. JARDINES
C. ADUANA
METROPOLIS BUILDING
CIRCULO DE BELLAS ARTES ❶
BANCO DE ESPAÑA
PALACIO DE CIBELES
CALLE DE ALARCÓN

ALCALÁ
Ⓜ Sevilla
CEDACEROS
C. MADRAZO
ZARZUELA THEATER
NAVAL MUSEUM
C. DE MONTALBÁN
CALLE DE ALFONSO XI
Retiro Park

ARLABÁN
C. DE ZORRILLA
CALLE JUAN DE MENA
PASEO DE ARGENTINA

CARR. DE SAN JERÓNIMO
Plaza de Canalejas
To Plaza Santa Ana
CONGRESO DIPUTADOS
THYSSEN MUSEUM
Plaza de la Lealtad
C. ANTONIO MAURA
MUSEO DEL EJÉRCITO
To Prado Museum
To Lake

GRAN VÍA WALK

For a walk down Spain's version of Fifth Avenue, stroll the Gran Vía. Built primarily between 1900 and the 1950s, this boulevard, worth ▲, affords a fun view of early-20th-century architecture and a chance to be on the street with workaday Madrileños. I've broken this self-guided walk into five sections, each of which was the ultimate in its day.

• *Start at the skyscraper at Calle de Alcalá #42 (Metro: Banco de España).*

❶ **Circulo de Bellas Artes:** This 1920s skyscraper has a venerable café on its ground floor (free entry) and the best rooftop view around. Ride the elevator to the seventh-floor roof terrace (€4, daily 11:00-14:00 & 17:00-21:00), and stand under a black, Art Deco statue of Minerva, perhaps put here to associate Madrid with this mythological protectress of culture and high thinking. Walk the perimeter of the rooftop from the far left for a clockwise tour.

Looking to the left, you'll see the gold-fringed dome of the landmark Metropolis building (inspired by Hotel Negresco in Nice), once the headquarters of an insurance company. It stands at the start of the Gran Vía and its cancan of proud facades celebrating the good times in pre-civil war Spain. On the horizon, the Guadarrama Mountains hide Segovia. Farther to the right, in the distance, skyscrapers mark the city's north gate, Puerta de Europa (with its striking slanted twin towers). The big traffic circle and fountain below are part of Plaza de Cibeles, with its ornate and bombastic cultural center and observation deck (Palacio de Cibeles). Behind that is the vast Retiro Park. Farther to the right, the big low-slung building surrounded by green is the Prado Museum. And, finally, at the far right (and hard to see), is the old town.

• *Descend the elevator and cross the busy boulevard immediately in front of Círculo de Belles Artes to reach the start of Gran Vía.*

❷ **1910s Gran Vía:** This first stretch, from the Banco de España Metro stop to the Gran Vía Metro stop, was built in the 1910s. While the people-watching and window-shopping can be enthralling, be sure to look up and enjoy the beautiful facades, too.

❸ **1920s Gran Vía:** The second stretch, from the Gran Vía Metro stop to the Callao Metro stop, starts where two recently pedestrianized streets meet up. To the right, Calle de Fuencarral is the trendiest pedestrian zone in town, with famous brand-name shops and a young vibe (the 14-story 1920s Telefónica skyscraper at the corner was one of the city's first). To the left, Calle de la Montera is notorious for its prostitutes. The action pulses from the McDonald's down a block or so. Some find it an eye-opening little detour.

❹ **1930s Gran Vía:** The final stretch, from the Callao Metro stop to Plaza de España, is considered the "American Gran Vía," built in the 1930s to emulate the buildings of Chicago and New York City. You'll see the Nebraska Cafeteria restaurant—a reminder that American food was trendy long before the advent of fast-food chains. This section is the Spanish version of Broadway, with all the big theaters and plays.

❺ **Plaza de España:** End your walk at Plaza de España (with a Metro station of the same name). Once the Rockefeller Plaza of Madrid, these days it's pretty tired. While statues of the epic Spanish characters Don Quixote and Sancho Panza (part of a Cervantes monument) are ignored in the park, two Franco-era buildings do their best to scrape the sky above. Franco wanted to show he could keep up with America, so he had the Spain Tower (shorter) and Madrid Tower (taller) built in the 1950s. But they succeed in reminding people more of Moscow than the USA.

Sights in Madrid

▲▲▲ROYAL PALACE (PALACIO REAL)

This is Europe's third-greatest palace, after Versailles and Vienna's Schönbrunn. It has arguably the most sumptuous original interior, packed with tourists and royal antiques.

The palace is the product of many kings over several centuries. Philip II (1527-1598) made a wooden fortress on this site his

governing center when he established Madrid as Spain's capital. When that palace burned down, the current structure was built by King Philip V (1683-1746). Philip V wanted to make it his own private Versailles, to match his French upbringing: He was born in Versailles—the grandson of Louis XIV—and ordered his tapas in French. His son, Charles III (whose statue graces Puerta del Sol), added interior decor in the Italian style, since he'd spent his formative years in Italy. These civilized Bourbon kings were trying to raise Spain to the cultural level of the rest of Europe. They hired foreign artists to oversee construction and established local Spanish porcelain and tapestry factories to copy works done in Paris or Brussels. Over the years, the palace was expanded and enriched, as each Spanish king tried to outdo his predecessor.

Today's palace is ridiculously supersized—with 2,800 rooms, tons of luxurious tapestries, a king's ransom of chandeliers, frescoes by Tiepolo, priceless porcelain, and bronze decor covered in gold leaf. While these days the royal family lives in a mansion a few miles away, this place still functions as the ceremonial palace, used for formal state receptions, royal weddings, and tourists' daydreams.

Cost and Hours: €11; open daily April-Sept 10:00-20:00, Oct-March 10:00-18:00, last entry one hour before closing; from Puerta del Sol, walk 15 minutes down pedestrianized Calle del Arenal (Metro: Ópera); palace can close for royal functions—confirm in advance.

Crowd-Beating Tips: The palace is most crowded on Wednesdays and Thursdays, when it's free for locals. On any day, arrive early or go late to avoid lines and crowds. Madrid Card holders get to skip the line: Enter around the right side at the group entry point, a block down, along Calle de Bailén.

Information: Short English descriptions posted in each room complement what I describe in my tour. The museum guidebook demonstrates a passion for meaningless data. Tel. 914-548-800, www.patrimonionacional.es.

Tours: You can wander on your own or join a €4 **guided tour.** Check the time of the next English-language tour and decide as you buy your ticket; the tours are dry, depart sporadically, and aren't worth a long wait. The excellent €4 **audioguide** is much more interesting.

Services: Free lockers and a WC are just past the ticket booth. Upstairs you'll find a more serious bookstore with good books on Spanish history.

MADRID

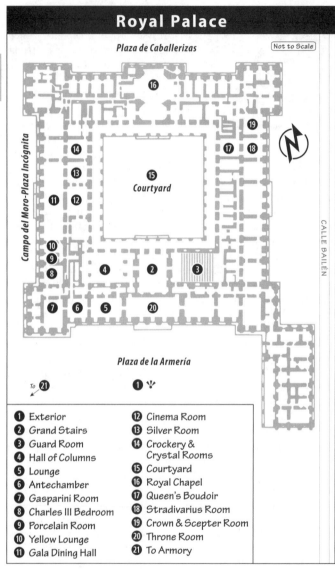

Royal Palace

Plaza de Caballerizas

Not to Scale

Campo del Moro-Plaza Incógnita

CALLE BAILÉN

16

19

14

17 **18**

13

15
Courtyard

11 **12**

10

9

4 **2** **3**

8

7 **6** **5** **20**

Plaza de la Armería

To **21**   **1**

1 Exterior	**12** Cinema Room
2 Grand Stairs	**13** Silver Room
3 Guard Room	**14** Crockery & Crystal Rooms
4 Hall of Columns	**15** Courtyard
5 Lounge	**16** Royal Chapel
6 Antechamber	**17** Queen's Boudoir
7 Gasparini Room	**18** Stradivarius Room
8 Charles III Bedroom	**19** Crown & Scepter Room
9 Porcelain Room	**20** Throne Room
10 Yellow Lounge	**21** To Armory
11 Gala Dining Hall	

Photography: Not allowed.

Eating: Though the palace has a refreshing air-conditioned cafeteria upstairs (with salad bar), I prefer to walk a few minutes and find a place near the Royal Theater or on Calle del Arenal. Another great option is **Café de Oriente,** boasting fin-de-siècle elegance immediately across the park from the Royal Palace. While its lunch special is good and reasonable—three courses for €15 (served

Mon-Fri 13:00-16:00)—the restaurant and terrace menus are pricey (Plaza de Oriente 2, tel. 915-413-974, www.cafedeoriente.es).

◒ Self-Guided Tour

You'll follow a simple one-way circuit on a single floor covering more than 20 rooms.

• *Buy your ticket, pass through the bookstore, stand in the middle of the vast open-air courtyard, and face the palace entrance.*

❶ **Palace Exterior:** The palace sports the French-Italian Baroque architecture so popular in the 18th century—heavy columns, classical-looking statues, a balustrade roofline, and false-front entrance. The entire building is made of gray-and-white local stone (very little wood) to prevent the kind of fire that leveled the previous castle. Imagine the place in its heyday, with a courtyard full of soldiers on parade, or a lantern-lit scene of horse carriages arriving for a ball.

• *Enter the palace and show your ticket.*

Palace Lobby: In the old days, horse-drawn carriages would drop you off here. Today, stretch limos do the same thing for gala events. (If you're taking a guided palace tour, this is where you wait to begin.) The modern black bust in the corner is of Juan Carlos I, a "people's king," who is credited with bringing democracy to Spain after 36 years under dictator Franco. (Juan Carlos passed the throne to his son in 2014.)

❷ **Grand Stairs:** Gazing up the imposing staircase, you can see that Spain's kings wanted to make a big first impression. Whenever high-end dignitaries arrive, fancy carpets are rolled down the stairs (notice the little metal bar-holding hooks). Begin your ascent, up steps that are intentionally shallow, making your climb slow and regal. Overhead, the white-and-blue ceiling fresco gradually opens up to your view. It shows the Spanish king, sitting on clouds, surrounded by female Virtues.

At the first landing, the burgundy coat of arms represents Felipe VI, the son of Spain's previous king, Juan Carlos. J. C. knew Spain was ripe for democracy after Francisco Franco's dictatorial regime. Rather than become "Juan the Brief" (as some were nicknaming him), he returned real power to the parliament. You'll see his (figure) head on the back of the Spanish €1 and €2 coins.

Continue up to the top of the stairs. Before entering the first room, look to the right of the door to find a white marble bust of J. C.'s great-great-g-g-g-great-grandfather Philip V, who began the Bourbon dynasty in Spain in 1700 and had this palace built.

❸ **Guard Room:** The palace guards used to hang out in this relatively simple room. Notice the two fake doors, added to give the room symmetry. The old clocks—still in working order—are part of a collection of hundreds amassed as a hobby by Spain's royal family. Throughout the palace, the themes chosen for the ceiling frescoes relate to the function of the room they decorate. In this room, the ceiling fresco is the first we'll see in a series by the great Venetian painter Giambattista Tiepolo (see sidebar). It depicts the legendary hero Aeneas (in red, with the narrow face of Charles III) standing in the clouds of heaven, gazing up at his mother Venus (with the face of Charles' own mother).

Notice the carpets in this room. Although much of what you see in the palace dates from the 18th century, the carpet on the left (folded over to show the stitching) is new, from 1991. It was produced by Madrid's royal tapestry factory, the same works that made the older original carpet (displayed next to the modern one). Though recently produced, the new carpet was woven the traditional way—by hand. The fine inlaid stone table in this room is important to Spaniards because it was here, in 1985, that the king signed the treaty finalizing Spain's entry into the European Union.

❹ **Hall of Columns:** Originally a ballroom and dining room, today this space is used for formal ceremonies and intimate concerts. This is where Spain formally joined the European Union in 1985 (the fancy table used to be in here) and honored its national soccer team after their 2010 World Cup victory. The tapestries (like most you'll see in the palace) are 17th-century Belgian, from designs by Raphael.

The central theme in the ceiling fresco (by Jaquinto, following Tiepolo's style) is Apollo driving the chariot of the sun, while Bacchus enjoys wine, women, and song with a convivial gang. This is a reminder that the mark of a good king is to drive the chariot of state as smartly as Apollo, while providing an environment where the people can enjoy life to the fullest.

• *The next several rooms were the living quarters of King Charles III (r. 1759-1788). First comes his* ❺ *lounge (with red walls), where the king would enjoy the company of a similarly great ruler—the Roman emperor Trajan—depicted "triumphing" on the ceiling. The heroics of Trajan, one of two Roman emperors born in Spain, naturally made the king feel good. Next, you enter the blue-walled...*

❻ **Antechamber:** This was Charles III's dining room. The four paintings—all originals by Francisco de Goya—are of Charles III's son and successor, King Charles IV (looking a bit like a dim-witted George Washington), and his wife, María Luisa (who wore the

MADRID

Charles III (1716-1788)

Of the many monarchs who've enlarged or redecorated the Royal Palace, it was Charles III who set the tone for its Baroque-Rococo interior. Charles' mother was Italian, and he spent his formative years in Italy. When he became Spain's king, he brought along sophisticated Italian artists to decorate his new home—the painter Tiepolo, the architect Sabatini, and the decorator Gasparini. They created some of the most elaborate, jaw-dropping rooms tourists see in the palace today.

Charles was an enlightened ruler who tried to reform Spain along democratic principles. He failed. After his death, Spain dwindled into repressive irrelevance. But over the centuries, each of his successors labored to top Charles in ostentatious decoration, making Madrid's Royal Palace his greatest legacy.

pants in the palace). María Luisa was famously hands-on, tough, and businesslike, while Charles IV was pretty wimpy as far as kings go. To meet the demand for his work, Goya made replicas of these portraits, which you'll see in the Prado.

The 12-foot-tall clock—showing Cronus, god of time, in porcelain, bronze, and mahogany—sits on a music box. Reminding us of how time flies, Cronus is shown both as a child and as an old man. The palace's clocks are wound—and reset—once a week (they grow progressively less accurate as the week goes on). The gilded decor you see throughout the palace is bronze with gold leaf. Velázquez's famous painting, *Las Meninas* (which you'll marvel at in the Prado), originally hung in this room.

❼ Gasparini Room: (Gasp!) The entire room is designed, top to bottom, as a single gold-green-pink ensemble: from the frescoed ceiling, to the painted stucco figures, silk-embroidered walls, chandelier, furniture, and multicolored marble floor. Each marble was quarried in, and therefore represents, a different region of Spain. Birds overhead spread their wings, vines sprout, and fruit bulges from the surface. With curlicues everywhere (including their reflection in the mirrors), the room dazzles the eye and mind. It's a

Tiepolo's Frescoes

In 1762, King Charles III invited Europe's most celebrated palace painter, Giambattista Tiepolo (1696-1770), to decorate three rooms in the newly built palace. Sixty-six-year-old Tiepolo made the trip from Italy with his two well-known sons as assistants. They spent four years atop scaffolding decorating in the fresco technique, troweling plaster on the ceiling and quickly painting it before it dried.

Tiepolo's translucent ceilings seem to open up to a cloud-filled heaven, where Spanish royals cavort with Greek gods and pudgy cherubs. Tiepolo used every trick to "fool the eye" (trompe l'oeil), creating dizzying skyscapes of figures tumbling at every angle. He mixes 2-D painting with 3-D stucco figures that spill over the picture frame. His colorful, curvaceous ceilings blend seamlessly with the flamboyant furniture of the room below. Tiepolo's Royal Palace frescoes are often cited as the final flowering of Baroque and Rococo art.

triumph of the Rococo style, with exotic motifs such as the Chinese people sculpted into the corners of the ceiling. (These figures, like many in the palace, were formed from stucco, or wet plaster.) The fabric gracing the walls was recently restored. Sixty people spent three years replacing the rotten silk fabric and then embroidering back on the silver, silk, and gold threads.

Note the micro-mosaic table—a typical royal or aristocratic souvenir from any visit to Rome in the mid-1800s. The chandelier, the biggest in the palace, is mesmerizing, especially with its glittering canopy of crystal reflecting in the wall mirrors.

The room was the king's dressing room. For a divine monarch, dressing was a public affair. The court bigwigs would assemble here as the king, standing on a platform—notice the height of the mirrors—would pull on his leotards and toy with his wig.

• *In the next room, the silk wallpaper is from modern times—the intertwined "J. C. S." indicates the former monarchs Juan Carlos I and Sofía. Pass through the silk room to reach...*

❽ **Charles III Bedroom:** Charles III died here in his bed in 1788. His grandson, Ferdinand VII, redid the room to honor the great man. The room's blue color scheme recalls the blue-clad monks of Charles' religious order. A portrait of Charles (in blue) hangs on the wall. The ceiling fresco shows Charles establishing his order, with its various (female) Virtues. At the base of the ceiling (near the harp player) find the baby in his mother's arms—that would be Ferdy himself, the long-sought male heir, preparing to continue Charles' dynasty.

The chandelier is in the shape of the fleur-de-lis (the symbol of the Bourbon family) capped with a Spanish crown. As you exit the room, notice the thick walls between rooms. These hid service corridors for servants, who scurried about mostly unseen.

❾ **Porcelain Room:** This tiny but lavish room is paneled with green-white-gold porcelain garlands, vines, babies, and mythological figures. The entire ensemble was disassembled for safety during the civil war. (Find the little screws in the greenery that hides the seams between panels.) Notice the clock in the center with Atlas supporting the world on his shoulders.

❿ **Yellow Lounge:** This was a study for Charles III. The properly cut crystal of the chandelier shows all the colors of the rainbow. Stand under it, look up, and sway slowly to see the colors glitter. This is not a particularly precious room. But its decor pops because the lights are generally left on. Imagine the entire palace as brilliant as this when fully lit. As you leave the room, look back at the chandelier to notice its design of a temple with a fountain inside.

• *Next comes the...*

⓫ **Gala Dining Hall:** Up to 12 times a year, the king entertains as many as 144 guests at this bowling lane-size table, which can be extended to the length of the room. The parquet floor was the preferred dancing surface when balls were held in this fabulous room. Note the vases from China, the tapestries, and the ceiling fresco depicting Christopher Columbus kneeling before Ferdinand and Isabel, presenting exotic souvenirs and his new, red-skinned friends. Imagine this hall in action when a foreign dignitary dines here. The king and queen preside from the center of the room. Find their chairs (slightly higher than the rest). The tables are set with fine crystal and cutlery (which we'll see a couple of rooms later). And the whole place glitters as the 15 chandeliers (and their 900 bulbs) are fired up. (The royal kitchens, where the gala dinners were prepared, may be open for viewing; ask the staff where to enter.)

• *Pass through the next room of coins and medals, known as the* ⓬ *Cinema Room because the royal family once enjoyed Sunday afternoons at the movies here. The royal string ensemble played here to entertain during formal dinners. From here, move into the...*

⓭ **Silver Room:** Some of this 19th-century silver tableware—knives and forks, bowls, salt and pepper shakers, and the big tureen—is used in the Gala Dining Hall on special occasions. If you look carefully, you can see quirky royal necessities, including a baby's silver rattle and fancy candle snuffers.

• *Head straight ahead to the...*

⓮ Crockery and Crystal Rooms: Philip V's collection of china is the oldest and rarest of the various pieces on display; it came from China before that country was opened to the West. Since Chinese crockery was in such demand, any self-respecting European royal family had to have its own porcelain works (such as France's Sèvres or Germany's Meissen) to produce high-quality knockoffs (and cutesy Hummel-like figurines). The porcelain technique itself was kept a royal secret. As you leave, check out Isabel II's excellent 19th-century crystal ware.

• *Exit to the hallway and notice the interior courtyard you've been circling one room at a time.*

⓯ Courtyard: You can see how the royal family lived in the spacious middle floor while staff was upstairs. The kitchens, garage, and storerooms were on the ground level. The new king, Felipe VI, married a commoner (for love) and celebrated their wedding party in this courtyard, which was decorated as if another palace room. Spain's royals take their roles and responsibilities seriously—making a point to be approachable and empathizing with their subjects—and are very popular.

• *Between statues of two of the giants of Spanish royal history (Isabel and Ferdinand), you'll enter the...*

⓰ Royal Chapel: This chapel is used for private concerts and funerals. The royal coffin sits here before making the sad trip to El Escorial to join the rest of Spain's past royalty. The glass case contains the entire body of St. Felix, given to the Spanish king by the pope in the 19th century. Note the "crying room" in the back for royal babies. While the royals rarely worship here (they prefer the cathedral adjacent to the palace), the thrones are here just in case.

• *Pass through the* **⓱** *Queen's Boudoir—where royal ladies hung out—and into the...*

⓲ Stradivarius Room: Of all the instruments made by Antonius Stradivarius (1644-1737), only 300 survive. This is the world's best collection and the only matching quartet set: two violins, a viola, and a cello. Charles III, a cultured man, fiddled around with these. Today, a single Stradivarius instrument might sell for $15 million.

• *Continue into the room at the far left.*

⓳ Crown and Scepter Room: The stunning crown and scepter of the last Habsburg king, Carlos II, are displayed in a glass case in the middle. Look for the 2014 proclamations of Juan Carlos' abdication of the crown and Felipe VI's acceptance as king of Spain. Notice which writing implement each man chose to sign with: Juan Carlos' traditional classic pen and Felipe VI's modern one.

• *Walk back through the Stradivarius Room and into the courtyard hallway. Continue your visit through the Antechamber, where ambassadors*

would wait to present themselves, and the Small Official Chambers,
where officials are received by royalty and have their photos taken. Walk
through two rooms, decorated in blue and red with tapestries and paint-
ings, to the grand finale, the...

❷⓿ **Throne Room:** This room, where the Spanish monarchs
preside, is one of the palace's most glorious. And it holds many
of the oldest and most precious things in the palace: silver-and-
crystal chandeliers (from Venice's Murano Island), elaborate lions,
and black bronze statues from the fortress that stood here before
the 1734 fire. The 12 mirrors, impressively large in their day, each
represent a different month.

The throne stands under a gilded canopy, on a raised platform,
guarded by four lions (symbols of power found throughout the palace). The coat of arms above the throne shows the complexity of the
Bourbon empire across Europe—which, in the 18th century, included Tirol, Sicily, Burgundy, the Netherlands, and more. Though
the room was decorated under Charles III (late 18th century), the
throne itself dates only from 1977. In Spain, a new throne is built
for each king or queen, complete with a gilded portrait on the back.
The room's chairs also indicate the previous monarchs—"JC I" and
"Sofía." With Juan Carlos' abdication, the chairs may not have
changed names yet.

Today, this room is where the king's guests salute him before
they move on to dinner. He receives them relatively informally...
standing at floor level, rather than seated up on the throne.

The ceiling fresco (1764) is the last great work by Tiepolo,
who died in Madrid in 1770. His vast painting (88 × 32 feet)
celebrates the vast Spanish empire—upon which the sun also
never set. The Greek gods look down from the clouds, oversee-
ing Spain's empire, whose territories are represented by the people ringing the edges of the ceiling. Find the Native American
(hint: follow the rainbow to the macho red-caped conquistador
who motions to someone he has conquered). From the near end
of the room (where tourists stand), look up to admire Tiepolo's
skill at making a pillar seem to shoot straight up into the sky.
The pillar's pedestal has an inscription celebrating Tiepolo's boss,
Charles III ("Carole Magna"). Notice how the painting spills over
the gilded wood frame, where 3-D statues recline alongside 2-D
painted figures. All of the throne room's decorations—the fresco,
gold garlands, mythological statues, wall medallions—unite in a
multimedia extravaganza.

• *Exit the palace down the same grand stairway you climbed at the start.*
Cross the big courtyard, heading to the far-right corner to the...

❷❶ **Armory:** Here you'll find weapons and armor belonging to
many great Spanish historical figures. While some of it was actually for fighting, remember that the great royal pastimes included

hunting and tournaments, and armor was largely for sport or ceremony. Much of this armor dates from Habsburg times, before this palace was built (it came here from the earlier fortress or from El Escorial). Circle the big room clockwise.

In the three glass cases on the left, you'll see the oldest pieces in the collection. In the central case (case III), the shield, sword, belt, and dagger belonged to Boabdil, the last Moorish king, who surrendered Granada in 1492. In case IV, the armor and swords belonged to Ferdinand, the husband of Isabel, and Boabdil's contemporary.

The center of the room is filled with knights in armor on horseback—mostly suited up for tournament play. Many of the pieces belonged to the two great kings who ruled Spain at its 16th-century peak, Charles I and his son Philip II.

The long wall on the left displays the personal armor wardrobe of Charles I (a.k.a. the Holy Roman emperor Charles V). At the far end, you'll meet Charles on horseback. The mannequin of the king wears the same armor and assumes the same pose as in Titian's famous painting of him (in the Prado).

The opposite wall showcases the armor and weapons of Philip II, the king who watched Spain start its long slide downward. Philip, who impoverished Spain with his wars against the Protestants, anticipated that debt collectors would ransack his estate after his death and specifically protected his impressive collection of armor by founding this armory.

The tapestry above the armor once warmed the walls of the otherwise stark palace that predated this one. Tapestries traveled ahead of royals to decorate their living space. They made many palaces "fit for a king" back when the only way to effectively govern was to be on the road a lot.

Downstairs is more armor, a mixed collection mostly from the 17th century. You'll find early guns and Asian armor. The pint-size armor you may see wasn't for children to fight in. It's training armor for noble youngsters, who as adults would be expected to ride, fight, and play gracefully in these clunky getups. Before you leave, notice the life-saving breastplates dimpled with bullet dents (to right of exit door).

• *Climb the steps from the armory exit to the viewpoint.*

View of the Gardens: Looking down from this high bluff, it's clear why rulers have built on this strategically located spot (great for protecting the historic capital, Toledo) since the ninth century. The vast palace backyard, once the king's hunting ground, is now a city park, dotted with fountains.

• *Walk to the center of the huge square and face the palace. Notice how the palace of the king faces the palace of the bishop (the cathedral). Whew. After all those rooms, frescoes, chandeliers, knickknacks, kings, and history, consider a final stop in the palace's upstairs café for a well-deserved rest.*

BETWEEN THE ROYAL PALACE AND PUERTA DEL SOL
Descalzas Royal Monastery (Monasterio de las Descalzas Reales)

Madrid's most visit-worthy monastery was founded in the 16th century by Philip II's sister, Joan of Habsburg (known to Spaniards as Juana and to Austrians as Joanna). She's buried here. The monastery's chapels are decorated with fine art, Rubens-designed tapestries, and the heirlooms of the wealthy women who joined the order (the nuns were required to give a dowry). Because this is still a working Franciscan monastery, tourists can enter only when the nuns vacate the cloister, and the number of daily visitors is limited. The scheduled tours often sell out—come in the morning to buy your ticket, even if you want an afternoon tour (plans are under way to sell advance tickets online; check www.patrimonionacional.es).

Cost and Hours: €7, visits guided in Spanish or English depending on demand, Tue-Sat 10:00-14:00 & 16:00-18:30, Sun 10:00-15:00, closed Mon, last entry one hour before closing, Plaza de las Descalzas Reales 1, near the Ópera Metro stop and just a short walk from Puerta del Sol, tel. 914-548-800.

MADRID'S MUSEUM NEIGHBORHOOD

Three great museums, all within a 10-minute walk of one another, cluster in east Madrid. The Prado is Europe's top collection of paintings. The Thyssen-Bornemisza sweeps through European art from old masters to moderns. And the Centro de Arte Reina Sofía has a choice selection of modern art, starring Picasso's famous *Guernica.*

Combo-Ticket: If visiting all three museums, you can save a few euros by buying the **Paseo del Arte** combo-ticket (€25.60, sold at all three museums, good for a year). Note that the Prado is free to enter every evening, the Reina Sofía has free hours every night but Tuesday (when it's closed), and the Thyssen-Bornemisza is free on Monday afternoons (see specifics in following listings).

▲▲▲Prado Museum (Museo Nacional del Prado)

With more than 3,000 canvases, including entire rooms of masterpieces by superstar painters, the Prado (PRAH-doh) is my vote for the greatest collection anywhere of paintings by the European masters. The Prado is *the* place to enjoy the great Spanish painter Francisco de Goya, and it's also the home of Diego Velázquez's *Las Meninas,* considered by many to be the world's finest painting, period. In addition to Spanish works, you'll find paintings by Italian

and Flemish masters, including Hieronymus Bosch's fantastical *Garden of Earthly
Delights* altarpiece.

MADRID

Cost: €14, additional (obligatory) fee
for occasional temporary exhibits, free
Mon-Sat 18:00-20:00 and Sun 17:00-
19:00, under age 18 always free.

Hours: Mon-Sat 10:00-20:00, Sun
10:00-19:00, last entry 30 minutes before
closing.

Crowd-Beating Tips: It's generally
less crowded at lunchtime (13:00-16:00),
when there are fewer groups, and on
weekdays. It can be busy on free evenings and weekends. Ticket-
buying lines can be long. Here are your time-saving options:

1. Use the ticket machines at the Goya entrance (credit cards
only).

2. Book an entry time in advance online or by phone (www.
museodelprado.es, print out ticket; or tel. 902-107-077, get a reference
number). Same-day advance purchase is possible if space is available.

3. Buy a Paseo del Arte combo-ticket (described earlier) at the
less-crowded Thyssen-Bornemisza or Reina Sofía museums.

4. Get a Madrid Card beforehand.

Getting There: It's at the Paseo del Prado. The nearest Metro
stops are Banco de España (line 2) and Atocha (line 1), each a five-
minute walk from the museum. It's a 15-minute walk from Puerta
del Sol.

Getting In: While there are several entrances, you must buy
tickets at the Goya (north) entrance. (Even at free-entry times, you
need to pick up a gratis ticket at the Goya ticket window.) Once
you have your ticket, you can enter at the Goya, Jerónimos, or Velázquez entrance. Those who book in advance or have a Madrid
Card can pick up their tickets at the adjacent Jerónimos entrance,
skipping the main line. The Murillo entrance is generally reserved
for student groups. Your bags will be scanned as you enter.

Information: Tel. 913-302-800, www.museodelprado.es.

Tours: The €3.50 audioguide is a helpful supplement to my
self-guided tour. Given the ever-changing locations of paintings
(making my tour tough to follow), the audioguide is a good investment, allowing you to wander and dial up commentary on 250
masterpieces.

Services: The Jerónimos entrance has an information desk,
bag check, audioguides, bookshop, WCs, and café. Larger bags
must be checked. No drinks, food, backpacks, or large umbrellas
are allowed inside.

Photography: Not allowed.

MADRID

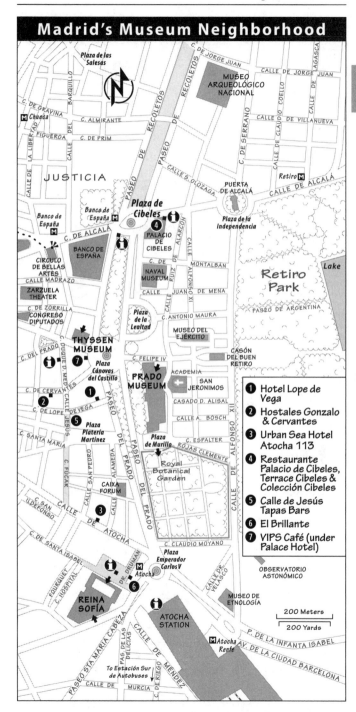

Madrid's Museum Neighborhood

Plaza de las Salesas

MUSEO ARQUEOLÓGICO NACIONAL

C. DE JORGE JUAN

CALLE DE JORGE JUAN

C. DE SERRANO

CALLE DE CLAUDIO COELLO

CALLE DE SERRANO

CALLE DE VILLANUEVA

C. DE GRAVINA

Chueca

C. ALMIRANTE

C. DE PRIM

CALLE DEL BARQUILLO

CALLE DE LA LIBERTAD

FIGUEROA

JUSTICIA

PASEO DE RECOLETOS

RECOLETOS

CALLE S. OLOZAGA

Retiro

PUERTA DE ALCALÁ

CALLE DE ALCALÁ

Banco de España

Banco de España

Plaza de Cibeles

C. DE ALCALÁ

BANCO DE ESPAÑA

CÍRCULO DE BELLAS ARTES

CALLE MADRAZO

ZARZUELA THEATER

C. DE ZORRILLA

CONGRESO DIPUTADOS

PALACIO DE CIBELES

C. DE ALARCÓN

MONTALBÁN

CALLE RUIZ DE ALFONSO XI

CALLE JUAN DE MENA

C. ANTONIO MAURA

Plaza de la Independencia

Retiro Park

Lake

PASEO DE ARGENTINA

NAVAL MUSEUM

Plaza de la Lealtad

MUSEO DEL EJÉRCITO

THYSSEN MUSEUM

C. DEL PRADO

C. DE CERVANTES

C. DE LOPE DE VEGA

C. SANTA MARÍA

Plaza Cánovas del Castillo

C. FELIPE IV

CALLE DE VEGA

PASEO DEL PRADO

PRADO MUSEUM

ACADEMIA

SAN JERÓNIMOS

CASADO D. ALISAL

CALLE A. BOSCH

C. ESPALTER

CASÓN DEL BUEN RETIRO

CALLE ALFONSO XII

Plaza Platería Martínez

C. SAN PEDRO

CAIXA FORUM

Plaza de Murillo

ROJAS CLEMENTE

Royal Botanical Garden

C. SAN ILDEFONSO

C. DE SANTA ISABEL

C. DE ATOCHA

C. CLAUDIO MOYANO

Plaza Emperador Carlos V

Atocha

OBSERVATORIO ASTONÓMICO

FOURQUET

C. DE HOSPITAL

REINA SOFÍA

PAS. DE LAS DELICIAS

ATOCHA STATION

MUSEO DE ETNOLOGÍA

CALLE DR. VELASCO

Atocha Renfe

P. DE LA INFANTA ISABEL

AV. DE LA CIUDAD BARCELONA

To Estación Sur de Autobuses

PASEO STA MARÍA CABEZA

CALLE DE RIEGO

CALLE DE MENDEZ

MURCIA

1 Hotel Lope de Vega

2 Hostales Gonzalo & Cervantes

3 Urban Sea Hotel Atocha 113

4 Restaurante Palacio de Cibeles, Terrace Cibeles & Colección Cibeles

5 Calle de Jesús Tapas Bars

6 El Brillante

7 VIPS Café (under Palace Hotel)

200 Meters

200 Yards

MADRID

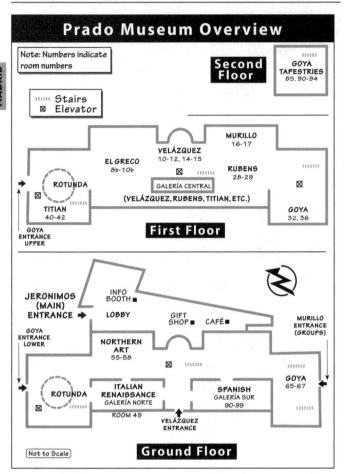

Cuisine Art: The self-service cafeteria and restaurant are open daily (Mon-Sat 10:00-19:30, Sun 10:00-18:30, €9 main dishes, €6 salads and sandwiches, hot dishes served only 12:30-16:00). A block west of the Prado, you'll find **VIPS**, a bright, popular chain restaurant, handy for a cheap and filling salad. Engulfed in a shop selling books and candy, this is a high-energy, no-charm eatery (daily 9:00-24:00, across the boulevard from northern end of Prado at Plaza de Canova del Castillo, under Palace Hotel). Next door is Spain's first Starbucks, opened in 2001. A strip of wonderful tapas bars is just a few blocks east of the museum, lining Calle de Jesús. If you want to take a break outside the museum for lunch, you can reenter the museum on the same ticket as long as you get it stamped at a desk marked "*Educación*," near the Jerónimos entrance.

MADRID

➔ Self-Guided Tour

Thanks to Gene Openshaw for writing the following tour.

Centuries of powerful kings (and lots of New World gold) funded the Prado, the greatest painting museum in the world. You'll see first-class Italian Renaissance art (especially Titian), Northern art (Bosch, Rubens, Dürer), and Spanish art (El Greco, Velázquez, Goya). This huge museum is not laid out chronologically, so this tour will not be chronological. Instead, we'll hit the highlights with a minimum of walking. Paintings are moved around frequently—if you can't find a particular one, ask a guard.

• *Pick up a museum map as you enter. Once inside, make your way to the main gallery on the ground floor. Plans are in the works to renumber the rooms. Compare the map in this book with the museum's printed map. Even if the room numbers are different, the paintings should be in the same physical locations. Follow your map and signs to Sala 49. Look for the following paintings in Room 49 and the adjoining galleries.*

Italian Renaissance

During its Golden Age (the 1500s), Spain may have been Europe's richest country, but Italy was still the most cultured. Spain's kings loved how Italian Renaissance artists captured a three-dimensional world on a two-dimensional canvas, bringing Bible scenes to life and celebrating real people and their emotions.

Raphael (1483-1520) was the undisputed master of realism. When he painted *Portrait of a Cardinal* (*El Cardenal,* c. 1510), he showed the sly Vatican functionary with a day's growth of beard and an air of superiority, locking eyes with the viewer. The cardinal's slightly turned torso is as big as a statue. Nearby are Raphael's *Holy Family* and other paintings.

Fra Angelico's *The Annunciation* (*La Anunciación,* c. 1426) is in nearby Room 56b. It's half medieval piety, half Renaissance re-

alism. In the crude Garden of Eden scene (on the left), a scrawny, sinful First Couple hovers unrealistically above the foliage, awaiting eviction. The angel's Annunciation to Mary (right side) is more Renaissance, both with its upbeat message (that Jesus will be born to redeem sinners like Adam and Eve) and in the budding photorealism, set beneath 3-D arches. (Still, aren't the receding bars of the porch's ceiling a bit off? Painting three dimensions wasn't that easy.)

Also in Room 56b, the tiny *Dormition of the Virgin (El Transito de la Virgen),* by **Andrea Mantegna** (c. 1431-1506), shows his mastery of Renaissance perspective. The apostles crowd into the room to mourn the last moments of the Virgin Mary's life. The receding floor tiles and open window in the back create the subconscious effect of Mary's soul finding its way out into the serene distance.

• *Find examples of Northern European art, including Dürer, in Room 55b.*

Northern Art

Albrecht Dürer's *Self-Portrait (Autorretrato)*, from 1498, is possibly the first time an artist depicted himself. The artist, age 26, is

German, but he's all dolled up in a fancy Italian hat and permed hair. He'd recently returned from Italy and wanted to impress his country-men with his sophistication. Dürer (1471-1528) wasn't simply vain. He'd grown accustomed, as an artist in Renaissance Italy, to being treat-ed like a prince. Note Dürer's sig-nature, the pyramid-shaped "A. D." (D inside the A), on the windowsill.

Dürer's 1507 panel paintings of Adam and Eve are the first full-size nudes in Northern European art. Like Greek statues, they pose in their separate niches, with three-dimensional, anatomically correct bodies. This was a bold humanist proclamation that the body is good, man is good, and the things of the world are good.

• *Backtrack through Room 56b, and go through Rooms 57b and 57 to Room 58.*

Descent from the Cross (El Descendimiento) by **Rogier van der Weyden** (c. 1399-1464) is a masterpiece. The Flemish painter reveals the psychological drama of this biblical event by placing the characters of real people in a contemporary (1435) scene. The Flemish were masters of detail, as you can see in the cloth, jewels, faces, and even tears. These effects are all enhanced by the artist's choice of oil paint, a relatively new and vibrant medium especially suited to conveying textural realism and intense color. The cre-ative composition suggests that, in losing her son, Mary suffered along with Jesus, which is conveyed by showing their bodies in the same position. Note the realism, especially in the mournful faces, and the gorgeous arc of Mary Magdalene's pose (far right). As the Netherlands was then a part of the Spanish empire, this painting ended up in Madrid.

• *Continue to Room 56a.*

Hieronymus Bosch (c. 1450-1516), in his cryptic triptych *The Garden of Earthly Delights* (*El Jardín de las Delicias,* c. 1505), relates the message that the pleasures of life are fleeting, and we'd better avoid them or we'll wind up in hell.

This is a triptych—a three-paneled altarpiece, with a central image and two hinged outer panels. When the panels are closed, another image is revealed on their back side. All four images work together to teach a religious message. First notice the back side of this otherwise colorful work. It's a black-and-white scene depicting Creation on Day Three—before God added animals and humans to the mix. So, imagine the altarpiece closed. All is mellow. Then open it up, bring on the people, and splash into the colorful *Garden of Earthly Delights.*

On the left is Paradise, showing naked Adam and Eve before original sin. Everything is in its place, with animals behaving vir-

tuously. Innocent Adam and Eve get married, with God himself performing the ceremony.

The central panel is a riot of hedonistic men and women on a perpetual spring break. Men on horseback ride round and round, searching for but never reaching the elusive Fountain of Youth. Others frolic in earth's "Garden," oblivious to where they came from (left) and where they may end up (exit...right).

Now, go to Hell (right panel). It's a burning Dante's Inferno-inspired wasteland where genetic-mutant demons torture sinners. Everyone gets their just desserts, like the glutton who is eaten and re-eaten eternally, the musician strung up on his own harp, and the gamblers with their table forever overturned. In the center, hell

is literally frozen over. A creature with a broken eggshell body hosting a tavern, tree-trunk legs, and a hat featuring a bag-pipe (symbolic of hedonism) stares out—it's the face of Bosch himself.

If you like this Bosch, you'll enjoy the others in this gallery. The table in the center features his *Seven Deadly Sins (Los Pecados Capitales,* late 15th century). Each of the four corners has a theme: death, judgment, paradise, and hell. The fascinating wheel, with Christ in the center, names the sins in Latin (lust, envy, gluttony, and so on), and illustrates each with a vivid scene that works as a slice of 15th-century Dutch life.

Another triptych, *The Hay Wain* (*El Carro de Heno,* c. 1516), hangs nearby. Like *The Garden of Earthly Delights,* and with the same vivid imagery, it teaches morality in what must have been a very effective and frightening way back when Bosch painted it.

Nearby, **Pieter Bruegel** the Elder's (c. 1525-1569) work chronicles the 16th century's violent Catholic-Protestant wars in *The Triumph of Death (El Triunfo de la Muerte).* The painting is one big, chaotic battle, featuring skeletons attacking helpless mortals. Bruegel's message is simple and morbid: No one can escape death.

• *But you can escape this room. Continue through the next few galleries (55a and 55) and into the red lobby. Find the elevators on the right, and go up to level 1. Exiting the elevator, turn left into Room 11. This is one of several rooms with work by Velázquez, but* Las Meninas *is around the corner to the right in the large, lozenge-shaped Room 12.*

Spanish Masters

Diego Velázquez (vel-LAHTH-keth, 1599-1660) was the photojournalist of court painters, capturing the Spanish king and his court in formal portraits that take on aspects of a candid snapshot. Room 12 is filled with the portraits Velázquez was called on to produce.

Kings and princes prance like Roman emperors. Get up close and notice that his remarkably detailed costumes are nothing but a few messy splotches of paint—the proto-Impressionism Velázquez helped pioneer.

The room's centerpiece, and perhaps the most important painting in the museum, is Velázquez's *Maids of Honor* (*Las Meninas,* c. 1656). It's a peek at nannies caring for Princess Margarita and, at the same time, a behind-the-scenes look at Velázquez at work. One hot summer day in 1656, Velázquez (at left, with paintbrush and Dalí moustache) stands at his easel and stares out at the people he's painting—the king and queen. They would have been standing about where we are, and we see only their reflection in the mirror at the back of the room. Their daughter (blonde hair, in center) watches her parents being painted, joined by her servants *(meninas),* dwarves, and the family dog. At that very moment, a man happens to pass by the doorway at back and pauses to look in. Why's he there? Probably just to give the painting more depth.

This frozen moment is lit by the window on the right, splitting the room into bright and shaded planes that recede into the distance. The main characters look right at us, making us part of the scene, seemingly able to walk around, behind, and among the characters. Notice the exquisitely painted mastiff.

If you stand in the center of the room, the 3-D effect is most striking. This is art come to life.

• *Facing this painting, leave to the left and go back into Room 11.*

Look around this gallery and see how Velázquez enjoyed capturing light—and capturing the moment. *The Feast of Bacchus* (*Los*

Borrachos, c. 1628) is a cell-phone snapshot in a blue-collar bar, with a couple of peasants mugging for a photo-op with a Greek god—Bacchus, the god of wine. This was an early work, before Velázquez got his court-painter gig. A personal homage to the hardworking farmers enjoying the fruit of their labor, it shows how Velázquez had a heart for real people and believed they deserved portraits, too. Notice the almost-sacramental presence of the ultrarealistic bowl of wine in the center, as Bacchus, with the honest gut,

crowns a fellow hedonist.

• *Backtrack through the big gallery with* Las Meninas *to Room 14.*

Velázquez's boss, King Philip IV, had an affair, got caught, and repented by commissioning the *Crucified Christ* (*Cristo Crucificado,* c. 1632). Christ hangs his head, humbly accepting his punishment. Philip would have been left to stare at the slowly dripping blood, contemplating how long Christ had to suffer to atone for Philip's sins. This is an interesting death scene. There's no anguish, no tension, no torture. Light seems to emanate from Jesus as if nothing else matters. The crown of thorns and the cloth wrapped around his waist are particularly vivid. Above it all, a sign reads in three languages: "*Jesus of Nazareth, King of the Jews.*"

• *The nearby rooms (16 and 17) are filled with Murillo paintings. Look for a couple of his immaculately conceived virgins.*

Bartolomé Murillo (1618-1682) put a human face on the abstract Catholic doctrine that Mary was conceived and born free of original sin. Murillo painted several versions of the *Immaculate Conception,* of which the Prado has five that sometimes rotate. *The Immaculate Conception of Los Venerables* (*La Inmaculada Concepción de los Venerables,* c. 1678) hangs in Room 16, and another version is installed in Room 17. Murillo's "immaculate" virgin floats in a cloud of Ivory Soap cleanliness, radiating youth and wholesome goodness. She wears the usual colors of the Virgin Mary—white for purity and blue for divinity. Sweet and escapist, Murillo's work was a hit, and it must have been very comforting to the wretched

people of post-plague Sevilla (his hometown was hit hard in 1647-1652).
• *Return to the main gallery (Rooms 28 and 29) for lots of fleshy excitement, courtesy of Peter Paul Rubens.*

Northern Baroque

A native of Flanders, **Peter Paul Rubens** (1577-1640) painted Baroque-style art meant to play on the emotions, titillate the senses,

and carry you away. His paintings surge with Baroque energy and ripple with waves of figures. Surveying his big, boisterous canvases, you'll notice his trademarks: sex, violence, action, emotion, bright colors, and ample bodies, with the wind machine set on full. Gods are melodramatic, and nymphs flee half-human predators. Rubens painted the most beautiful women of his day—well-fed, no tan lines, squirt-gun breasts, and very sexy.

Rubens' *The Three Graces* (*Las Tres Gracias,* c. 1630-1635) celebrates cellulite. The ample, glowing bodies intertwine as the women exchange meaningful glances. The Grace at the left is Rubens' young second wife, Hélène Fourment, who shows up regularly in his paintings.

• *From the main gallery with the Rubens, look to the near end of the hall, where Goya's royal portraits hang. We'll end up there. But first, head the other way to Titian and El Greco. Titians line the main gallery, and the El Grecos are in Rooms 8b, 9b, and 10b.*

Spanish Mystic

El Greco (1541-1614) was born in Greece (his name is Spanish for "The Greek"), trained in Venice, then settled in Toledo—60 miles from Madrid. His paintings are like Byzantine icons drenched in Venetian color and fused in the fires of Spanish mysticism. The El Greco paintings displayed here rotate, but they all glow with his unique style.

In *Christ Carrying the Cross* (*Cristo Abrazado a la Cruz*, c. 1602), Jesus accepts his fate, trudging toward death with blood running down his neck. He hugs the cross and directs his gaze along the cross-bar. His upturned eyes (sparkling with a streak of white paint) lock onto his next stop—heaven.

The Adoration of the Shepherds (*La Adoración de los Pastores*, c. 1614), originally painted for El Greco's own burial chapel in Toledo, has the artist's typical two-tiered composition—heaven above, earth below. The long, skinny shepherds are stretched unnaturally in between, flickering like flames toward heaven.

The Nobleman with His Hand on His Chest (*El Caballero de la Mano al Pecho*, c. 1580) shows an elegant and somewhat arrogant man whose hand has the middle fingers touching—El Greco's trademark way of expressing elegance (or was it the 16th-century symbol for "Live long and prosper"?). The signature is on the right in faint Greek letters—"Doménikos Theotokópoulos," El Greco's real name.

• *Return to the main gallery. Spot several Titian paintings in Rooms 25-26, and meander through the Italian wing, including Venetian portraits in Rooms 40-44 (this collection may have moved into the main gallery—Rooms 24-27—by the time you visit). Continue down the main gallery to the center, under the dome (and opposite* Las Meninas*), where Charles I sits royally on horseback.*

Venetian Painter to the Court

Spain's Golden Age kings Charles I (a.k.a. Charles V) and Philip II were both staunch Catholics, but that didn't stop them from amassing this sometimes surprisingly racy collection. Both kings sat for portraits by the Venetian master **Titian** (c. 1485-1576).

In *The Emperor Charles V at Mühlberg* (*Carlos V en la Batalla de Mühlberg*, 1548), the king rears on his horse, raises his lance, and rides out to crush an army of Lutherans. Charles, having inherited many kingdoms and baronies through his family connections, was the world's most powerful man in the 1500s. (You can see the suit of armor depicted in the painting in the Royal Palace.)

In contrast (just to the left), Charles I's son, *Philip II* (*Felipe II*, c. 1550-1551), looks pale, suspicious, and lonely—a scholarly and complex figure. He built the austere, monastic palace at El Escorial, but also indulged himself with Titian's bevy of Renaissance Playmates—a sampling of which is here in the Prado.

These are the faces of the Counter-Reformation. While father and son ruled very differently, both had underbites, a product of royal inbreeding (which Titian painted...but very delicately).

• *Now walk to the far end of the main gallery and enter the round Room 32, where you'll see royal portraits by Goya. The museum's exciting Goya collection is on three levels at this end of the building: classic Goya (royal portraits and* La Maja*), on this floor; early cartoons, upstairs; and his dark and political work, downstairs.*

Painter of Kings and Demons

Follow the complex **Francisco de Goya** (1746-1828) through the stages of his life—from dutiful court painter, to political rebel and scandal maker, to the disillusioned genius of his "black paintings."

In the group portrait *The Family of Charles IV* (*La Familia de Carlos IV,* 1800), the royals are all decked out in their Sunday best.

Goya himself stands at his easel to the far left, painting the court (a tribute to Velázquez in *Las Meninas*) and revealing the shallowness beneath the fancy trappings. Charles, with his ridiculous hairpiece and goofy smile, was a vacuous, henpecked husband. His toothless yet domineering queen upstages him, arrogantly stretching her swanlike neck. The other adults, with their bland faces, are bug-eyed with stupidity.

Surrounding you in this same room are other portraits of the king and queen. Also notice the sketch paintings, quick studies done with the subjects posing for Goya. He used these for reference to complete his larger, more finished canvases.

• *Exit to the right across a small hallway and enter Room 36, where you'll find Goya's most scandalous work.*

Rumors flew that Goya was fooling around with the vivacious Duchess of Alba, who may have been the model for two

similar paintings, **Nude Maja** (*La Maja Desnuda,* c. 1800) and **Clothed Maja** (*La Maja Vestida,* c. 1808). A *maja* was a trendy, working-class girl. Whether she's a duchess or a *maja*, Goya painted a naked lady—an actual person rather than some mythic Venus. And that was enough to risk incurring the wrath of the Inquisition. The nude stretches in a Titian-esque pose to display her charms, the pale body with realis-

MADRID

tic pubic hair highlighted by cool green sheets. (Notice the artist's skillful rendering of the transparent fabric on the pillow.) According to a believable legend, the two paintings were displayed in a double frame, with the *Clothed Maja* sliding over the front to hide the *Nude Maja* from Inquisitive minds.

• *Find the nearby staircase and elevator, and head up to level 2 to Rooms 85 and 90–94 for more Goya.*

These rooms display Goya's **designs for tapestries** (known as "cartoons") for nobles' palaces. As you stroll around, the scenes

make it clear that, while revolution was brewing in America and France, Spain's lords and ladies were playing, blissfully ignorant of the changing times. Dressed in their "Goya-style" attire, they're picnicking, dancing, flying kites, playing paddleball and Blind Man's Bluff, or just relaxing in the sun—as in the well-known *The Parasol* (*El Quitasol*, Room 85).

• *For more Goya, take the stairs or elevator down to level 0. Room 66 leads into Goya's final paintings, with a darker edge. But first go to Room 65, which takes you to powerful military scenes.*

Goya became a political liberal, a champion of democracy. He was crushed when France's hero of the French Revolution, Napo-

leon, morphed into a tyrant and invaded Spain. In the **Second of May, 1808** (*El 2 de Mayo de 1808*, 1814), Madrid's citizens rise up to protest the occupation in Puerta del Sol, and the French send in their dreaded Egyptian mercenaries. They plow through the dense tangle of Madrileños, who have nowhere to run. The next day, the **Third of May, 1808** (*El 3 de Mayo de 1808*, 1814), the French rounded up ringleaders and executed them. The colorless firing squad—a faceless machine of death—mows them down, and they fall in bloody, tangled heaps. Goya throws a harsh prison-yard floodlight on the main victim, who spreads his arms Christ-like to ask, "Why?"

Politically, Goya was split—he was a Spaniard, but he knew France was leading Europe into the modern age. His art, while political, has no Spanish or French flags. It's a universal comment on the horror of war. Many consider Goya the last classical and first modern painter...the first painter with a social conscience.

• *About-face to the "black paintings" in Room 67.*

Depressed and deaf from syphilis, Goya retired to his small home and smeared its walls with his "**black paintings**"—dark in color and in mood. During this period in his life, Goya would paint his nightmares...literally. The style is considered Romantic—emphasizing emotion over beauty—but it foreshadows 20th-century Surrealism with its bizarre imagery, expressionistic and thick brushstrokes, and cynical outlook.

Stepping into Room 67, you are surrounded by art from Goya's dark period. These paintings are the actual murals from the walls of his house, transferred onto canvas. Imagine this in your living room. Goya painted what he felt with a radical technique unburdened by reality—a century before his time. And he painted without being paid for it—perhaps the first great paintings done not for hire or for sale. We know frustratingly little about these works because Goya wrote nothing about them.

Dark forces convened continually in Goya's dining room, where *The Great He-Goat* (*El Aquelarre/El Gran Cabrón*, c. 1820-1823) hung. The witches, who look like skeletons, swirl in a frenzy around a dark, Satanic goat in monk's clothing who presides over the obscene rituals. The black goat represents the Devil and stokes the frenzy of his wild-eyed subjects. Amid this adoration and lust, a noble lady (far right) folds her hands primly in her lap ("I thought this was a Tupperware party!"). Or, perhaps it's a pep rally for her execution, maybe inspired by the chaos that accompanied Plaza Mayor executions. Nobody knows for sure.

In *Fight to the Death with Clubs* (*Duelo a Garrotazos*, c. 1820-1823), two giants stand face-to-face, buried up to their knees, and flail at each other with clubs. It's a standoff between superpowers in the never-ending cycle of war—a vision of a tough time when people on the streets would kill for a piece of bread.

In *Saturn* (*Saturno*, c. 1820-1823), the king of the Roman gods—fearful that his progeny would overthrow him—eats one of his offspring. Saturn, also known as Cronus (Time), may symbolize how time devours us all. Either way, the painting brings new meaning to the term "child's portion."

The Drowning Dog (*Perro Semihundido*, c. 1820-1823) is, according to some, the hinge between classical art and modern art. The dog, so full of feeling and sadness, is being swallowed by quicksand...much as, to Goya, the modern age was overtaking a more classical era. And look closely at the dog. It also can be seen as a turning point for Goya. Perhaps he's bottomed out—he's been overwhelmed by depression, but his spirit has survived. With the portrait of this dog, color is returning.

• *Head back to Room 66, and look on the right.*

The last painting we have by Goya is *The Milkmaid of Bordeaux* (*La Lechera de Burdeos,* c. 1827). Somehow, Goya pulled out of his depression and moved to France, where he lived until his death at 82. While painting as an old man, color returned to his palette. His social commentary, his passion for painting what he felt (more than what he was hired to do), and, as you see here, the freedom of his brushstrokes explain why many consider Francesco de Goya to be the first modern artist.

• *There's lots more to the Prado, but there's also lots more to Madrid. The choice is yours.*

▲▲Thyssen-Bornemisza Museum (Museo del Arte Thyssen-Bornemisza)

Locals call this stunning museum simply the Thyssen (TEE-sun). It displays the impressive collection that Baron Thyssen (a wealthy German married to a former Miss Spain) sold to Spain for $350 million. The museum offers a unique chance to enjoy the sweep of all of art history—including a good sampling of the "isms" of the 20th century—in one collection. It's basically minor works by major artists and major works by minor artists. (Major works by major artists are in the Prado.) But art lovers appreciate how the good baron's art complements the Prado's collection by filling in where the Prado is weak—such as Impressionism, which is the Thyssen's forte.

After purchasing your ticket, continue down the wide main hall past larger-than-life paintings of former monarchs Juan Carlos I and Sofía, and then paintings of the baron (who died in 2002) and his art-collecting baroness, Carmen. At the info desk, pick up a museum map. Each of the three floors is divided into two separate areas: the permanent collection (numbered rooms) and additions from the baroness since the 1980s (lettered rooms). Ascend to the top floor and work your way down, taking a delightful walk through art history. Visit the rooms on each floor in numerical order, from Primitive Italian (Room 1) to Surrealism and Pop Art (Room 45-47).

Cost and Hours: €10, up to €11 more for optional special exhibits, free for kids under age 12, free on Mon; open Mon 12:00-16:00, Tue-Sun 10:00-19:00, Sat until 21:00 in summer (exhibits only), last entry 45 minutes before closing; audioguide-€4; kitty-corner from the Prado at Paseo del Prado 8 in Palacio de Villahermosa (Metro: Banco de España); tel. 902-760-511, www.museothyssen.org.

Services: The museum has free baggage storage (bags must fit through a small x-ray machine), a cafeteria and restaurant, and a shop/bookstore.

Connecting the Thyssen and Reina Sofía: If you're heading to the Reina Sofía and you're tired, hail a cab at the gate to zip straight there, or take bus #27, which stops in the square with the Neptune fountain, in front of the Starbucks (ride to the end of Paseo del Prado, get off at the McDonald's, and cross the street, going away from the Royal Botanical Garden, to Plaza Sánchez Bustillo and the museum).

▲▲▲Centro de Arte Reina Sofía

Home to Picasso's *Guernica,* the Reina Sofía is one of Europe's most enjoyable modern art museums. Its exceptional collection of

20th-century art is housed in what was Madrid's first public hospital. The focus is on 20th-century Spanish artists—Picasso, Dalí, Miró, Gris, and Tàpies—but you'll also find plenty of works by Kandinsky, Braque, and many other giants of modern art.

The curator, who has a passion for cinema, has paired paintings with films from the same decade, which play continuously in nearby rooms. This provides a fascinating insight into the social context that inspired the art of Spain's tumultuous 20th century. Those with an appetite for modern and contemporary art can spend several delightful hours in this museum.

Cost: €8 (includes most temporary exhibits), €3 if you're under 18 or over 65, free Mon and Wed-Sat 19:00-21:00, Sun 15:00-19:00 (free times are often crowded, and you must pick up a ticket).

Hours: Mon and Wed-Sat 10:00-21:00, Sun 10:00-19:00 (fourth floor not accessible Sun after 15:00), closed Tue.

Getting There: It's a block from the Atocha Metro stop, on Plaza Sánchez Bustillo (at Calle de Santa Isabel 52). In the Metro station, follow signs for the Reina Sofía exit. Emerging from the Metro, walk straight ahead a half-block and look for an opening between the group of buildings. You'll see the tall, exterior glass elevators that flank the museum's main entrance.

A second entrance in the newer section of the building sometimes has shorter lines, especially during the museum's free hours.

Facing the glass elevators, walk left around the old building to the large gates of the red-and-black Nouvel Building.

Information: Tel. 917-741-000, www.museoreinasofia.es.

Tours: The hardworking audioguide is €4.

Services: Bag storage is free. The *librería* just outside the Nouvel wing has a larger selection of Picasso and Surrealist reproductions than the main gift shop at the entrance.

Photography: Photos are not allowed in the room containing *Guernica* or in the surrounding rooms. Otherwise, photos without flash are OK.

Cuisine Art: The museum's café (a long block around the left from the main entrance) is a standout for its tasty cuisine. The square immediately in front of the museum is ringed by fine places for a simple meal or drink. My favorite is **El Brillante,** a classic dive offering pricey tapas and baguette sandwiches. But everyone comes for the fried squid sandwiches (evidenced by the older *señoras* with mouthfuls of *calamares*). Sit at the simple bar or at an outdoor table (long hours daily, two entrances—one on Plaza Sánchez Bustillo, the other at Plaza del Emperador Carlos V 8, tel. 915-286-966). Also nearby is my favorite strip of tapas bars, on Calle de Jesús.

➲ Self-Guided Tour

Pick up a free map and use the good information sheets to supplement this tour.

The permanent collection is divided into three groups: art from 1900 to 1945 (second floor), art from 1945 to 1968 (fourth floor), and art from 1962 to 1982 (adjoining Nouvel wing, which also has space for bigger installations). Temporary exhibits are on the first and third floors.

While the collection is roughly chronological, it's displayed thematically. The second-floor grand hallway leads around a courtyard connecting a series of rooms, each clearly labeled with a theme. For a good first visit, ride the fancy glass elevator to level 2 and tour that floor clockwise (Goya, Surrealism, Cubism, Picasso's *Guernica*), and then finish with post-WWII art on level 4.

• *Begin in Room 201, with examples of...*

Proto-Modern Goya

The installations at many museums can leave you scratching your head in frustration. But the wonderful curator of the Reina Sofía insightfully begins your look at modern art with Goya engravings. That's because Goya is a proto-modernist—the first painter with a social conscience, the first to show inner feelings, and the first to deal with social reality. He painted because he had something to say, not just to get a paycheck.

• *Browse through the next rooms, whose underlying theme is the conflict between tradition (the powerful Church) and progress (social modernization). Find your way to Room 205 and...*

Surrealism and Salvador Dalí

In 1914 a generation marched enthusiastically into combat, believing the Great War would be the "war to end all wars." Many artists embraced this fight, volunteered to serve, and died for the cause. But when it was over, it was clear: World War I brought no lasting change. Frustrated, many survivors turned their backs on society.

In the postwar years, a class of artists abandoned the outer world and looked inside (with inspiration from Freud). They painted mindscapes rather than landscapes. They had learned that reality is deeper than what you first "see." These were the Surrealists. To "see" their art, you need to vary your position: your physical perspective and your mental perspective. See it happy, sad, before coffee, after coffee.

In the Dalí room, you'll see the artist's distinct, Surrealist, melting-object style. Dalí places familiar items in a stark landscape, creating an eerie effect. Figures morph into misplaced faces and body parts. Background and foreground play mind games—is it an animal (seen one way) or a man's face? A waterfall or a pair of legs? It's a wide shot...no, it's a close-up. Look long at paintings like Dalí's *Endless Enigma* (1938) and *The Invisible Man* (c. 1933); they take different viewers to different places.

The Great Masturbator (1929) is psychologically exhausting, depicting in its Surrealism a lonely, highly sexual genius in love with his muse, Gala (while she was still married to a French poet). This is the first famous Surrealist painting.

During this productive period, Dalí was working on the classic Surrealist film *Un Chien Andalou* (*The Andalusian Dog*, 1928) with his collaborator Luis Buñuel (the film plays in Room 203). Both men were members of the Generation of '27, a group of nonconformist Spanish bohemians whose creative interests had a huge influence on art and literature in their era.

• *Skirt back around the courtyard to find Room 210 and...*

Cubism

Cubism was born in the first decade of the 20th century. You could make a good case that the changes in society in the year 1900 were more profound than those we lived through in 2000. Trains and cars brought speed to life. Electricity brought light. Einstein introduced us to abstract ideas. Photography captured reality. And art broke away. At the turn of the century there were two ways to express art: line (Picasso) and color (Matisse)—but it was still in two dimensions. With Cubism, three dimensions are shown in two. Imagine walking around a statue to take in all the angles, and then attempting to put it on a 2-D plane. With Cubism, everyone sees things differently. To appreciate it, take your time and free your imagination.

Room 210 shows the birth of Cubism—a movement in which Spaniards were very much at the forefront (with works by Picasso, Braque, Léger, and Gris). To literally see a 2-D picture plane leap to life, watch the Lumière brothers' early film *Partie d'Écarté* (c. 1898).

• *In Room 206, you come to what is likely the reason for your visit...*

Picasso's *Guernica*

Perhaps the single most impressive piece of art in Spain is Pablo Picasso's *Guernica* (1937). The monumental canvas—one of Europe's must-see sights—is not only a piece of art but a piece of history, capturing the horror of modern war in a modern style.

While it's become a timeless classic representing all war, it was born in response to a specific conflict—the civil war (1936-1939), which pitted the democratically elected Second Republican government against the fascist general Francisco Franco. Franco won and ended up ruling Spain with an iron fist for the next 36 years. At the time Franco cemented his power, *Guernica* was touring internationally as part of a fund-raiser for the Republican cause. With Spain's political situation deteriorating and World War II looming, Picasso in 1939 named New York's Museum of Modern Art as the depository for the work. It was only after Franco's death, in 1975, that *Guernica* ended its decades of exile. In 1981 the painting finally arrived in Spain (where it had never before been), and it now stands as Spain's national piece of art.

Guernica—The Bombing: On April 26, 1937, Guernica—a Basque market town in northern Spain and an important Republican center—was the target of the world's first saturation-bombing raid on civilians. Franco gave permission to his fascist confederate Hitler to use the town as a guinea pig to try out Germany's new air force. The raid leveled the town, causing destruction that was unheard of at the time (though by 1944 it would be commonplace).

News of the bombing reached Picasso in Paris, where coincidentally he was just beginning work on a painting commission awarded by the Republican government. Picasso scrapped his earlier plans and immediately set to work sketching scenes of the destruction as he imagined it. In a matter of weeks he put these bomb-shattered shards together into a large mural (286 square feet). For the first time, the world could see the destructive force of the rising fascist movement—a prelude to World War II.

MADRID

Guernica—**The Painting:** The bombs are falling, shattering the quiet village. ❶ A woman looks up at the sky (far right), ❷ horses scream (center), and ❸ a man falls from a horse and dies, while ❹ a wounded woman drags herself through the streets. She tries to escape, but her leg is too thick, dragging her down, like trying to run from something in a nightmare. ❺ On the left, a bull—a symbol of Spain—ponders it all, watching over ❻ a mother and her dead baby...a modern *pietà*. ❼ A woman in the center sticks her head out to see what's going on. The whole scene is lit from above by the ❽ stark light of a bare bulb. Picasso's painting threw a light on the brutality of Hitler and Franco, and suddenly the whole world was watching.

Picasso's abstract, Cubist style reinforces the message. It's as if he'd picked up the shattered shards and pasted them onto a canvas. The black-and-white tones are as gritty as the black-and-white newspaper photos that reported the bombing. The drab colors create a depressing, almost nauseating mood.

Picasso chose images with universal symbolism, making the work a commentary on all wars. Picasso himself said that the central horse, with the spear in its back, symbolizes humanity succumbing to brute force. The fallen rider's arm is severed and his sword is broken, more symbols of defeat. The bull, normally a proud symbol of strength and independence, is impotent and frightened. Between the bull and the horse, the faint dove of peace can do nothing but cry.

The bombing of Guernica—like the entire civil war—was an exercise in brutality. As one side captured a town, it might systematically round up every man, old and young—including priests—line them up, and shoot them in revenge for atrocities by the other side.

Thousands of people attended the Paris exhibition, and *Guernica* caused an immediate sensation. They could see the horror of modern war technology, the vain struggle of the Spanish Republicans, and the cold indifference of the fascist war machine. Picasso vowed never to return to Spain while Franco ruled (the dictator outlived him).

With each passing year, the canvas seemed more and more prophetic—honoring not just the hundreds or thousands who died in Guernica, but also the estimated 500,000 victims of Spain's bitter civil war and the 55 million worldwide who perished in World War II. Picasso put a human face on what we now call "collateral damage."

• After seeing Guernica, view the additional exhibits that put the painting in its social context.

Other Picasso Exhibits

On the back wall on the *Guernica* room is a line of **photos** showing the evolution of the painting, from Picasso's first concept to the final mural. The photos were taken in his Paris studio by Dora Maar, Picasso's mistress-du-jour (and whose portrait by Picasso hangs nearby). Notice how his work evolved from the defiant fist in early versions to a broken sword with a flower.

The room behind *Guernica* contains **studies** Picasso did for the painting. These studies are filled with motifs that turn up in the final canvas—iron-nail tears, weeping women, and screaming horses. Picasso returned to these images in his work for the rest of his life. He believed that everyone struggles internally with aspects of the horse and bull: rationality and brutality, humanity and animalism. The Minotaur—half-man and half-bull—powerfully captures Picasso's poet/rapist vision of man. Having lived through the brutality of the age—World War I, the Spanish Civil War, and World War II—his outlook is understandable.

In the far end of this hall, you'll also find a **model of the Spanish Pavilion** at the 1937 Paris exposition where *Guernica* was first displayed (look inside to see Picasso's work). Picasso originally toyed with painting an allegory on the theme of the artist's studio for the expo. But the bombing of Guernica jolted him into the realization that Spain was a country torn by war. Thanks to *Guernica*, the pavilion became a vessel for propaganda and a fund-raising tool against Franco.

Nearby the Spanish Pavilion, you'll see posters and political cartoons that are pro-communist and anti-Franco. Made the same year as *Guernica* and the year after, these touch on timeless themes related to rich elites, industrialists, agricultural reform, and the military industrial complex versus the common man, as well as promoting autonomy for Catalunya and the Basque Country.

The remaining rooms display pieces from contemporary artists reacting to the conflict of the time, whether through explicit commentary or through new, innovative styles inspired by the changing political and social culture.

• Head up to level 4, where the permanent collection continues.

Post-WWII Art

After World War II, the center of the art world moved from Paris to New York City. Spain was ruled by a dictatorship, and the avant-garde could not be so *avant*. The organizing theme in this part of the museum is "Art in a Divided World." On this floor, especially, you'll want to take full advantage of the English information sheets in each room and the narration provided by your audioguide.

You'll see Kandinsky as a bridge into abstract art and the Abstract Expressionism of Jackson Pollock and company. Room 419 is especially interesting, with late works by Picasso and Miró (from the 1960s and 1970s). On this floor, you can see photographs and watch films documenting Spain's slow recovery from its devastating civil war. The physical and psychological damage of the war weighed on Spain for decades afterward.

• *End your visit in the...*

Nouvel Wing

The newest wing of the museum features art from the 1960s through the 1980s, with a thematic focus on the complexity and plurality of modern times. While these galleries have fewer household names, the pieces displayed demonstrate the many aesthetic directions of more recent modern art.

NEAR THE PRADO (AND BEYOND)

Several other worthy sights are located in and around the museum neighborhood. This is also where my self-guided bus tour along Paseo de la Castellana to the modern skyscraper part of Madrid starts.

▲Retiro Park (Parque del Buen Retiro)

Once the private domain of royalty, this majestic park has been a favorite of Madrid's commoners since Charles III decided to share it with his subjects in the late 18th century. Siesta in this 300-acre green-and-breezy escape from the city. At midday on Saturday and Sunday, the area around the lake becomes a street carnival, with jugglers, puppeteers, and lots of local color. These peaceful gardens offer great picnicking and people-watching (closes at dusk). From the Retiro Metro stop, walk to the big lake (El Estanque), where you can rent a rowboat. Past the lake, a grand boulevard of statues leads to the Prado.

▲Royal Botanical Garden (Real Jardín Botánico)

After your Prado visit, you can take a lush and fragrant break in this sculpted park. Wander among trees from around the world, originally gathered by—who else?—the enlightened King Charles III. This garden was established when the Prado's building housed the natural science museum. A flier in English explains that this is actually more than a park—it's a museum of plants.

Cost and Hours: €3, daily 10:00-21:00, shorter hours off-season, last entry 30 minutes before closing, entrance is opposite the Prado's Murillo/south entry, Plaza de Murillo 2, tel. 914-203-017.

▲Naval Museum (Museo Naval)

This museum tells the story of Spain's navy, from 1492 to today, in a plush and fascinating-to-boat-lovers exhibit. Given Spain's importance in maritime history, there's quite a story to tell. Because this is a military facility, you'll need to show your passport or driver's license to get in. A good English brochure is available.

Cost and Hours: €3, Tue-Sun 10:00-19:00, until 15:00 in Aug, closed Mon, a block north of the Prado, across boulevard from Thyssen-Bornemisza Museum, Paseo del Prado 5, tel. 915-238-789.

CaixaForum

Across the street from the Prado and Royal Botanical Garden, this impressive exhibit hall has sleek architecture and an outdoor hanging garden—a bushy wall festooned with greens designed by a French landscape artist. The forum, funded by La Caixa Bank, features world-class art exhibits—generally 20th-century art, well-described in English and changing three times a year. Ride the elevator to the top, where you'll find a café with a daily €13 fixed-price meal and sperm-like lamps swarming down from the ceiling; from here, explore your way down.

Cost and Hours: €4, daily 10:00-20:00, audioguide-€2, Paseo del Prado 36, tel. 913-307-300.

Palacio de Cibeles

This former post-office headquarters was recently converted to a cultural center—featuring mostly empty exhibition halls, an auditorium, and public hang-out spaces—and renamed the Cibeles CentroCentro of Culture and Citizenship. (Say that five times fast!) The temporary exhibits can be skipped. The real attraction lies in the gorgeous 360-degree rooftop views from the eighth-floor observation deck (ticket office outside to the right of the main entrance). Visit the recommended sixth-floor Restaurante Palacio de Cibeles and bar for similar views from its two terraces.

Cost and Hours: €2 elevator ride to observation deck, visiting the Palacio itself is free—take advantage of its air-conditioning and free Wi-Fi; building open Tue-Sun 10:00-20:00, terrace visits possible every half hour 10:30-13:30 & 16:00-19:00, closed Mon, Plaza de Cibeles 1, tel. 914-800-008, www.centrocentro.org.

▲▲National Archaeological Museum (Museo Arqueológico Nacional/MAN)

Reopened in 2014 after a major renovation, this museum is like a little British Museum. You'll follow a chronological walk through the story of Iberia. With a well-curated, rich collection of artifacts and tasteful multimedia displays, the museum shows off the wonders of each age: Celtic pre-Roman, Roman, a fine and rare Visigothic section, Moorish, Romanesque, and beyond. A highlight is the Lady of Elche (Room 13), a prehistoric Iberian female bust and a symbol of Spanish archaeology. You may also find underwhelming replica artwork from northern Spain's Altamira Caves (big on bison), giving you a faded peek at the skill of the cave artists who created the originals 14,000 years ago.

Cost and Hours: €3, free on Sat 14:00-20:00 and all day Sun; open Tue-Sat 9:30-20:00, Sun 9:30-15:00, closed Mon; €2 multimedia guide (also available as mobile app—MAN Museo Arqueológico Nacional); 20-minute walk north of the Prado at Calle Serrano 13, Metro: Serrano or Colón, tel. 915-777-912, www.man.es.

Royal Tapestry Factory (Real Fábrica de Tapices)

Take this factory tour for a look at traditional tapestry-making. You'll also have the chance to order a tailor-made tapestry (starting at $10,000).

Cost and Hours: €4, by tour only, tours depart on the half-hour—some in English; open Mon-Fri 10:00-14:00, closed Sat-Sun and Aug, last entry at 13:30; south of Retiro Park at Calle Fuenterrabia 2, Metro: Menendez Pelayo, take Gutenberg exit, tel. 914-340-550, www.realfabricadetapices.com.

▲Museum of the Americas (Museo de América)

Thousands of pre-Columbian and colonial artworks and artifacts make up the bulk of this worthwhile museum, though it offers few English explanations. Covering the cultures of the Americas (North and South), its exhibits focus on language, religion, and art, and provide a new perspective on the cultures of our own hemisphere. Highlights include one of only four surviving Mayan codices (ancient books) and a section about the voyages of the Spanish explorers, with their fantastical imaginings of mythical creatures awaiting them in the New World.

Cost and Hours: €3, free on Sun; open Tue-Sat 9:30-15:00, Thu until 19:00, Sun 10:00-15:00, closed Mon; Avenida de los Reyes Católicos 6, Metro: Moncloa, tel. 915-492-641, museodeamerica.mcu.es.

Getting There: The museum is a 15-minute walk from the Moncloa Metro stop: Take the Calle de Isaac Peral exit, cross Plaza de Moncloa, and veer right to Calle de Fernández de los Ríos. Follow that street (toward the shiny Faro de Moncloa tower), and turn left on Avenida de los Reyes Católicos. Head around the base of the tower, which stands at the museum's entrance.

▲Clothing Museum (Museo del Traje)

This museum shows the history of clothing from the 18th century until today. In a cool and air-conditioned chronological sweep, the museum's one floor of exhibits includes regional ethnic costumes, a look at how bullfighting and the French influenced styles, accessories through the ages, and Spanish flappers. The only downside of this marvelous, modern museum is that it's a long way from anything else of interest.

Cost and Hours: €3, free on Sat 14:30-19:00 and all day Sun; open Tue-Sat 9:30-19:00, Thu until 22:30 in July-Aug, Sun 10:00-15:00, closed Mon, last entry 30 minutes before closing; Avenida de Juan Herrera 2; Metro: Moncloa and a longish walk, bus #46, or taxi; tel. 915-497-150, museodeltraje.mcu.es.

▲Hermitage of San Antonio de la Florida (Ermita de San Antonio de la Florida)

In this simple little Neoclassical chapel from the 1790s, Francisco de Goya's tomb stares up at a splendid cupola filled with his own proto-Impressionist frescoes. He used the same unique technique that he employed for his "black paintings" (described earlier, under the Prado Museum listing). Use the mirrors to enjoy the drama and energy he infused into this marvelously restored masterpiece.

Cost and Hours: Free, Tue-Sun 9:30-20:00, closed Mon, Glorieta de San Antonio de la Florida 5; Metro: Príncipe Pío, then eight-minute walk down Paseo de San Antonio de la Florida; tel. 915-420-722, www.madrid.es/ermita.

Temple of Debod (Templo de Debod)

In 1968, Egypt gave Spain its own ancient temple. It was a gift of the Egyptian government, which was grateful for the Spanish dictator Franco's help in rescuing monuments that had been threatened by the rising Nile waters above the Aswan Dam. Consequently, Madrid is the only place I can think of in Europe where you can actually wander through an intact original Egyptian temple—complete with fine carved reliefs from 200 B.C. Set in a romantic park that locals love for its great city views (especially at sunset), the temple—as well as its art—is well-described. The much-touted but uninspiring "grand Madrid view" only causes me to wonder why anyone would build a city here.

Cost and Hours: Free; Tue-Fri 10:00-14:00 & 18:00-20:00 in summer, shorter hours off-season, closed Mon year-round; last entry 15 minutes before closing; in Parque de Montaña, north of the Royal Palace, tel. 913-667-415, www.madrid.es (search for "Templo de Debod").

Sorolla Museum (Museo Sorolla)

Painter Joaquín Sorolla (1863-1923) is known for his portraits, landscapes, and use of light. It's a relaxing experience to stroll through the rooms of his former house and studio, especially to see the lazy beach scenes of his hometown, Valencia. The museum is best experienced when daylight streams through the house, which is how the artist intended for people to view his work. Take a break after your visit to reflect in the small garden in front of his house.

Cost and Hours: €3, free on Sat 14:00-20:00 and all day Sun; open Tue-Sat 9:30-20:00, Sun 10:00-15:00, closed Mon; €5 refundable deposit for use of museum guidebook, audioguide-€2; General Martínez Campos 37, Metro: Iglesia, tel. 913-101-584, museosorolla.mcu.es.

Madrid History Museum (Museo de Historia de Madrid)

This museum covers the history of Madrid in old paintings and interesting models. The entrance features a fine Baroque door by architect Pedro de Ribera, with a depiction of St. James the Moor-Slayer. The museum has been undergoing major renovations, though all rooms should reopen by the time you visit (but smart to confirm with the TI or call before you make the trip).

Cost and Hours: Free, Tue-Sun 11:00-14:00 & 16:00-19:00, closed Mon, Calle de Fuencarral 78, Metro: Tribunal, tel. 917-011-863.

Experiences in Madrid

▲▲Self-Guided Bus Tour: Paseo de la Castellana

Tourists risk leaving Madrid without ever seeing the modern "Manhattan" side of town. But it's easy to find. From the museum neighborhood, bus #27 makes the trip straight north along Paseo del Prado and then Paseo de la Castellana, through the no-nonsense skyscraper part of this city of more than three million. The line ends at the leaning towers of Puerta de Europa (Gate of Europe). This trip is simple and cheap. If starting from the Prado, catch the bus from the museum side to head north; from the Reina Sofía, the stop is a couple of blocks away at the Royal Botanical Garden, at the end of the garden fence (€1.50, buses run every 10 minutes, sit on the right if possible, beware of pickpockets). You just joyride for 30 minutes to the last stop (longer if it's rush hour), get out at the end of the line when everyone else does, ogle the skyscrapers, and catch the Metro for a 20-minute ride back to the city's center. At twilight, when fountains and facades are floodlit, the ride is particularly enjoyable.

Historic District: Bus #27 rumbles from Atocha Station past the Royal Botanical Garden (opposite McDonald's) and the Velázquez entrance to the Prado (right). From here look out for these landmarks: a square with a fountain of Neptune (left); an obelisk and war memorial to those who have died for Spain (right, with the stock market behind it); the Naval Museum (right); Plaza de Cibeles—with the fancy City Hall and cultural center, the Bank of Spain (left), and other huge buildings; and then the National Library (right).

Modern District: The roundabout and square with a statue of Columbus in the middle and a giant Spanish flag mark the end of the historic town and the beginning of the modern city. At this point the boulevard changes its name (and the sights I mention are much more spread out). This street used to be named for Franco; now it's named for the people he no longer rules—*la Castellana* (Castilians). Next, just after an underpass with several sculptures, comes the American Embassy (hard to see behind its fortified wall, right) and some circa 1940s buildings that once housed Franco's ministries (left, typical fascist architecture, with large colonnades). Continuing up the boulevard, look left to see the Picasso Tower, resembling one of New York's former World Trade Center towers (designed by the same architect), the huge Bernabéu soccer stadium (right, home of Real Madrid, Europe's most successful soccer team, described later), and the Ministry of Defense (large building with the flag, left).

Your trip ends at Plaza de Castilla, where you can't miss the avant-garde Puerta de Europa, consisting of the twin "Torres Kios," office towers that lean at a 15-degree angle (look for the big green sign BANKIA, for the Bank of Madrid). In the distance, you can see four of the tallest buildings in Spain. The plaza sports a futuristic golden obelisk by contemporary Spanish architect Santiago Calatrava.

It's the end of the line for the bus—and for you. You can return directly to Puerta del Sol on the Metro, or cross the street and ride bus #27 along the same route back to the Prado Museum or Atocha Station.

▲Electric Minibus Joyride and the Lavapiés District

For a relaxing ride through the characteristic old center of Madrid, hop the little electric **minibus #M1** (€1.50, 5/hour, 20-minute trip, Mon-Sat 8:00-20:00, none on Sun). These are designed especially for the difficult-to-access streets in the historic heart of the city, and they're handy for seniors who could use a lift (offer your seat if there's a senior standing). Catch the minibus at the Sevilla Metro stop and simply ride it to the end (Metro: Embajadores). Enjoy this gritty slice of workaday Madrid—both people and architecture—

as you roll slowly through Plaza Santa Ana, down a bit of the pe-destrianized Calle de las Huertas, past gentrified Plaza Tirso de Molina (its junkies now replaced by a faded family-friendly flower market), and through Plaza de Lavapiés and a barrio of African and Bangladeshi immigrants. Jump out along the way to explore La-vapiés on foot, or stay on until you get to Embajadores. From there, you can catch the next #M1 minibus back to the Sevilla Metro stop (it returns along a different route) or descend into the subway system.

In the Lavapiés neighborhood, the multiethnic tapestry of Madrid enjoys seedy-yet-fun-loving life on the streets. Neighbor-hoods like this typically experience the same familiar evolution: Initially they're so cheap that only immigrants, the downtrodden, and counter-culture types live there. The diversity and color they bring attracts those with more money. Businesses erupt to cater to those bohemian/trendy tastes. Rents go up. Those who gave the area its colorful energy in the first place can no longer afford to live there. They move out...and here comes Starbucks.

For now, Lavapiés is still edgy, yet comfortable enough for most. To help rejuvenate the area, the city built the big Centro Dramático Nacional theater just downhill from Lavapiés' main square.

The district has almost no tourists. (Some think it's too scary.) Old ladies with their tired bodies and busy fans hang out on their tiny balconies as they have for 40 years, watching the scene. Shady types lurk on side streets (don't venture off the main drag, don't show your wallet or money, and don't linger late on Plaza de La-vapiés).

If you're walking, start from Plaza de Antón Martín (Metro: Antón Martín) or Plaza Santa Ana. Find your way to Calle del Ave María (on its way to becoming Calle del Ave Allah) and on to Plaza de Lavapiés (Metro: Lavapiés), where elderly Madrileños hang out with the swarthy drunks and drug dealers; a mosaic of cultures treat this square as a communal living room. Then head up Calle de Lavapiés to the remodeled Plaza Tirso de Molina (Metro stop). This square was once plagued by druggies, but is now home to flower kiosks and a playground. This is a good example of Ma-drid's vision for reinvigorating its public spaces.

For food, you'll find plenty of tapas bars plus gritty Indian (almost all run by Bangladeshis) and Moroccan eateries. For Span-ish fare try Bar Melos, a thriving dive jammed with a hungry and nubile crowd. It's famous for its giant patty melts called *zapatillas de lacón y queso* (because they're the size and shape of a *zapatilla*, or slipper; €11, feeds at least two, closed Sun-Mon, Calle del Ave María 44). Nuevo Café Barbieri, one of a dying breed of mirrored cafés with a circa-1940 ambience, offers classical music in the afternoon and jazz in the evening (closed Sun-Mon, Calle del Ave María 45). The Indian places line Calle de Lavapiés.

▲▲Bullfight

Madrid's Plaza de Toros hosts Spain's top bullfights on some Sundays and holidays from March through mid-October, and nearly

every day during the San Isidro festival (May-early June—often sold out long in advance). Fights start between 17:00 and 21:00 (early in spring and fall, late in summer). The bullring is at the Ventas Metro stop (a 25-minute Metro ride from Puerta del Sol, tel. 913-562-200, www.las-ventas.com).

Getting Tickets: Bullfight tickets range from €5 to €150. There are no bad seats at Plaza de Toros; paying more gets you in the shade and/or closer to the gore. (The action often intentionally occurs in the shade to reward the expensive-ticket holders.) To be close to the bullring, choose areas 8, 9, or 10; for shade: 1, 2, 9, or 10; for shade/sun: 3 or 8; for the sun and cheapest seats: 4, 5, 6, or 7. Note these key words: *corrida*—a real fight with professionals; *novillada*—rookie matadors, younger bulls, and cheaper tickets. Getting tickets through your hotel or a booking office is convenient, but they add 20 percent or more and don't sell the cheap seats. There are two booking offices; call both before you buy: at Plaza del Carmen 1 (Mon-Sat 9:00-13:00 & 16:30-19:00, Sun 9:30-14:00, tel. 915-319-131, or buy online at www.bullfightticketsmadrid.com; run by José and his English-speaking son, also José, who also sells soccer tickets) and at Calle Victoria 3 (Mon-Fri 10:00-14:00 & 17:00-19:00, Sat-Sun 10:00-13:00, tel. 915-211-213).

To save money, you can stand in the ticket line at the bullring. Except for important bullfights—or during the San Isidro festival—there are generally plenty of seats available. About a thousand tickets are held back to be sold in the five days leading up to and on the day of a fight. Scalpers hang out before the popular fights at the Calle Victoria booking office. Beware: Those buying scalped tickets are breaking the law and can lose the ticket with no recourse.

For a dose of the experience, you can buy a cheap ticket and just stay to see a couple of bullfights. Each fight takes about 20 minutes, and the event consists of six bulls over two hours. Or, to keep your distance but get a sense of the ritual and gore, tour the bull bar on Plaza Mayor.

Bullfighting Museum (Museo Taurino): This museum, located at the back of the bullring, is not as good as the ones in Sevilla or Ronda (free, Sun 10:00-13:00, Mon-Fri 9:30-14:30, closed Sat, closes early on fight days, tel. 917-251-857).

"Football" and Bernabéu Stadium

Madrid, like most of Europe, is enthusiastic about soccer (which they call *fútbol*). The Real ("Royal") Madrid team plays to a spirited crowd Saturdays and Sundays from September through May (tickets from €50—sold at bullfight box offices listed earlier). One of the most popular sightseeing activities among European visitors to Madrid is touring the 80,000-seat stadium. The €19 unguided visit includes the box seats, dressing rooms, technical zone, playing field, trophy room, and a big panoramic stadium view (Mon-Sat 10:00-19:00, Sun 10:30-18:30, shorter hours on game days, Metro: Santiago Bernabéu, tel. 913-984-300, www.realmadrid.com). Even if you can't catch a game, you'll see plenty of Real Madrid's all-white jerseys and paraphernalia around town.

Shopping in Madrid

Madrileños have a passion for shopping. It's a social event, often incorporated into their afternoon paseo, which eventually turns into drinks and dinner. Most shoppers focus on the colorful pedestrian area between and around Gran Vía and Puerta del Sol. Here you'll find shops like H&M and Zara clothing, Imaginarium toys, FNAC books and music, and a handful of small local shops. The fanciest big-name shops (Gucci, Prada, and the like) tempt strollers along Calle Serrano, northwest of Retiro Park. For trendier chain shops and local fashion, head to pedestrian Calle Fuencarral, Calle Augusto Figueroa, and the streets surrounding Plaza Chueca (north of Gran Vía, Metro: Chueca). Here are some other places to check out:

El Corte Inglés Department Store

The giant El Corte Inglés, a block off Puerta del Sol, is a handy place to pick up just about anything you need (Mon-Sat 10:00-22:00, Sun 11:00-21:00).

▲El Rastro Flea Market

Europe's biggest flea market is a field day for shoppers, people-watchers, and pickpockets (Sun only, 9:00-15:00). It's best before 11:00, though bargain shoppers like to go around 14:00, when vendors are more willing to strike end-of-day deals. Thousands of stalls titillate more than a million browsers with mostly new junk. Locals have lamented the tackiness of El Rastro lately—on the

main drag, you'll find cheap under-
wear and bootleg CDs, but no real
treasures.

For an interesting market day
(Sun only), start at Plaza Mayor,
where Europe's biggest stamp and
coin market thrives. Enjoy this genteel delight as you watch old-timers
paging lovingly through each other's
albums, looking for win-win trades.
When you're done, head south or
take the Metro to Tirso de Molina. Walk downhill, wandering off on the side streets to browse antiques, old furniture, and
garage-sale-style sellers who often simply throw everything out
on a sheet.

A typical Madrileño's Sunday could involve a meander
through the Rastro streets with several stops for *cañas* (small
beers) at the gritty bars along the way, then a walk to the Cava
Baja area for more beer and tapas. El Rastro offers a fascinating
chance to see gangs of young thieves overwhelming and ripping
off naive tourists with no police anywhere in sight. Seriously:
Don't even bring a wallet. The pickpocket action is brutal, and
tourists are targeted.

Specialty Shops
These places are fun to browse for Spanish specialties and locally
made goods.

Ceramics: Antigua Casa Talavera has sold hand-made ceramics from Spain's family craftsmen since 1904. They can explain
the various regional styles and colors of pottery and tiles, based on
traditional designs from the 11th to 19th century (Mon-Fri 10:00-
13:30 & 17:00-20:00, Sat 10:00-13:30, closed Sun, Calle Isabel La
Católica 2, tel. 915-473-417, www.antiguacasatalavera.com).

Leather: Taller Puntera is a workshop and store where the
new generation carries on a longtime family tradition of Madrileño
leather artisans. They design and create all of their products on-
site, from bags to shoes and more (Mon-Sat 10:00-14:00 & 17:00-
21:00, closed Sun, Plaza Conde de Barajas 4, tel. 913-642-926,
www.puntera.com).

Shoes: For *the* shoe street in Madrid head up Calle Fuencarral
and take a right on to Calle Augusto Figueroa. Walk a couple of
blocks down to find one local *zapatería* after another. On Gran Vía,
you'll also find Camper shoes, launched in 1975 on the Spanish
island of Mallorca. This popular brand is now relatively easy to find
around the world, though here in Madrid you may see more styles
(daily, Calle Preciados 23, tel. 915-317-897, www.camper.com).

MADRID

Souvenirs: Casa de Diego sells *abanicos* (fans), *mantones* (typical Spanish shawls), *castañuelas* (castanets), *peinetas* (hair combs), and umbrellas. Even if you're not in the market, it's fun to watch the women flip open their final fan choices before buying (Mon-Sat 9:30-20:00, closed Sun, Puerta del Sol 12, tel. 915-226-643).

Guitars: Spain makes some of the world's finest classical guitars. Several of the top workshops, within an easy walk of Puerta del Sol, offer inviting little showrooms that give a peek at their craft and an opportunity to strum the final product. Consider the workshops of José Romero (Calle de Espoz y Mina 30, tel. 915-214-218) and José Ramirez (Calle de la Paz 8, tel. 915-314-229). Union Musical is a popular guitar shop off Puerta del Sol (Carrera de San Jerónimo 26, tel. 914-293-877). If you're looking to buy, be prepared to spend €1,000.

Nightlife in Madrid

Those into clubbing may have to wait until after midnight for the most popular places to even open, much less start hopping. Spain has a reputation for partying very late and not stopping until offices open in the morning. (Spaniards, who are often awake into the wee hours of the morning, have a special word for this time of day: *la madrugada*.) If you're out early in the morning, it's actually hard to tell who is finishing their day and who's just starting it. Even if you're not a party animal after midnight, make a point to be out with the happy masses, luxuriating in the cool evening air between 22:00 and midnight. The scene is absolutely unforgettable.

▲▲▲Paseo

Just walking the streets of Madrid seems to be the way the Madrileños spend their evenings. Even past midnight on a hot summer night, entire families with little kids are strolling, enjoying tiny beers and tapas in a series of bars, licking ice cream, and greeting their neighbors. Good areas to wander include along Gran Vía (from about Plaza de Callao to Plaza de España), perhaps following my "Gran Vía Walk" suggested earlier; from Puerta del Sol to Plaza Mayor and down Calle del Arenal until you hit Plaza de Isabel II; the pedestrianized Calle de las Huertas from Plaza Mayor to the Prado; and, to window shop with the young and trendy, from Gran Vía up Calle de Fuencarral (keep going until you hit traffic).

▲Zarzuela

For a delightful look at Spanish light opera that even English speakers can enjoy, try zarzuela. Guitar-strumming Napoleons in red capes; buxom women with masks, fans, and castanets; Spanish-speaking pharaohs; melodramatic spotlights; and aficionados clapping and singing along from the cheap seats, where the acoustics are best—this is zarzuela...the people's opera. Originating in Madrid, zarzuela is known for its satiric humor and surprisingly good music. Performances occur evenings at Teatro de la Zarzuela, which alternates between zarzuela, ballet, and opera throughout the year. The TI's monthly guide has a special zarzuela section.

Getting Tickets: Prices range from €16-40, 50 percent off for Wed shows and anytime for those over 65, Teatro de la Zarzuela box office open Mon-Fri 12:00-18:00 and Sat-Sun 15:00-18:00 for advance tickets or until show time for same-day tickets, near the Prado at Jovellanos 4, Metro: Sevilla or Banco de España, tel. 915-245-400, teatrodelazarzuela.mcu.es. To purchase tickets online, go to www.entradasinaem.es and click on *"Espacios"* ("Spaces") to find Teatro de la Zarzuela; you will receive an email with your tickets, which you need to print before you arrive at the theater.

▲▲Flamenco

Although Sevilla is the capital of flamenco, Madrid has a few easy and affordable options. And on summer evenings, Madrid puts on live flamenco events in the Royal Palace gardens (ask TI for details). Among the listings below, Casa Patas is grumpy, while Carboneras is friendlier—but Casa Patas has better-quality artists and a riveting seriousness. Considering that prices at Las Carboneras essentially match those at Casa Patas, the "House of Feet" is the better value.

Taberna Casa Patas attracts big-name flamenco artists. You'll quickly understand why this intimate venue (30 tables, 120 seats) is named "House of Feet." Since this is for locals as well as tour groups, the flamenco is contemporary and may be jazzier than your notion—it depends on who's performing (€36 includes cover and first drink, Mon-Thu at 22:30, Fri-Sat at 21:00 and 24:00, closed Sun, 1.25-1.5 hours, reservations smart, no flash cameras, Cañizares 10, tel. 913-690-496, www.casapatas.com). Its restaurant is a logical spot for dinner before the show (€30 dinners, Mon-Sat from 20:00). Or, since it's three blocks south of the recommended Plaza Santa Ana tapas bars, this could be your pre- or post-tapas-crawl entertainment.

Las Carboneras, more downscale, is an easygoing, folksy little place a few steps from Plaza Mayor with a nightly hour-long flamenco show (€36 includes entry and a drink, €69 gets you a table up front with dinner and unlimited cheap drinks if you reserve ahead, manager Enrique promises a €5/person discount if you book directly and show this book in 2016, daily at 20:30, also Mon-Thu at 22:30 and Fri-Sat at 23:00, reservations recommended, Plaza del Conde de Miranda 1, tel. 915-428-677, www.tablaolascarboneras.com). Dinner is served one hour before showtime.

Las Tablas Flamenco offers a less expensive nightly show respecting the traditional art of flamenco. You'll sit in a plain room with a mix of tourists and cool, young Madrileños in a modern, nondescript office block just over the freeway from Plaza de España (€27 with drink, reasonable drink prices, shows daily at 20:00 and 22:00, 1.25 hours, corner of Calle de Ferraz and Cuesta de San Vicente at Plaza de España 9, tel. 915-420-520, www. lastablasmadrid.com).

More Flamenco: Regardless of what your hotel receptionist may want to sell you, other flamenco places—such as Arco de Cuchilleros (Calle de los Cuchilleros 7), Café de Chinitas (Calle Torija 7, just off Plaza Mayor), Corral de la Morería (Calle de Morería 17), and Torres Bermejas (off Gran Vía)—are filled with tourists and pushy waiters.

Mesones

These long, skinny, cave-like bars, famous for customers drinking and singing late into the night, line the lane called Cava de San Miguel, just west of Plaza Mayor. If you were to toss lowbrow barflies, Spanish karaoke, electric keyboards, crass tourists, cheap sangria, and greasy calamari into a late-night blender and turn it on, this is what you'd get. They're generally lively only on Friday and Saturday.

Bars and Jazz

If you're just picking up speed at midnight and looking for a place filled with old tiles and a Gen-X crowd, power into **Bar Viva Madrid** (daily 13:00-late, downhill from Plaza Santa Ana at Calle Manuel Fernández y González 7, tel. 914-293-640). The same street has other bars filled with music. Or hike on over to Chocolatería San Ginés for a dessert of *churros con chocolate*.

For live jazz, **Café Central** is the old town favorite. Since 1982 it's been known as the place where rising stars get their start (€14, nightly at 21:00—stop by to reserve your table or come early to score one of the unreserved seats by the bar, food and drinks available, great scene, Plaza del Ángel 10, tel. 913-694-143, www. cafecentralmadrid.com).

Movies

During the dictatorial days of Franco, movies were always dubbed in Spanish, making them easier to censor. (One famously awkward example: Franco's censors were scandalized by a film depicting a man and a woman having an implied affair, so they edited the voiceover to make the characters brother and sister. But the onscreen chemistry was still sexually charged—so they wound up turning a questionable relationship into an incestuous one.) As a result, movies in Spain remain about the most often dubbed in Europe. To see a movie with its original soundtrack, look for "V.O." (meaning "original version"). **Cine Ideal**, with nine screens, is a good place for the latest films in V.O. (assigned seats during most days and showings, good to get tickets early on weekends, 5-minute walk south of Puerta del Sol at Calle del Dr. Cortezo 6, tel. 913-692-518 for info, www.yelmocines.es). For extensive listings, see the *Guía del Ocio* entertainment guide or a local newspaper.

Sleeping in Madrid

Madrid has plenty of centrally located budget hotels and *pensiones*. Most of the accommodations I've listed are within a few minutes' walk of Puerta del Sol.

You should be able to find a sleepable double for €60, a good double for €90, and a modern, air-conditioned double with all the comforts for €120. Prices vary throughout the year at bigger hotels, but remain about the same for the smaller hotels and *hostales*. It's almost always easy to find a place. Anticipate full hotels only during May (the San Isidro festival, celebrating Madrid's patron saint with bullfights and zarzuelas—especially around his feast day on May 15) and September (when conventions can clog the city). During the hot months of July and August, prices can be soft—ask for a discount.

With all of Madrid's street noise, I'd request the highest floor possible. Also, twin-bedded rooms are generally a bit larger than double-bedded rooms for the same price. Remember, you may find good deals by emailing several hotels (including business-class hotels) to ask for their best price. And during slow times, drop-ins can often score a room in business-class hotels for just a few euros more than the budget hotels (which don't have prices that fluctuate as wildly with demand).

Smoking bans have changed the atmosphere in hotel reception areas and hallways, but things aren't completely smoke-free, as hotels are still allowed to designate up to 10 percent of their rooms for smokers.

MID-RANGE AND FANCIER PLACES

These mostly business-class hotels are good values (especially Hotel Europa) for those willing to spend a little more. Their formal prices may be inflated, but most offer weekend and summer discounts when it's slow. Drivers pay about €24 a day in garages.

Near Puerta del Sol and Gran Vía

These hotels are located in and around the pedestrian zone north

MADRID

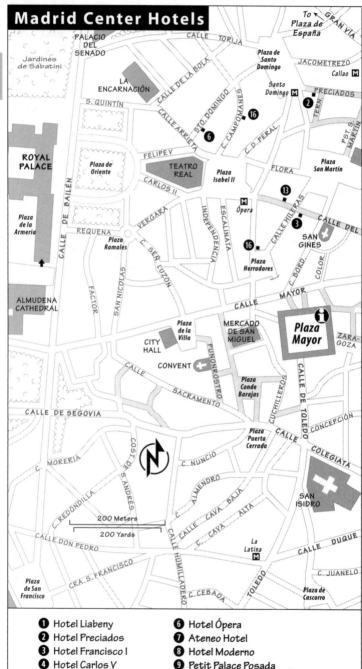

Madrid Center Hotels

- ❶ Hotel Liabeny
- ❷ Hotel Preciados
- ❸ Hotel Francisco I
- ❹ Hotel Carlos V
- ❺ Hotel Europa
- ❻ Hotel Ópera
- ❼ Ateneo Hotel
- ❽ Hotel Moderno
- ❾ Petit Palace Posada del Peine

MADRID

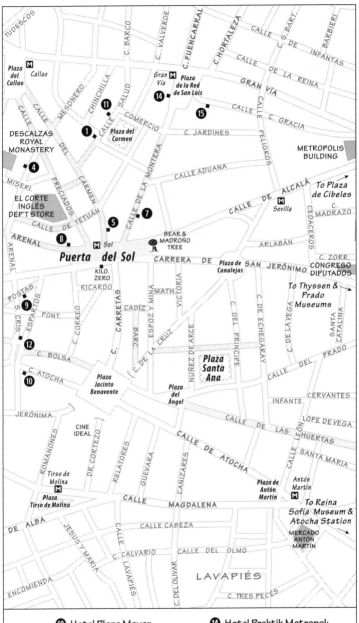

10 Hotel Plaza Mayor

11 Hostales Acapulco & Triana; Pensión Arcos

12 Hostal Santa Cruz

13 Hostales Mayrit & Ivor

14 Hotel Praktik Metropol; Hostales Residencia Luis XV & Jerez

15 Hostal Aliste

16 Launderettes (2)

Sleep Code

Abbreviations   (€1=about $1.10, country code: 34)
S=Single, **D**=Double/Twin, **T**=Triple, **Q**=Quad, **b**=bathroom
Price Rankings
  $$$ Higher Priced—Most rooms €120 or more
  $$ Moderately Priced—Most rooms €70-120
  $ Lower Priced—Most rooms €70 or less
Unless otherwise noted, credit cards are accepted, breakfast is not included, free Wi-Fi and/or a guest computer is generally available, and English is spoken. Some hotels include the 10 percent IVA tax in the room price; others tack it onto your bill. Prices change; verify current rates online or by email. For the best prices, always book directly with the hotel.

and west of Puerta del Sol. Use Metro: Sol for these listings unless noted otherwise.

$$$ Hotel Liabeny rents 220 plush, spacious, business-class rooms offering all the comforts (Sb-€108, Db-€127, Tb-€165, 10 percent cheaper mid-July-Aug, prices vary widely according to demand, breakfast-€16, air-con, elevator, sauna, gym, off Plaza del Carmen at Salud 3, tel. 915-319-000, www.liabeny.es, reservas@hotelliabeny.com).

$$$ Hotel Preciados, a four-star business hotel, has 100 welcoming, sleek, and modern rooms as well as elegant lounges. It's well-located and reasonably priced for the luxury it provides (Db-€125-160, prices often soft, checking Web specials in advance or dropping in will likely enable you to snag a room for around €100, breakfast-€18, free mini-bar, air-con, elevator, gym, parking-€21/day, just off Plaza de Santo Domingo at Calle Preciados 37, Metro: Callao, tel. 914-544-400, www.preciadoshotel.com, preciadoshotel@preciadoshotel.com).

$$$ Hotel Francisco I is a big, quiet, and well-run place with 60 rooms, nicely situated midway between the Royal Theater and Puerta del Sol (Sb-€115, Db-€160, Tb-€200, breakfast-€8, prices fluctuate—book a month or more in advance to save 30-35 percent, air-con, showers only—no tubs, elevator, Calle del Arenal 15, tel. 915-480-204, www.hotelfrancisco.com, info@hotelfrancisco.com).

$$$ Hotel Carlos V is a Best Western with 67 high-ceilinged and somewhat worn-out rooms and a pleasant lounge (Sb-€80-120, standard Db-€100-173, Tb-€115-200, rates depend on demand and season, elegant breakfast-€10, air-con, nonsmoking floors, elevator, Maestro Victoria 5, tel. 915-314-100, www.hotelcarlosv.com, recepcion@hotelcarlosv.com).

$$ Hotel Europa, with sleek marble, red carpet runners along the halls, happy Muzak charm, and an attentive staff, is a tremendous value. It rents 100 squeaky-clean rooms, many with balconies overlooking the pedestrian zone or an inner courtyard. The hotel has an honest ethos and offers a straight price (Sb-€79, Db-€99, Db with view-€119, Tb-€142, Qb-€168, Quint/b-€190, sometimes cheaper with Web specials, air-con, elevator, gym, Calle del Carmen 4, tel. 915-212-900, www.hoteleuropa.eu, info@ hoteleuropa.eu, run by Antonio and Fernando Garaban and their helpful and jovial staff, Javi and Jim). The recommended Europa cafeteria-restaurant next door is a lively and convivial scene—fun for breakfast.

$$ Hotel Ópera, a serious and contemporary hotel with 79 classy rooms, is located just off Plaza Isabel II, a four-block walk from Puerta del Sol toward the Royal Palace (Db-€85-110 but prices spike wildly with demand, 10 percent discount if you reserve direct with this year's book, includes breakfast, air-con, elevator, sauna and gym, ask for a higher floor—there are nine—to avoid street noise, Cuesta de Santo Domingo 2, Metro: Ópera, tel. 915-412-800, www.hotelopera.com, reservas@hotelopera.com). Hotel Ópera's cafeteria is deservedly popular. Consider their "singing dinners"—great operetta music with a delightful dinner—offered nightly (around €60, reservations smart, call 915-426-382 or reserve at hotel).

$$ Ateneo Hotel, just steps off Puerta del Sol, lacks public spaces and character, but its 38 rooms are close to business-class (Db-€75-90, occasionally less or more, can be as high as €115, 5 percent discount if you book directly with the hotel with this year's book, air-con, elevator, Calle de la Montera 22, tel. 915-212-012, www.hotel-ateneo.com, info@hotel-ateneo.com).

$$ Hotel Moderno, renting 97 rooms in a quiet, professional, and friendly atmosphere, has a comfy first-floor lounge and is just steps off Puerta del Sol (Db-€74-129, extra person-€25, breakfast-€11, air-con, Calle del Arenal 2, tel. 915-310-900, www.hotel-moderno.com, info@hotel-moderno.com).

Near Plaza Mayor
Both of these are a block off Plaza Mayor.

$$$ Petit Palace Posada del Peine feels like part of a big, modern chain (which it is), but fills its well-located old building with fresh, efficient character. Behind the ornate Old World facade is a comfortable and modern business-class hotel with 67 rooms (Db-€80-160 depending on demand, breakfast-€10, air-con, free use of iPads, Calle Postas 17, tel. 915-238-151, www.petitpalace. com, posadadelpeine@petitpalace.com).

$$ Hotel Plaza Mayor, with 41 solidly outfitted rooms, is tastefully decorated and beautifully situated a block off Plaza Mayor (Sb-€40-90, Db-€50-100, superior Db-€60-120, Tb-€80-140, breakfast-€8, air-con, elevator, Calle de Atocha 2, tel. 913-600-606, www.h-plazamayor.com, info@h-plazamayor.com). Director Leo offers a free breakfast to travelers who book directly with the hotel (by email or phone—not through different websites), pay the rates listed earlier, and show a copy of this year's book.

Near the Prado
$$ Hotel Lope de Vega offers good business-class hotel value near the Prado. It is a "cultural-themed" hotel inspired by the 17th-century writer Lope de Vega. With 59 rooms, it feels cozy and friendly for a formal hotel (Sb-€97, Db-€69-117, extra person-€20, rates can vary wildly based on demand, cheaper July-Aug, one child under 12 sleeps free, air-con, elevator, limited parking-€25/day—request ahead, Calle Lope de Vega 49—see map on page 47, tel. 913-600-011, www.accor.com, H9618@accor.com).

CHEAP SLEEPS
Near Plaza del Carmen
These three are all in the same building at Calle de la Salud 13, north of Puerta del Sol. The building overlooks Plaza del Carmen—a little square with a sleepy, almost Parisian ambience.

$ Hostal Acapulco rents 16 bright rooms with air-conditioning and all the big hotel gear. The neighborhood is quiet enough that it's smart to request a room with a balcony (Sb-€49-54, Db-€59-64, Tb-€77-80, show this book for a 5 percent discount at check-in, elevator, fourth floor, reasonable laundry service, overnight luggage storage, limited parking available—ask when you reserve, tel. 915-311-945, www.hostalacapulco.com, hostal_acapulco@yahoo.es, Ana, Marco, and Javier).

$ Hostal Triana, also a good deal, is bigger—with 40 rooms—and offers a little less charm for a little less money (Sb-€38, Db-€53, Tb-€69, rooms facing the square have air-con and cost €3 extra, other rooms have fans, elevator and some stairs, first floor, tel. 915-326-812, www.hostaltriana.com, triana@hostaltriana.com, Victor González).

$ Pensión Arcos is tiny, granny-run, and old-fashioned—it's been in the Hernández family since 1936. You can reserve by phone (in Spanish), and you must pay in cash—but its five rooms are clean, extra quiet, and served by an elevator. You also have access to a tiny roof terrace and a nice little lounge. For cheap beds in a great locale, assuming you can communicate, this place is unbeatable (D-€36, Db-€40, air-con, closed Aug, fifth floor, tel. 915-324-994, Anuncia and Sabino).

Near Puerta del Sol
$ Hostal Santa Cruz, simple and well-located (but with a smoky

office), has 16 rooms at a good price (Sb-€40, Db-€55, Tb-€70, air-con, elevator, Plaza de Santa Cruz 6, second floor, tel. 915-222-441, www.hostalsantacruz.com, info@hostalsantacruz.com).

$ Hostal Mayrit and **Hostal Ivor** rent 28 rooms with thoughtful touches on pedestrianized Calle del Arenal (Sb-€40-55, Db-€55-65, air-con, elevator, near Metro: Ópera at Calle del Arenal 24, reception on third floor, tel. 915-480-403, www.hostalivor.com, reservas@hostalivor.com).

At the Top of Calle de la Montera

These places are a few minutes' walk from Puerta del Sol and a stone's throw from Gran Vía at the top of Calle de la Montera, which some dislike because of the prostitutes who hang out here. They're legal, and the zone is otherwise safe and comfortable.

$$ Hotel Praktik Metropol sports plaid-and-striped hipster decor in its 70 fresh, modern rooms. Many rooms are tiny and on the building's interior—ask for a corner room or pay extra for the bigger superior double. The spectacular views from the top-floor "skyline" rooms are worth the extra money, too. All guests have access to a rooftop terrace with views (interior Sb-€55-89, standard interior Db-€65-99, superior exterior Db-€75-109, skyline Db-€81-130, higher rates Thu-Sat, breakfast-€4, air-con, elevator, reception on first floor, Calle de la Montera 47, tel. 915-212-935, www.hotelpraktikmetropol.com, reservas@hotelpraktikmetropol.com).

$ Hostal Aliste rents 11 decent rooms in a dreary-yet-secure building at a great price (Sb-€29, Db-€39, extra bed-€15, these prices for Rick Steves readers in 2016 who book directly with the hotel and show this book at check-in, air-con-€5, elevator, third floor, Caballero de Gracia 6, tel. 915-215-979, www.hostalaliste.net, info@hostalaliste.net, Rachel and Eduardo).

$ Hostal Residencia Luis XV is a big, plain, well-run, and clean place offering a good value. It's on a quiet eighth floor (Sb-€45, Db-€59, Tb-€75, air-con, elevator, Calle de la Montera 47, tel. 915-221-021, www.hostalluisxvmadrid.com, reservas@hrluisxvmadrid.com). They also run the 36-room **Hostal Jerez**—similar in every way—on the sixth floor (tel. 915-327-565, www.hostaljerezmadrid.com/en, reservas@hrjerez.net). Both properties are completely nonsmoking.

Near the Prado

For locations of the following places, see the map on page 47.

Two fine budget *hostales* are at Cervantes 34 (Metro: Antón Martín—but not handy to Metro). Both are homey, with inviting lounge areas; neither serves breakfast. **$ Hostal Gonzalo** has 15 spotless, comfortable rooms on the third floor and is well-run by friendly and helpful Javier. It's deservedly in all the guidebooks, so reserve in advance (Sb-€45, Db-€60, Tb-€75, air-con, elevator, tel. 914-292-714, www.hostalgonzalo.com, hostal@hostalgonzalo. com). Downstairs, the nearly as polished **$ Hostal Cervantes** also has 15 rooms (Sb-€35-40, Db-€45-50, Tb-€55-60, cheaper when slow and for longer stays, some rooms with air-con, tel. 914-298-365, www.hostal-cervantes.com, correo@hostal-cervantes.com, Fabio).

$ Urban Sea Hotel Atocha 113 is a basic but contemporary option that is nicely located between the Prado and the Reina Sofía, near Atocha Station (Sb-€40-45, Db-€50-75, rates vary on demand, includes self-service snacks, small rooftop terrace, Calle de Atocha 113, tel. 913-692-895, www.urbanseahotels.com, recepcionatocha@blueseahotels.es).

Hostel

$ Madrid Municipal Youth Hostel (Albergue Juvenil Madrid) is fairly new and decidedly big, with 132 beds. A Metro ride north of downtown, it has four to six beds per room with lockers, modern bathrooms, and lots of extras, such as a laundry room, billiards, and movies (dorm bed-about €22, includes sheets and breakfast, coed rooms, towels-€3, free guest computer, 24-hour reception; Metro: Tribunal, then walk 2 minutes down Calle de Barceló to Calle de Mejia Lequerica 21; tel. 915-939-688, www.ajmadrid.es, info@ ajmadrid.es).

Eating in Madrid

In Spain, only Barcelona rivals Madrid for taste-bud thrills. You have three dining choices: a memorable, atmospheric sit-down meal in a well-chosen restaurant; a forgettable, basic sit-down meal; or a meal of tapas at a bar or two...or four. Unless otherwise noted, restaurants start serving lunch at 13:00 or 13:30 and dinner around 20:30. Depending on what time you show up, the same place may seem forlorn, touristy, or thriving with local eaters. Many restaurants close in August. Madrid has famously good tap water, and waiters willingly serve it free—just ask for *agua del grifo*. Restaurants and bars in Spain are smoke-free.

I've broken my recommended choices into groups: serious dining establishments, tapas places, and simple, economical venues. For suggestions on where to eat near the Royal Palace, Prado, and Reina Sofía, see their individual sight listings.

FINE DINING

D'Fábula, as its name indicates, offers a fairy tale of a menu and an elegant, peaceful setting. Its chef lovingly concocts weird and experimental tapas. Sit at the bar (to get help ordering) and go into orbit with inverted *patatas bravas,* delightful croquettes, "Planet Mars" (needs instruction), and so on. Prices are the same at the bar, in the dining room, and on the wonderful terrace (€3-8 tapas, €10-18 plates, daily from 20:00, just below Mercado de San Miguel but out of the rat race at Plaza Conde de Barajas 3, tel. 913-664-962).

Restaurante Casa Paco is a Madrid tradition. Check out its old walls plastered with autographed photos of Spanish celebrities who have enjoyed their signature dish—ox grilled over a coal fire. Though popular with tourists, the place is authentic, confident, and uncompromising. It's a worthwhile splurge if you want to dine out well and carnivorously (€15-25 plates, ox sold by weight, 200 grams—which is almost half a pound—is a hearty steak, closed Mon, Plaza de la Puerta Cerrada 11, tel. 913-663-166, www. casapaco1933.com).

Sobrino del Botín is a hit with many Americans because "Hemingway ate here." It's grotesquely touristy, pricey, and the last place "Papa" would go now...but still, people love it and go for the roast suckling pig, their specialty. I'd eat upstairs for a still-traditional, but airier style over the darker downstairs (€40-50 meals, daily 13:00-16:00 & 20:00-24:00, a block downhill from Plaza Mayor at Cuchilleros 17, tel. 913-664-217).

Casa Lucio is a favorite splurge for traditional specialties among power-dressing Madrileños. Juan Carlos and Sofía, the former king and queen of Spain, eat in this formal place, but it's accessible to commoners. This is a good restaurant for a special night out and a full-blown meal, but you pay extra for this place's fame (€50 for dinner, daily 13:00-16:00 & 20:30-24:00, closed Aug, Calle Cava Baja 35; unless you're the king or queen, reserve several days in advance—and don't even bother on weekends; tel. 913-653-252, www.casalucio.es).

Restaurante Palacio de Cibeles is on the sixth floor of the Palacio de Cibeles and features an outdoor terrace with spectacular views. The elegant restaurant of highly respected Toledo-based chef Adolfo features an extensive wine list and a fresh, creative Spanish menu that changes frequently based on season and availability (€50-60 for dinner, daily 13:00-16:00 & 20:00-24:00). The neighboring **Terrace Cibeles** serves drinks and light bites late into the night (daily 13:00-24:00), and the first-floor **Colección Cibeles,** though lacking views, serves an excellent €19 tapas *menu* with three "magnum" tapas (just about a half-*ración*) and two glasses of wine, or a €15 fixed-price meal (daily 10:00-24:00, Plaza de Cibeles 1—see map on page 47, central tel. 915-231-454).

El Caldero ("The Pot") is a romantic spot and *the* place for paella and other rice dishes. A classy, in-the-know crowd appreciates its subdued elegance and crisp service. The house specialty, *arroz*

MADRID

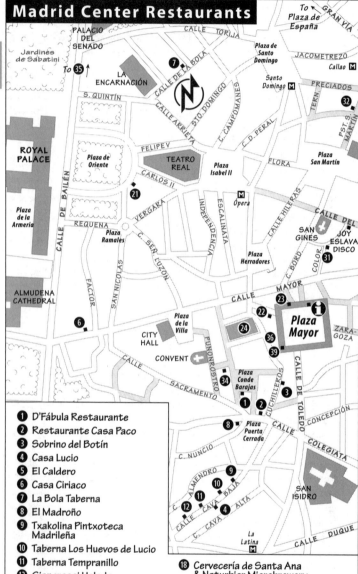

Madrid Center Restaurants

❶ D'Fábula Restaurante
❷ Restaurante Casa Paco
❸ Sobrino del Botín
❹ Casa Lucio
❺ El Caldero
❻ Casa Ciriaco
❼ La Bola Taberna
❽ El Madroño
❾ Txakolina Pintxoteca Madrileña
❿ Taberna Los Huevos de Lucio
⓫ Taberna Tempranillo
⓬ Giangrossi Helado Artesanal
⓭ Museo del Jamón & Lhardy Pastelería
⓮ La Taurina
⓯ La Casa del Abuelo
⓰ La Oreja de Jaime
⓱ Casa Toni
⓲ Cervecería de Santa Ana & Naturbier Microbrewery
⓳ La Vinoteca
⓴ Casa Gonzalez Wine & Cheese Shop
㉑ Café de Oriente
㉒ Casa Rúa
㉓ La Torre del Oro Bar Andalú

MADRID

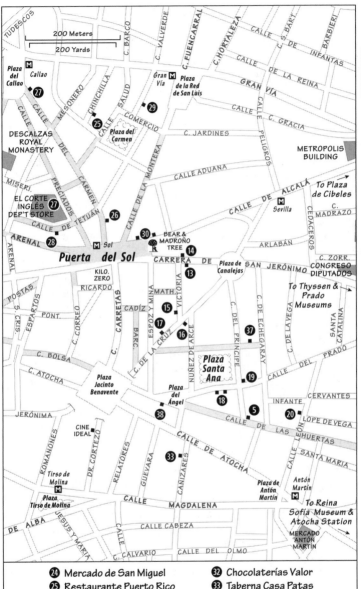

24 Mercado de San Miguel
25 Restaurante Puerto Rico
26 Rest.-Cafeteria Europa
27 El Corte Inglés Cafeterias (2)
28 Casa Labra Taberna Rest.
29 Artemisia II Veggie Rest.
30 Rodilla; Pans & Co.
31 Chocolatería San Ginés

32 Chocolaterías Valor
33 Taberna Casa Patas (Flamenco)
34 Las Carboneras (Flamenco)
35 To Las Tablas (Flamenco)
36 Mesones ("Cave Bars")
37 Bar Viva Madrid
38 Café Central Jazz Bar
39 Cervecería Pulpito

caldero (a variation on paella), is served with panache from a caul-dron hanging from a tripod. Most of the formal rice dishes come in pots for two, including the €30-per-couple paella (€26 with sea-food, closed for dinner Sun-Mon, Calle de las Huertas 15, tel. 914-295-044). Wash it all down with the house sangria.

Casa Ciriaco is a tired but classic old place, popular with Madrileños who appreciate good traditional cooking—like stews—served with no affectation (€35 meals, €20 soup and steak specials, €20 fixed-price lunch, closed Wed and Aug, Calle Mayor 84, tel. 915-480-620). It was from this building in 1906 that an anarchist bombed King Alfonso XIII and his bride on their wedding day; the royal couple survived, but many others were killed (for the story, see page 27). Photos of the carnage are inside the front door.

La Bola Taberna, touristy but friendly and tastefully elegant, specializes in *cocido Madrileño*—Madrid stew. The stew, made of various meats, carrots, and garbanzo beans in earthen jugs, is a winter dish, prepared here for the tourists all year. It's served as two courses: First enjoy the broth as a soup, then dig into the meat and veggies. Curious about how it's made? Ask to take a peek in the kitchen (€20 stew, about €35/person for full meal, cash only, daily lunch seatings at 13:30 and 15:30, dinner 20:30-23:00, closed Sun in July-Aug, midway between Royal Palace and Gran Vía at Calle Bola 5, tel. 915-476-930).

Treating Tapas Bars as Restaurants: Of the many recom-mended *tabernas* and tapas bars along Calle Cava Baja and Calle de Jesús (see listings later), several have tables and menus that lend themselves to fine dining. If you don't mind the commotion of the nearby bar action, you can order high on the menu in these places and, I'd say, eat better and more economically than in the more formal restaurants listed above.

TAPAS-HOPPING FROM BAR TO BAR

For maximum fun, people, and atmosphere, go mobile for dinner: Do the *tapeo*, a local tradition of going from one bar to the next, munching, drinking, and socializing. If done properly, a pub crawl can be a highlight of your trip. While tiny tapas plates are standard in Andalucía, these days most of Madrid's bars offer bigger plates for around €6 (vegetables) to €15 (fish). Called *raciones*, these are ideal for a small group to share. The real action begins late (around 21:00). But for beginners, an earlier start, with less commotion, can be easier.

In Madrid, any proper bar gives a **free tapa** to anyone ordering a drink. But if you order any food with your drink, you won't get the free dish. If you care (and you should), always order the drink alone first and expect a tapa. If you don't get one, ask, *"Tapa?"* as if expecting the little bonus. Once you get it, order additional food as you like.

There are tapas bars almost everywhere, but three areas in the city center are particularly rewarding for a bar-crawl meal. Calle de Jesús (near the Prado) is the easiest, with several wonderful and diverse places in a two-block row. Trendy Calle Cava Baja has fancier offerings and feels most energetic, and the area between Puerta del Sol and Plaza Santa Ana is most central.

The Great Tapas Row on Calle de Jesús

This two-block stretch of tapas bars offers an amazing variety of fun places. Each has its own personality, and many have small and inviting sections with tables. Make the circuit and eyeball each place to see which appeals—you'll see that there's no reason to spend all your time and appetite at your first stop. Calle de Jesús stretches between Calle de Cervantes and Calle de las Huertas, behind the Palace Hotel (across the boulevard from the Prado, see map on page 47). In the middle is the Plaza de Jesús, so named because this is the location of the Basilica of Jesús de Medinaceli (home to a relic that attracts huge crowds of pilgrims on special days). Start near the church at the first recommended bar, Cervecería Cervantes. I haven't given the nitty-gritty specifics for these places as they are mostly open every day for long hours.

Cervecería Cervantes serves hearty *raciones,* specializes in octopus, and has both a fine bar and good restaurant seating (intersection of Plaza de Jesús and Calle de Cervantes, tel. 914-296-093).

Taberna de la Daniela Medinaceli has a lovely dining area if you want to settle in for a while. It's popular for its specialty *cocido madrileño,* a rich chickpea-based soup (Plaza de Jesús 7, tel. 913-896-238).

La Dolores, with a rustic little dining area, has been a hit since 1908 and is still extremely popular. Its canapés (€2.50 little sandwiches) are listed on the wall (Plaza de Jesús 4, tel. 914-292-243).

Cervezas La Fabrica packs in seafood lovers at the bar; there's a quieter back room for those preferring a table. Prices are the same in both spots (Calle de Jesús 2, tel. 913-690-671).

Cervecería Los Gatos is a kaleidoscope of Spanish culture, with chandeliers swinging above wine barrels in the bar area and characteristic tables below (Calle de Jesús 2, tel. 914-293-067).

La Anchoíta is named "the little anchovy" for its top-notch *anchoas* (cured anchovies) and *boquerones* (uncured anchovies). When these tasty little tidbits share a slice of bread, it's a "matrimonio." The three taps serve regular beer, "sin" (nonalcoholic) beer, and *vermut* (vermouth) from a tap shaped like a shrimp. If drinking white wine, get it in a frozen glass—ask for *"copa fría"* (Calle de Jesús 4, tel. 913-601-674).

MADRID

El Olivar seems humble, but serves particularly tasty *racio-nes*—especially their *pimientos de Padrón*—little green peppers (Calle de Jesús 6, tel. 645-575-784).

Cervecería El Diario, while a tavern dating from 1879, feels the most formulaic. They're known for their *calamares* (intersection of Calle de las Huertas and Calle de Jesús, tel. 914-292-800).

Taberna Maceira may be your favorite of the bunch. A bit farther down the strip, it's a Galician place with a wonderfully woody and rustic energy. It's a restaurant (not a bar), and it special-izes in octopus, codfish, *pimientos de Padrón* (green peppers), and *caldo Gallego* (white bean soup)—all classic Galician specialties of northwest Spain. Every day, the sign reads, *no hay Coca-Cola*—"no Coke" (Tue-Sun 13:00-16:00 & 20:30-24:00, closed Mon, cash only, Calle de Jesús 7, tel. 914-291-584). Taberna Maceira has two sister restaurants—Maceiras and Belesar—around the corner at Calle de las Huertas 64 and 66. Both are open long hours daily and accept credit cards.

An Irish bar marks the end of Calle de Jesús.

Tapas on Calle Cava Baja

Just a few minutes' walk south of Plaza Mayor, Calle Cava Baja fills each evening with mostly young, professional Madrileños prowling for chic tapas and social fun. Come at night only and treat the en-tire street as a destination. I've listed a few standards, but excellent new eateries are always opening up. For a good, authentic Madrid dinner experience, take time to survey the many options along this street and then choose your favorites. Remember, it's easier and touristy early, jammed with locals later. (If you want a formal din-ing experience on this street, survey the lot and pick one you like with tables in the back, or see the places recommended under "Fine Dining," earlier.) These tapas bars, listed in the order you'll reach them as you walk from Plaza Mayor up Calle Cava Baja, are worth special consideration.

El Madroño ("The Berry Tree," a symbol of Madrid) is more of a cowboy bar, a block to the right (with your back to Plaza Mayor) off the top of Calle Cava Baja. Preserving a bit of old Madrid, a tile copy of Velázquez's famous *Drinkers* grins from its facade. Inside, look above the stairs for photos of 1902 Madrid. Study the coats of arms of Madrid through the centuries as you try a *vermut* (ver-mouth) on tap and a €4 sandwich. Or ask to try the *licor de madroño;* a small glass *(chupito)* costs €2. Indoor seating is bright and color-ful; the sidewalk tables come with great people-watching. Munch *raciones* at the bar or front tables to be in the fun scene, or have a quieter sit-down meal at the tables in the back (closed Mon, Plaza de la Puerta Cerrada 7, tel. 913-645-629).

Txakolina Pintxoteca Madrileña is a thriving bar serving Basque-style *pinchos* (fancy sandwiches—*pintxo* in Basque) to a young crowd (€3/*pincho*, Calle Cava Baja 26, tel. 913-664-877).

Taberna Los Huevos de Lucio, owned by the same family as the reputable Casa Lucio (described earlier, under "Fine Dining"), is a jam-packed bar serving good tapas, salads, *huevos estrellados* (scrambled eggs with fried potatoes), and wine. If you'd like to make it a sit-down meal, head to the tables in the back. Their basement is much less atmospheric (Calle Cava Baja 30, tel. 913-662-984).

Taberna Tempranillo, ideal for hungry wine lovers, offers fancy tapas and fine wine by the glass (see listing on the board or ask for their English menu). While there are a few tables, the bar is just right for hanging out. With a spirit of adventure, use their fascinating menu to assemble your dream meal. When I order high on their menu, I'm generally very happy. This place is typically packed and full of commotion—the crowds can be overwhelming. Arrive by 20:00 or plan to wait (closed Mon lunch and Aug, Calle Cava Baja 38, tel. 913-641-532).

Ice Cream Finale: **Giangrossi Helado Artesanal** serves Argentinean-style ice cream, considered to be some of Madrid's best. With a wide, open lounge and lots of great flavors, this hipster ice cream shop offers a sweet way to finish your dining experience in this area (they also serve cocktails, becoming part of the bar scene late at night). Enjoy a couple of free tastes before you choose (at the end of Calle Cava Baja at #40, 50 yards from La Latina Metro stop, tel. 913-660-272).

Central Pub-Crawl Tapas Route

The little streets between Puerta del Sol, San Jerónimo, and Plaza Santa Ana hold tasty surprises. Here I've described a five-stop tapa crawl. These places are good, but don't be afraid to make some discoveries of your own.

• *Start at the intersection of Carrera de San Jerónimo and Calle Victoria.*

The atmospheric **Museo del Jamón** (Museum of Ham), festooned with ham hocks, is a fun place to see—unless you're a pig (or a vegetarian). Its frenetic, cheap, stand-up bar (with famously rude service) is an assembly line of fast-and-simple *bocadillos* and *raciones.* If you order anything, get only a cheap sandwich, because the staff is not honest. Take advantage of the easy photo-illustrated menus that show various dishes and their prices. The best ham is the pricey *jamón ibérico*—from pigs who led stress-free lives in acorn-strewn valleys. Point clearly to what you want, and be very specific to avoid being served a pricier meal than you intended. For instance, if you're on a budget, don't let them sell you the *jamón ibérico*, which costs €10; a plate of low-end *jamón blanco* costs just €2.50. For a small sandwich, ask for a *chiquito* (€1.50, or €4 for *ibérico;* daily 9:00-24:00, sit-down restaurant upstairs, air-con).

• *Across the street is the touristy and overpriced bull bar,* **La Taurina.** *(I wouldn't eat here, but you're welcome to ponder the graphic photos that celebrate the gory art of bullfighting.) And next door take a detour from your pub crawl with something better for grandmothers.*

Lhardy Pastelería offers a genteel taste of Old World charm in this district of rowdy pubs. This place has been a fixture since 1839 for Madrileños wanting to duck in for a cup of soup or a light snack. Step right in, and pretend you're an aristocrat back between the wars. Serve yourself. You'll pay as you leave (on the honor system). Help yourself to the silver water dispenser (free), a line of elegant bottles (each a different Iberian fortified wine: sherry, port, and so on, €2.80/glass), a revolving case of meaty little pastries (€1.40 each), and a fancy soup dispenser (chicken broth consommé-€2.60, or €3 with a splash of sherry...local style—bottles in the corner, help yourself; daily 10:00-22:00, Sun until 15:00; Carrera de San Jerónimo 8, tel. 915-222-207).

• *Next, forage up Calle Victoria.*

La Casa del Abuelo is where seafood lovers savor sizzling plates of tasty little *gambas* (shrimp) and *langostinos* (prawns), with bread to sop up the delightful juices. As drinks are cheap and dishes are small and pricey, you might just want to share a *ración* or sample some wine. For about €11, try *gambas a la plancha* (grilled shrimp) or *gambas al ajillo* (ah-HEE-yoh, a small clay dish of shrimp cooked in oil and garlic); wash it down with a €2.30 glass of sweet red house wine. They serve gazpacho May through September (daily 12:00-24:00, Calle Victoria 12).

• *Head around the corner onto Calle de la Cruz.*

At **La Oreja de Jaime** (not to be confused with another eatery called La Oreja de Oro), the specialty is sautéed pigs' ears (*oreja,* €5). While pig ears are a Madrid dish (fun to try, hard to swallow), this place is Galician—they serve *pimientos de Padrón* (sau-

Breakfast in Madrid

Most hotels don't include breakfast (and many don't even serve it), so you may be out on the streets first thing looking for a place to eat. Nontouristy cafés only offer a hot drink and a pastry, with perhaps a potato omelet and sandwiches (toasted cheese, ham, or both). Touristy places will have a *desayuno* menu with various ham-and-eggs deals. Try *churros* once (see the listings on page 98 for my favorite places); if you're not in the mood for heavy chocolate in the morning, go local and dip your *churros* in a *café con leche*. If all else fails, a Starbucks is often nearby (just like home). Get advice from your hotel staff for their favorite breakfast place. My typical breakfast, found at any corner bar: *café con leche, tortilla española* (a slice of potato omelet), and *zumo de naranja natural* (fresh-squeezed orange juice).

téed miniature green peppers—quite possibly the tastiest plate of the entire crawl, €4.50) and the distinctive *ribeiro* (ree-BAY-roh) wine, served Galician-style, in characteristic little ceramic bowls to disguise its lack of clarity (Calle de la Cruz 12, tel. 647-293-693).

• *For a finale, continue up Calle de la Cruz.*

Memorable little **Casa Toni** is my favorite stop on this crawl. Run by Toni, it has a helpful English menu and several fun, classic dishes to try: *patatas bravas* (fried potatoes in a spicy sauce, €4.20), *berenjena* (deep-fried slices of eggplant, €5.20), *champiñones* (sautéed mushrooms, €5.70), and gazpacho—the cold tomato-and-garlic soup (€2.50) that is generally served only during the hot season, but available here year-round just for you (closed 16:00-19:00 and July, Calle de la Cruz 14, tel. 915-322-580).

More Options: If you're hungry for more, and want a trendy, up-to-date, pricier tapas experience, head for Plaza Santa Ana, with lively bars spilling out onto the square. Survey the entire scene. Consider **Cervecería de Santa Ana** (tasty tapas with two zones: rowdy, circa-1900 beer hall and classier sit-down) or **Naturbier,** a local microbrewery. **La Vinoteca,** at the downhill end of the square, has an inviting menu of tapas and fine wines by the glass (indoor and outdoor seating). **Casa Gonzalez,** a venerable gourmet cheese and wine shop with a circa-1930s interior, offers a genteel opportunity to enjoy a plate of first-class cheese and a fine glass of wine with friendly service and a fun setting recalling the happy days of the Republic of Spain—after the monarchy but before Franco. Their €17 assortment of five Spanish cheeses—more than enough for two—is a cheese lover's treat (40 wines by the glass, Mon-Sat 9:30-24:00, Sun 11:00-18:00, three blocks past Plaza Santa Ana at Calle de León 12, tel. 914-295-618, Francisco and Luciano).

EATING CHEAPLY
On or near Plaza Mayor

Madrileños enjoy a bite to eat on Plaza Mayor (without its high costs) by grabbing food to go from a nearby bar and just planting themselves somewhere on the square to eat (squid sandwiches are popular). But for many tourists, dinner at a sidewalk café right on Plaza Mayor is worth the premium price (consider Cervecería Pulpito, southwest corner of the square at #10).

Squid Sandwiches: Plaza Mayor is famous for its *bocadillos de calamares*. For a tasty €2.80 squid-ring sandwich, line up at **Casa Rúa** at Plaza Mayor's northwest corner, a few steps up Calle Ciudad Rodrigo (daily 11:00-23:00). Hanging up behind the bar is a photo-advertisement of Plaza Mayor from the 1950s, when the square contained a park.

Bullfighting Bar: The walls of **La Torre del Oro Bar Andalú** are lined with grisly bullfight photos. This place is good for drinks,

but you pay a premium for the tapas and food...the cost of munching amidst all that bullephenalia while enjoying their excellent Plaza Mayor outdoor seating (daily 8:00-15:00 & 18:00-24:00, closed in Jan).

Mercado de San Miguel: This early-20th-century market sparkles after a recent renovation and bustles with a trendy food circus of eateries (daily 10:00-24:00). While it's expensive and touristy, it's also fun and accessible. You can stroll while you munch, hang out at bars, or take a break at one of the market's food-court-style tables.

Near Puerta del Sol

Restaurante Puerto Rico, a simple, no-nonsense place, serves good meals for great prices to smart Madrileños in a long, congested hall (€13 three-course fixed-price meal, long hours daily, Chinchilla 2, between Puerta del Sol and Gran Vía, tel. 915-219-834).

Restaurante-Cafeteria Europa is a fun, high-energy scene with a mile-long bar, old-school waiters, great people-watching, local cuisine, and a fine €11 fixed-price lunch (offered daily 13:00-16:00, inside only). The menu lists three price levels: bar (inexpensive), table (generally pricey), or terrace (sky-high but with good people-watching). Your best value is to stick to the lunch menu if you're sitting inside, or order off the plastic *barra* menu if you sit at the bar—the €3 ham-and-egg toast or the homemade *churros* make a nice breakfast (daily 7:00-24:00, next to Hotel Europa, 50 yards off Puerta del Sol at Calle del Carmen 4, tel. 915-212-900).

El Corte Inglés' top-floor cafeterias (in both of its buildings) are fresh, modern, and popular, though not particularly cheap. One is just off Puerta del Sol at the intersection of Calle de Preciados and Calle de Tetuán, but the better one is near Plaza del Callao: Its snazzy Gourmet Experience houses a specialty grocery mart and 10 different mini-restaurants with cuisines ranging from Mexican to Chinese. The lunch hour is busy, though it's worth the wait for its great views of Gran Vía and Plaza de España. Take a seat at any of the indoor tables, or out on the open terrace (Mon-Sat 10:00-24:00, Sun 11:00-24:00, shorter hours at Puerta del Sol location).

Casa Labra Taberna Restaurante is famous as the birthplace of the Spanish Socialist Party in 1879...and as a spot for great cod. Packed with Madrileños, it manages to be both dainty and rustic. It's a wonderful scene with three distinct sections: the stand-up bar (cheapest, with two lines: one for munchies, the other for drinks), a peaceful little sit-down area in back (a little more expensive but still cheap; €6 salads), and a fancy restaurant (€20 fixed-price lunch). Their tasty little €1.40 *tajada de bacalao* cod dishes put them on the map. The waiters are fun to joke around with (daily 11:00-15:30 & 18:00-23:00, a block off Puerta del Sol at Calle Tetuán 12, tel. 915-310-081).

Vegetarian: **Artemisia II** is a hit with vegetarians and vegans, who like good, healthy food without the typical hippie ambience that comes with most veggie places (great €12 three-course fixed-price lunch Mon-Fri only, open daily 13:30-16:00 & 21:00-24:00, north of Puerta del Sol at Tres Cruces 4, a few steps off Plaza del Carmen, tel. 915-218-721).

Other Budget Options

Fast-Food Sandwich Joints: For an easy, light, and cheap meal, look for the Spanish answers to Subway: **Rodilla** and **Pans & Company** (open daily 9:00-23:00). You'll see them on Puerta del Sol and nearly every square, offering all the ambience of a McDonald's and a good selection of fresh sandwiches and prepackaged salads.

Picnic: The department store **El Corte Inglés** has well-stocked meat and cheese counters in its lower-level grocery store (Mon-Sat 10:00-22:00, Sun 11:00-21:00).

Churros con Chocolate

Those not watching their cholesterol will want to try the deep-fried doughy treats called *churros* (or the thicker *porras*), best enjoyed by dipping them in pudding-like hot chocolate. Though many *chocolaterías* offer the dunkable fritters, *churros* are most delicious when consumed fresh out of the greasy cauldron at a place that actually fries them. Two of my favorites are near Puerta del Sol.

Chocolatería San Ginés is a classy institution, much beloved by Madrileños for its *churros con chocolate* (€4). Dunk your *churros* into the warm chocolate pudding, as locals have done here for more than 100 years. Though quiet before midnight, it's packed with the disco crowd in the wee hours; the popular dance club Joy Eslava is next door (open 24 hours; from Puerta del Sol, take Calle del Arenal 2 blocks west, turn left on bookstore-lined Pasadizo de San Ginés, and you'll see the café at #5; tel. 913-656-546).

Chocolaterías Valor, a modern chain and Spanish chocolate maker, does *churros* with pride and gusto. A few minutes' walk from nearly all my hotel recommendations, it's a fine place for breakfast. With a website like www.amigosdelchocolate.com, you know where their heart is. You can also buy powdered Valor chocolate at supermarkets (like the one at El Corte Inglés) to make the drink at home (€4.30 *churros con chocolate,* daily 8:00-22:30, Fri-Sat until 24:00, a half-block below Plaza del Callao and Gran Vía at Postigo de San Martín 7, tel. 915-229-288).

Madrid Connections

BY TRAIN

Madrid has two main train stations: Chamartín and Atocha. Both stations offer long-distance trains *(largo recorridos)* as well as smaller local trains (*regionales* and *cercanías*) to nearby destinations. You can **buy tickets** at the stations, at travel agencies, or online. (For all the details, see the Practicalities chapter.) While travel agencies add a small fee, they can be a good place to buy tickets, especially during the high season or holidays, when the station's ticket counters have long lines. Convenient locations include the El Corte Inglés travel agency at Atocha (Mon-Fri 8:00-22:00, Sat-Sun 10:00-18:00, on ground floor of AVE side at the far end) and the El Corte Inglés department store at Puerta del Sol (see "Travel Agencies" on page 13).

Chamartín Station

The TI is near track 20. The impressively large information, tickets, and customer-service office is at track 11. You can relax in the Sala VIP Club if you have a first-class rail pass and first-class seat or sleeper reservations (between tracks 13 and 14, cooler of free drinks). Luggage storage *(consigna)* is across the street, opposite track 17. The station's Metro stop is also called Chamartín (not "Pinar de Chamartín"). Train connections from here are listed later.

Atocha Station

The station is split in two: an AVE side (mostly long-distance trains) and a *cercanías* side (mostly local trains to the suburbs—known as *cercanías*—and the Metro for connecting into downtown). These two parts are connected by a corridor of shops. Each side of the station has separate schedules and customer-service offices. The TI, which is on the AVE arrivals side, offers tourist info, but no train info (Mon-Sat 8:00-20:00, Sun 9:00-14:00, tel. 915-284-630). To get to Atocha, use the "Atocha RENFE" Metro stop (not "Atocha").

Ticket Offices: The *cercanías* side has two offices—a small one for local trains and a big one for major trains (such as AVE). The AVE side has a pleasant, airy office that sells tickets for AVE and other long-distance trains (two lines: "Tickets in Advance" or "Selling Out Today"/"Departures Today"). A ticket counter will sometimes open up to sell tickets for trains departing soon—if you need to make a last-minute purchase, look for your destination and departure time, and get in line at that counter. If the line at one office is long, check the other offices. To secure your place in line, grab a number from a machine, usually located in the middle of the office by a sign with an image of a ticket. Ticket machines outside and around the office require a chip-and-PIN credit card.

AVE Side: Located in the towering old-station building, this half of the station boasts a lush, tropical garden filling its grand

hall. It has the AVE trains, other fast trains (Grandes Líneas), a pharmacy (daily 8:00-22:00, facing garden), and the wicker-elegant Samarkanda— both an affordable cafeteria (daily 13:00-20:00) and a pricey restaurant (daily from 21:00, tel. 915-309-746). Luggage storage *(consigna)* is below Samarkanda (daily 6:00-22:20). In the departure lounge on the upper floor, TV monitors announce track numbers. (A few trains, such as those for Toledo, Alicante, and Valencia, depart from the lower floor.) For information, try the *Información* counter (daily 6:30-22:30), next to Centro Servicios AVE (which handles only AVE changes and problems). The *Atención al Cliente* office deals with problems on Grandes Líneas (daily 6:30-23:30). Also on the AVE side is the Club AVE/Sala VIP, a lounge reserved solely for AVE business-class travelers and for first-class ticket-holders or Eurailers with a first-class reservation (upstairs, past the security check on right; free drinks, newspapers, showers, and info service).

Cercanías Side: This is where you'll find the local *cercanías* trains, *regionales* trains, some eastbound faster trains, and the "Atocha RENFE" Metro stop. The *Atención al Cliente* office in the

MADRID

cercanías section has information only on trains to destinations near Madrid. During busy times, some AVE trains will pull in on this side—clearly marked signs lead you to the Metro, taxi stand, or back to the AVE side.

Terrorism Memorial: The terrorist bombings of March 11, 2004, took place in Atocha and on local lines going into and out of the station. Security is understandably tight here. A moving memorial is in the *cercanías* part of the station near the Atocha RENFE Metro stop. Walk inside and under the cylinder to read the thousands of condolence messages in many languages (daily 11:00-14:00 & 17:00-19:00). The 36-foot-tall cylindrical glass memorial towers are visible from outside on the street.

AVE Trains

Spain's bullet train opens up some good itinerary options. You can get from Madrid's Atocha Station to **Barcelona** in about three hours, with trains running almost hourly. The AVE train is generally faster and easier than flying, but not necessarily cheaper. Basic second-class tickets are about €110-130 one-way for most departures; first-class tickets are €180. Advance purchase discounts (40-60 days ahead) are available through the national rail company (RENFE), but sell out quickly. Save by not traveling on holidays.

The AVE is also handy for visiting **Sevilla** (and, on the way, **Córdoba**). The basic Madrid-Sevilla second-class AVE fare is €75, depending upon departure time; first-class AVE costs €130 and comes with a meal. Consider this exciting day trip: 7:00-depart Madrid, 8:45-12:40-in Córdoba, 13:30-20:45-in Sevilla, 23:15-back in Madrid.

Other AVE destinations include **Toledo, Segovia,** and **Valencia.** Prices vary with times, class, date of purchase—RENFE discounts unsold AVE tickets as departure dates near. Eurail Pass holders pay a seat reservation fee (for example, Madrid to Sevilla is €13 second-class, but only at RENFE ticket windows—discount not available at ticket machines). Reserve each AVE segment ahead (tel. 902-320-320 for Atocha AVE info). For the latest, pick up the AVE brochure at the station, or check www.renfe.com.

Train Connections

Below I've listed both non-AVE and (where available) AVE trains to help you compare your options. General train info: tel. 902-320-320; international journeys: tel. 902-243-402; www.renfe.com.

From Madrid by Train to: Toledo (AVE or cheaper Avant: nearly hourly, 30 minutes, from Atocha), **El Escorial** (2/hour, but bus is better—see page 107), **Segovia** (AVE: 8-10/day, 30 minutes plus 20-minute shuttle bus into Segovia center, from Chamartín, take train going toward Valladolid; slower *cercanías* trains: 9/day,

2 hours, from both Chamartín and Atocha), **Ávila** (nearly hourly until 22:30, 1.5-2 hours, more frequent departures from Chamartín than Atocha), **Salamanca** (7/day, 3 hours, from Chamartín), **Valencia** (AVE: nearly hourly, 2 hours, from Atocha; in Valencia, AVE passengers arrive at Joaquín Sorolla Station), **Santiago de Compostela** (4/day, 5.5-8.5 hours, most transfer in Ourense, includes night train, from Chamartín), **Barcelona** (AVE: at least hourly, 2.5-3 hours from Atocha), **San Sebastián** (4/day, 5.5-7.5 hours, from Chamartín), **Bilbao** (2-3/day, 5-6.5 hours, some transfer in Zaragoza, from Chamartín), **Pamplona** (3/day direct, 3 hours, more with transfer in Zaragoza, from Atocha), **Burgos** (5/day, 2.5-5 hours, from Chamartín), **León** (8/day, 3-4.5 hours, from Chamartín), **Granada** (2/day on Altaria, 4.5 hours; also 2/day with transfer to AVE in Málaga, 4 hours), **Sevilla** (AVE: hourly, 2.5 hours, departures from 16:00-19:00 can sell out far in advance, from Atocha), **Córdoba** (AVE: 2-3/hour, 2 hours; Altaria trains: 4/day, 2 hours; all from Atocha), **Málaga** (AVE: 9/day, 2.5-3 hours, from Atocha), **Algeciras** (3/day, one with transfer in Antequera, 5.5-6 hours, from Atocha), **Lisbon** (1/night, 10.5 hours, from Chamartín).

BY BUS

Madrid has several major bus stations with good Metro connections. Multiple bus companies operate from these stations, including Alsa (tel. 902-422-242, www.alsa.es), Avanza and Auto-Res (tel. 902-020-052, www.avanzabus.com), and La Sepulvedana (tel. 901-119-699, www.lasepulvedana.es). If you take a taxi from any bus station, you'll be charged a legitimate €3 supplement (not levied for trips to the station).

Plaza Elíptica Station: Served by Alsa. Buses to Toledo leave from here (2/hour, 1-1.5 hours, *directo* faster than *ruta*, Metro: Plaza Elíptica).

Estación Sur de Autobuses (South Station): Served by Alsa, Socibus, and Avanza. From here, buses go to **Ávila** (9/day, 6/day on weekends, 1.5 hours, Avanza), **Salamanca** (hourly express, 2.5-3 hours, Avanza), **León** (10/day, 3.5-4.5 hours, Alsa), **Santiago de Compostela** (5/day, 8-11 hours, includes 1 night bus, Alsa), **Granada** (nearly hourly, 5-6 hours, Alsa), and **Lisbon** (2/day, 9 hours, Avanza). The station sits squarely on top of the Méndez Álvaro Metro (has TI, tel. 914-684-200, www.estacionautobusesmadrid.com).

Príncipe Pío Station: Príncipe Pío is the old North train station, which has now morphed into a trendy mall and a bus hub for local lines including Segovia (2/hour departing on half-hour from platforms 6 or 7, 1.5 hours, runs from around 6:30-21:30, service starts later on Sat-Sun). From Metro: Príncipe Pío, follow signs to *terminal de autobuses* or follow pictures of a bus. Buy a ticket from the Sepulvedana window (platform 4). Reservations are rarely necessary.

Moncloa Station: This station, in the Moncloa Metro station, serves **El Escorial** (4/hour, fewer on weekends, 1 hour; for details, see page 107). To reach the **Valley of the Fallen,** it's best to connect via El Escorial (see page 115 for details).

Avenida de América Station: Served by Alsa. Located at the Avenida de América Metro, buses go to **Burgos** (hourly, 3 hours) and **Pamplona** (7/day, 5-7.5 hours).

BY PLANE
Madrid's Adolfo Suárez Barajas Airport

Ten miles east of downtown, Madrid's modern airport has four terminals. Terminals 1, 2, and 3 are connected by long indoor walkways (about an 8-minute walk apart) and serve airlines including Delta, United, US Airways, and Air Canada. The newer Terminal 4 serves airlines including Iberia, Vueling, Ryanair, British, and American, and also has a separate satellite terminal called T4S. To transfer between Terminals 1-3 and Terminal 4, you can take a 10-minute shuttle bus (free, leaves every 10 minutes from departures level), or take the Metro (stops at Terminals 2 and 4). Make sure to allow enough time if you need to travel between terminals (and then for the long walk within Terminal 4 to the gates). For more information about navigating this massive airport, go to www.aena-aeropuertos.es (airport code: MAD).

International flights typically use Terminals 1 and 4. At the Terminal 1 arrivals area, you'll find a helpful, though privately run, English-speaking Turismo Madrid **TI** (marked *Oficina de Información Turística*, Mon-Sat 8:00-20:00, Sun 9:00-14:00, tel. 913-058-656), **ATMs,** a **flight info office** (marked simply *Information* in airport lobby, open daily 24 hours, tel. 902-353-570), a **post-office** window, a pharmacy, lots of phones (buy a phone card from the nearby machine), a few scattered **Internet** terminals (small fee), **eateries,** a **RENFE office** (where you can get train info and buy long-distance train tickets, long hours daily, tel. 902-320-320), and on-the-spot **car-rental agencies.** The super-modern Terminal 4 offers essentially the same services. **Luggage storage** *(consigna)* is in Terminal 2, near the Metro exit. Some buses leave from the airport to far-flung destinations, such as Pamplona (see www.alsa.es; buy ticket online or from the driver).

Consider flying between Madrid and other cities in Spain (see "Flights" in the Practicalities chapter). Domestic airline Vueling (www.vueling.com) is popular for its discounts (e.g., Madrid-Barcelona flight as cheap as €30 if booked in advance).

Getting Between the Airport and Downtown

By Public Bus: The yellow **Exprés Aeropuerto** runs between the airport (all terminals) and Atocha Station (€5, pay driver in cash, departing from arrivals level every 15-20 minutes, ride takes about 40 minutes, runs 24 hours a day; from 23:30-6:00, the bus only goes to Plaza de Cibeles, not all the way to Atocha). From Atocha, you can take a taxi or the Metro to your hotel. The bus back to the airport leaves Atocha from near the taxi stand on the *cercanías* side (from 23:30-6:00, it departs downtown from Plaza de Cibeles).

Bus #200 (from all terminals) is less handy than the express bus because it leaves you farther from downtown (at the Metro stop at Avenida de América, northeast of the historical center). This bus departs from the arrivals level about every 10 minutes and takes about 20 minutes to reach Avenida de América (runs 6:00-24:00, buy €1.50 ticket from driver; or get a shareable 10-ride Metrobus ticket at a tobacco shop).

By Cercanías Train: From Terminal 4, passengers can ride a *cercanías* train to either of Madrid's stations (€2.60, 2/hour, 25 minutes to Atocha, 12 minutes to Chamartín). The bus is still a more convenient choice for arriving or departing from the other airport terminals.

By Metro: Considering the ease of riding the Exprés Aeropuerto bus in from the airport, I'd rather bus than Metro. The subway involves two transfers to reach the city; it's not difficult, but usually involves climbing some stairs (€4.50-6; or add a €3 supplement to your 10-ride Metrobus ticket). The airport's futuristic "Aeropuerto T-1, T-2, T-3" Metro stop (notice the ATMs, subway info booth, and huge lighted map of Madrid) is in Terminal 2. Access the Metro at the check-in level; to reach the Metro from Terminal 1's arrivals level, stand with your back to the baggage claim, then go to your far right, up the stairs, and follow red-and-blue Metro diamond signs to the station (8-minute walk). The Terminal 4 stop is the end of the line. To get to Puerta del Sol, take line 8 for 12 minutes to Nuevos Ministerios, then continue on line 10 to Tribunal, then line 1 to Puerta del Sol (30 minutes more total); or exit at Nuevos Ministerios and take a €5 taxi or bus #150 straight to Puerta del Sol.

By Minibus Shuttle: The AeroCity shuttle bus provides door-to-door transport in a seven-seat minibus with up to three hotel stops en route. It's promoted by hotels, but if you want door-to-door service, simply taking a taxi generally offers a better value.

By Taxi: With cheap and easy alternatives available, there's not much reason to take a taxi unless you have lots of luggage or just want to go straight to your hotel. If you do take a taxi between the airport and downtown, the flat rate is €30. There is no charge for luggage. Plan on getting stalled in traffic.

MADRID

BY CAR

Avoid driving in Madrid. If you're planning to rent a car, do it when you depart the city.

Renting a Car: It's cheapest to make car-rental arrangements before you leave home. In Madrid, consider **Europcar** (central reservations tel. 902-105-030, San Leonardo 8 office tel. 915-418-892, Atocha Station tel. 902-105-055, Chamartín Station tel. 912-035-070, airport tel. 902-105-055), **Hertz** (central reservations tel. 902-402-405, Plaza de España 18 tel. 915-425-805, Chamartín Station tel. 917-330-400, airport tel. 913-228-331), **Avis** (central reservations tel. 933-443-700, Gran Vía 60 tel. 915-484-204, airport tel. 902-200-162), and **Enterprise Atesa** (central reservations tel. 902-100-101). Ask about free delivery to your hotel. At the airport, most rental cars are returned at Terminal 1. For more on renting a car and driving in Spain, see page 189 of the Practicalities chapter.

Route Tips for Drivers: To leave Madrid from Gran Vía, simply follow signs for *A-6* (direction *Villalba* or *A Coruña*) for Segovia, El Escorial, or the Valley of the Fallen (see next chapter for details).

NORTHWEST OF MADRID

El Escorial • Valley of the Fallen • Segovia • Ávila

Before slipping out of Madrid, consider several fine side-trips northwest of Spain's capital city, all conveniently reached by car, bus, or train.

Spain's lavish, brutal, and complicated history is revealed throughout Old Castile. This region, where the Spanish language originated, is named for its many castles—battle scars from the long-fought Reconquista.

An hour from Madrid, tour the imposing and fascinating palace at El Escorial, headquarters of the Spanish Inquisition. Nearby, at the awe-inspiring Valley of the Fallen, pay tribute to the countless victims of Spain's bloody civil war.

Segovia, with its remarkable Roman aqueduct and romantic castle, is another worthwhile side-trip. At Ávila you can walk the perfectly preserved medieval walls.

PLANNING YOUR TIME

You can see El Escorial and the Valley of the Fallen in less than a day, but don't go on a Monday, when both sights are closed. By car,

see them en route to Segovia; by bus, make them a day trip from Madrid.

Segovia, worth a half-day of sightseeing, is easy to reach from Madrid. If you have time, spend the night—the city is a joy in the evenings. Ávila, while charming, merits only a quick stop (if you're driving and in the area) to marvel at its medieval walls and, perhaps, check out St. Teresa's finger (1.5 hours

NORTHWEST OF MADRID

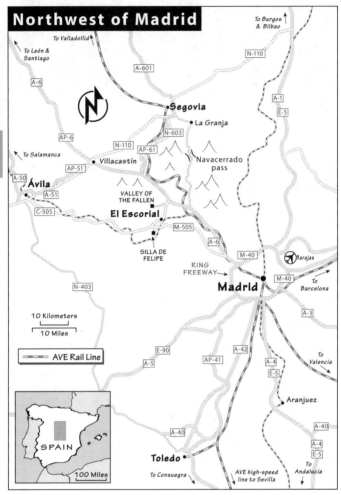

from Madrid, also a logical stop on the way to/from Salamanca by train).

In total, these sights are worth two days if you're in Spain for less than a month. If you're a history buff in Spain for just a week, squeeze in a quick side-trip from Madrid to El Escorial and the Valley of the Fallen.

Monasterio de San Lorenzo de El Escorial

The Monasterio de San Lorenzo de El Escorial, worth ▲▲▲, is a symbol of power rather than elegance. This 16th-century palace, 30

miles northwest of Madrid, was built at a time when Catholic Spain felt threatened by Protestant "heretics," and its construction dominated the Spanish economy for a generation (1562-1584). Because of this bully in the national budget, Spain has almost nothing else to show from this most powerful period of her history. El Escorial gives us a better feel for the Counter-Reformation and the Inquisition than any other building.

GETTING TO EL ESCORIAL

Most people visit El Escorial from Madrid. By public transportation, the bus is most convenient (since it gets you closer to the palace than the train does). Remember that it makes sense to combine El Escorial with a visit to the nearby Valley of the Fallen.

By Bus: Buses leave from the Moncloa bus station, which is in the basement of Madrid's Moncloa Metro station (4/hour, fewer on weekends, 1 hour, €4.20 one-way, buy ticket from driver; in Madrid take bus #664 or slower #661 from Moncloa's platform 11, Herranz Bus, tel. 918-969-028). The bus drops you downtown in San Lorenzo de El Escorial, a pleasant 10-minute stroll from the palace (see map): Exit the bus station from the back ramp that leads over the parked buses (noting that return buses to Madrid leave from platform 3 or 4 below this ramp; bus schedule posted by information counter inside station), turn left, and follow the cobbled pedestrian lane, Calle San Juan. This street veers to the right and becomes Calle Juan de Leyva. In a few short blocks, it dead-ends at Duque de Medinaceli, where you'll turn left and see the palace. Stairs lead past several decent eateries, through a delightful square, past the TI (Tue-Sat 10:00-14:00 & 15:00-18:00, Sun 10:00-14:00, closed Mon; tel. 918-905-313), and directly to the tourist entry of the immense palace/monastery.

By Train: Local trains (*cercanías* line C-8A) run at least twice an hour from Madrid's Atocha and Chamartín stations to El Escorial. From the station, walk 20 minutes uphill through Casita del Príncipe park, straight up from the station. Or you can take a shuttle bus from the station (2/hour, usually timed with arrival of

NORTHWEST OF MADRID

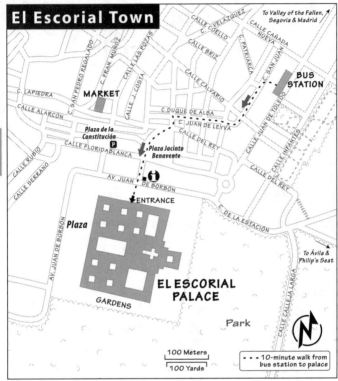

El Escorial Town

To Valley of the Fallen,
Segovia & Madrid

CALLE VELAZQUEZ
CALLE COELLO
CALLE CAÑADA NUEVA
CALLE BRIZ
CALLE CALVARIO
C. FRAN MUÑOZ
CALLE LAS ROZAS
SAN PEDRO REGALADO
C. J. COSTA
C. PATRIARCA
C. SAN JUAN

BUS STATION

C. LAPIEDRA
CALLE ALARCÓN
MARKET

C. DUQUE DE ALBA
C. JUAN DE LEYVA
CALLE DEL REY
CALLE JUAN DE TOLEDO

Plaza de la Constitución
P
CALLE FLORIDABLANCA
Plaza Jacinto Benavente

CALLE RUBIO
CALLE SERRANO

AV. JUAN DE BORBON

CALLE INFANTES
CALLE DEL REY

ENTRANCE

Plaza

AV. JUAN DE BORBON

C. DE LA ESTACIÓN

EL ESCORIAL PALACE

GARDENS

To Ávila & Philip's Seat

CALLE CALLEJA LARGA

Park

100 Meters
100 Yards

- - - 10-minute walk from bus station to palace

trains, €1.30) or a taxi (€7.50) to the San Lorenzo de El Escorial town center and the palace.

By Car: It's quite simple. Pick up or have your rental car delivered by 8:30, and ask for directions to highway A-6. From Gran Vía in central Madrid, follow signs to *A-6* (direction *Villalba* or *A Coruña*). The freeway leads directly out of town. Stay on A-6 past the first El Escorial exit. At kilometer 37 you'll see the cross marking the Valley of the Fallen ahead on the left. Exit 47 takes you to both the Valley of the Fallen (after a half-mile, a granite gate on right marks Valle de los Caídos turnoff) and El Escorial (follow *San Lorenzo de El Escorial* signs).

The nearby **Silla de Felipe** (Philip's Seat) is a rocky viewpoint where the king would come to admire his palace as it was being built. From El Escorial, follow directions to Ávila, then M-505 to Valdemorillo; look for a sign on your right after about a mile.

When you leave El Escorial for Madrid, Toledo, or Segovia, follow signs to *A-6 Guadarrama*. After about six miles you pass the Valley of the Fallen and hit the freeway.

ORIENTATION TO EL ESCORIAL

Cost and Hours: €10, April-Sept Tue-Sun 10:00-20:00, Oct-March Tue-Sun 10:00-18:00, closed Mon year-round, last entry one hour before closing, basilica closes 10 minutes before the rest of the sight.

Information: English descriptions are scattered within the palace. For more information, get the *Guide: Monastery of San Lorenzo El Real de El Escorial,* which follows the general route you'll take (€9, available at any of several shops in the palace). Tel. 918-905-904, www.patrimonionacional.es.

Tours: For an extra €4, a guided 1.5-hour **tour** takes you through the complex and covers other buildings on the grounds, including the Palace of the Bourbons (Palacio de los Borbones), House of the Infants (Casita del Infante), and House of the Prince (Casita del Príncipe). Unfortunately, there are so few tours in English that it generally isn't worth waiting around for one. Ask when the next tour in English is scheduled, and if nothing's running soon, go on your own: You can follow my self-guided tour, which covers the basics, or rent the €4 **audioguide.**

Eating: The **Mercado Público,** a four-minute walk from the palace, is the place to shop for a picnic (Mon-Wed and Fri 9:30-13:30 & 17:00-20:00, Thu and Sat 9:30-14:00, closed Sun, Calle del Rey 9). On **Plaza Jacinto Benavente and Plaza de la Constitución,** just two blocks north of the palace complex, you'll find a handful of nondescript but decent restaurants serving fixed-price lunches, often at shady outdoor tables (best on weekdays).

➋ SELF-GUIDED TOUR

The *monasterio* looks confusing at first, but the *visita* arrows and signs help guide you through one continuous path. This is the general order you'll follow.

• *Pass through the security scanner, buy your ticket, and then continue down the hall past the* consigna *baggage check (Sala 1) to the...*

Museum of Tapestries

This chamber is hung with 16th-century tapestries, including fascinating copies of Hieronymus Bosch's most famous and preachy paintings (which Philip II fancied). Don't miss El Greco's towering painting of the *Martyrdom of St. Maurice.* This was the artist's first commission after arriving in Spain from Venice. It was too subtle and complex for the king, so El Greco moved on to Toledo to find work.

• *Continue downstairs to the fascinating...*

NORTHWEST OF MADRID

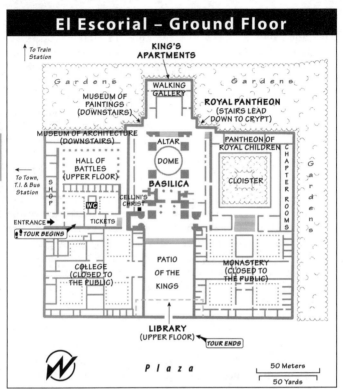

El Escorial – Ground Floor

To Train Station

KING'S APARTMENTS

Gardens

MUSEUM OF PAINTINGS (DOWNSTAIRS)

WALKING GALLERY

Gardens

ROYAL PANTHEON (STAIRS LEAD DOWN TO CRYPT)

MUSEUM OF ARCHITECTURE (DOWNSTAIRS)

ALTAR

DOME

PANTHEON OF ROYAL CHILDREN

CHAPTER ROOMS

HALL OF BATTLES (UPPER FLOOR)

To Town, T.I. & Bus Station

SHOP

BASILICA

CELLINI'S CHRIST

CLOISTER

Gardens

WC

ENTRANCE

TICKETS

TOUR BEGINS

COLLEGE (CLOSED TO THE PUBLIC)

PATIO OF THE KINGS

MONASTERY (CLOSED TO THE PUBLIC)

LIBRARY (UPPER FLOOR)

TOUR ENDS

Plaza

50 Meters

50 Yards

Museum of Architecture (Museo de Arquitectura)

It has long, parallel corridors of fine models of the palace and some of the actual machinery and tools used to construct it. Huge stone-pinching winches, fat ropes, and rusty mortar spades help convey the immensity of this 21-year project involving 1,500 workers. At the big model, you can see how the complex is shaped like a grill. San Lorenzo—St. Lawrence, a Christian Spaniard martyred by pagan Romans (A.D. 258)—was burned to death on a grill. Throughout the palace, you'll see this symbol associated with the saint. The grill's "handle" was the palace, or residence of the royal family. The monastery and school gathered around the huge basilica.

• *Next linger in the...*

Museum of Paintings

Consider the 15th- to 17th-century Flemish, Spanish, and Italian works. In the fourth room of paintings, contemplate Rogier van der Weyden's *Calvary*, with mourning Mary and St. John at the feet of the crucified Christ (may be away for restoration during your visit). It's interesting to compare it with Van der Weyden's similar *Descent from the Cross*, which hangs in the Prado in Madrid. For an in-the-moment comparison, check out artist Michiel Coxcie's copy on the nearby wall.

• *Pass through the peaceful and empty Courtyard of the Fountainheads (Patio de Mascarones), and go upstairs to the...*

Hall of Battles (Sala de Batallas)

Its paintings celebrate Spain's great military victories—including the Battle of San Quentin over France (1557) on St. Lawrence's feast day, which inspired the construction of El Escorial. The sprawling series, painted in 1590, helped teach the new king all the elements of warfare. Stroll the length for a primer on army skills.

• *Head back downstairs, following signs to* Palacio de los Austrias, *then follow a corridor lined with various family trees (some scrawny, others lush and fecund). The hall leads into the building's grill handle, the...*

King's Apartments

Immediately inside the first door, find the small portrait of Philip II flanked by two large paintings of his daughters. The palace was like Philip: austere. Notice the simple floors, plain white walls, and bare-bones chandelier. This was the bedroom of one of his daughters. The sheet warmer beside her bed was often necessary during the winter. If the bed curtains are drawn, bend down to see the view from her bed...of the high altar in the basilica next door. The entire complex of palace and monastery buildings was built around that altar.

In the next room, the **Guard's room,** notice the reclinable sedan chair that Philip II, thick with gout, was carried in (for seven days) on his last trip from Madrid to El Escorial. He wanted to be here when he died.

The **Audience Chamber** is now a portrait gallery filled with Habsburg royals painted by popular local artists. The portraits of unattractive people that line the walls provide an instructive peek at the consequences of mixing blue blood with more of the same blue blood (inbreeding among royals was a common problem throughout Europe in those days). The Spanish emperor Charles V (1500-1558) is over the fireplace mantel. Charles, Philip II's dad, was the most powerful man in Europe, having inherited not only the Spanish crown, but also control over Germany, Austria, the Low Countries (Belgium and the Netherlands), and much of Italy. When he announced his abdication in 1555, his son Philip II inherited much of this territory...plus the responsibility of managing it. Philip's draining wars with France, Portugal, Holland, and England—including the disastrous defeat of Spain's navy, the Spanish

History of El Escorial

The giant, gloomy building made of gray-black stone looks more like a prison than a palace. About 650 feet long and 500 feet wide, it has 2,600 windows, 1,200 doors, more than 100 miles of passages, and 1,600 over-whelmed tourists.

Four hundred years ago, the enigmatic, introverted, and extremely Catholic King Philip II (1527-1598) ruled his bulky empire and directed the Inquisition from here. To Philip, the building embod-ied the wonders of Catholic learn-ing, spirituality, and arts. To 16th-century followers of Martin Luther, it epitomized the evil of closed-minded Catholicism. To archi-tects, the building—built on the cusp between styles—exudes both Counter-Reformation grandeur and understated Renais-sance simplicity. Today it's a time capsule of Spain's "Golden Age," packed with history, art, and Inquisition ghosts. (And at an elevation of nearly 3,500 feet, it can be friggin' cold.)

The building was conceived by Philip II to serve several purposes: as a grand mausoleum for Spain's royal family, start-ing with his father, the Holy Roman emperor Charles V; as a monastery to pray (a lot) for the royal souls; as a small palace to use as a Camp David of sorts for Spain's royalty; and as a school to embrace humanism in a way that promoted the Catholic faith.

Spanish architect Juan Bautista de Toledo, who had stud-ied in Italy, was called by Philip II to carry out the El Escorial project, but he died before it was finished. His successor, Juan de Herrera, made extensive changes to Toledo's original de-sign and completed the palace in 1584.

Armada, by England's Queen Elizabeth I (1588)—knocked Spain from its peak of power and began centuries of decline. The guy with the red tights and good-looking legs to the right of Charles is his illegitimate son, Don Juan de Austria—famous for his hand-some looks, thanks to a little fresh blood. Other royal offspring weren't so lucky: When one king married his niece, the result was Charles II (1665-1700, opposite Charles V). His severe underbite (an inbred royal family trait) was the least of his problems. An epi-leptic before that disease was understood, poor "Charles the Mad" would be the last of the Spanish Habsburgs. He died without an heir in 1700, ushering in the continent-wide War of the Spanish Succession and the dismantling of Spain's empire.

In the **Walking Gallery,** the royals got their exercise privately, with no risk of darkening their high-class skins with a tan. Study the 16th-century maps along the walls. The slate strip on the floor is a sundial from 1755. It lined up with a (now plugged) hole in the wall so that at noon a tiny beam hit the middle of the three lines. Palace clocks were set by this. Where the ray crossed the strip indicated the date and sign of the zodiac.

As you enter the **King's Antechamber,** look back to study the fine inlaid-wood door (a gift from the German emperor that celebrates the exciting humanism of the age).

Philip II's bedroom is austere, like his daughter's. Look at the king's humble bed...barely queen-size. He too could view Mass at the basilica's high altar without leaving his bed. The red box next to his pillow holds the royal bedpan. But don't laugh—the king's looking down from the wall to your left. At age 71, Philip II, the gout-ridden king of a dying empire, died in this bed (1598).

• *From here his body was taken to our next stop, the...*

Royal Pantheon (Panteón Real)

This is the gilded resting place of 26 kings and queens...four centuries' worth of Spanish monarchy. All the kings are included—but the only queens here are the ones who became mothers of kings.

A post-mortem filing system is at work in the Pantheon. From the entrance, kings are on the left, queens on the right. (The only exception is Isabel II, since she was a ruling queen and her husband was a consort.) The first and greatest, Charles V and his Queen Isabel, flank the altar on the top shelf. Her son, Philip II, rests below Charles and opposite (only) one of Philip's four wives, and so on. There is a waiting process, too. Before a royal corpse can rest in this room, it needs to decompose for at least 25 years. The bones of the current king's (Felipe VI) great-grandmother, Victoria Eugenia (who died in 1964), were transferred into the crypt in late 2011. The two empty niches are already booked: Felipe's grandfather, Don Juan (who died in 1993), is on the waiting list...controversially. Technically, he was never crowned king of Spain—Generalísimo Francisco Franco took control of Spain before Don Juan could ascend to the throne, and he was passed over for the job when Franco reinstituted the monarchy. Felipe's grandmother is the most recent guest in the rotting room. So where does that leave Felipe's parents, Juan Carlos and Sofía, and monarchs still to come (and go)? This hotel is *todo completo.*

The next rooms are filled with the tombs of lesser royals: Each bears that person's name (in Latin), relationship to the king, and slogan or epitaph. From here, it's on to the wedding-cake **Pantheon of Royal Children** (Panteón de los Infantes), which holds the remains of various royal children who died before the age of seven (and their first Communion).

• *Head past the tiny gift shop and continue upstairs to the...*

Chapter Rooms (Salas Capitulares)

These rooms are where the monks met to do church business; they're also lined with big-name paintings by José Ribera, El Greco, Titian, and Velázquez. (More great paintings are in the monastery's Museum of Painting.) Continue to the final room to see some atypical Bosch paintings and the intricate, portable altar of Charles V.

• *Next find the...*

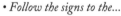

Cloister

The cloister glows with bright, restored paintings by Pellegrino Tibaldi. Off the cloister is the **Old Church** (Iglesia Vieja), which they used from 1571 to 1586, while finishing the basilica. During that time the bodies of several kings, including Charles V, were interred here. Among the many paintings, look for the powerful *Martyrdom of St. Lawrence* by Tiziano (Titian) above the main altar.

• *Follow the signs to the...*

Basilica

Find the flame-engulfed grill in the center of the altar wall that features San Lorenzo (the same St. Lawrence from the painting) meeting his famous death—and taking "turn the other cheek" to new extremes. Lorenzo was so cool, he reportedly told his Roman executioners, "You can turn me over now—I'm done on this side." With your back to the altar, go to the right corner for the artistic highlight of the basilica: Benvenuto Cellini's marble sculpture, *The Crucifixion*. Jesus' features are supposedly modeled after the Shroud of Turin. Cellini carved this from Carrara marble for his own tomb in 1562 (according to the letters under Christ's feet).

• *Cross the courtyard to enter the immense...*

Library (Biblioteca)

It's clear that education was a priority for the Spanish royalty.

Savor this room. The ceiling (by Tibaldi, depicting various disciplines labeled in Latin, the lingua franca of the multinational Habsburg Empire) is a burst of color. At the far end of the room, the armillary sphere—an elaborate model of the solar system—looks like a giant gyroscope, revolving unmistakably around the Earth, with a misshapen, underexplored North America. As you leave, look back above the wooden door. The plaque warns *"Excomunión..."*—you'll be excommunicated if you take a book without checking it out properly. Who needs late fees when you hold the keys to hell?

Valley of the Fallen

Six miles from El Escorial, high in the Guadarrama Mountains, is the Valley of the Fallen (Valle de los Caídos). A 500-foot-tall granite cross marks this immense and powerful underground monument to the victims of Spain's 20th-century nightmare—the Spanish Civil War (1936-1939).

GETTING TO THE VALLEY OF THE FALLEN

Most visitors side-trip to the Valley of the Fallen from El Escorial. If you don't have your own wheels, the easiest way to get between these two sights is to negotiate a deal with a **taxi** (to take you from El Escorial to Valley of the Fallen, wait 30-60 minutes, and then bring you back to El Escorial, €45 total). Or you can use the **bus** service between El Escorial and the Valley of the Fallen, though the timing isn't the most convenient (€11.20 includes entrance fee, 1/day Tue-Sun at 15:15, 15 minutes, return bus to El Escorial doesn't leave until 17:30—a long time to spend at this place).

ORIENTATION TO THE VALLEY OF THE FALLEN

Cost and Hours: €9; April-Sept Tue-Sun 10:00-19:00, Oct-March Tue-Sun 10:00-18:00, closed Mon year-round; last entry one hour before closing, basilica closes 30 minutes before site closes, ask about audioguide, tel. 918-905-611, www.valledeloscaidos.es.

Mass: You can enter the basilica during Mass, but you can't sightsee or linger afterward. One-hour services run Tue-Sat at 11:00 and Sun at 11:00, 13:00, and 17:30 (17:00 in winter). During services, the entire front of the basilica (altar and tombs) is closed. Mass is usually accompanied by the resident

The Spanish Civil War (1936-1939)

Thirty-three months of warfare killed roughly 500,000 Spaniards. Unlike America's Civil War, which split the US north and south, Spain's war was between classes and ideologies, dividing every city and village, and many families. It was especially cruel, with atrocities and reprisals on both sides.

The war began as a military coup to overthrow the democratically elected Republic, a government that the army and other conservative powers considered too liberal and disorganized. The rebel forces, called the Nationalists (Nacionalistas), consisted of the army, monarchy, Catholic Church, big business, and rural estates, with aid from Germany, Italy, and Portugal. Trying to preserve the liberal government were the Republicans (Republicanos), also called Loyalists: the government, urban areas, secularists, small business, and labor unions, with aid from the United States (minimal help) and the "International Brigades" of communists, socialists, and labor organizers.

In the summer of 1936, the army rebelled and took control of its own garrisons, rejecting the Republic and pledging allegiance to Generalísimo Francisco Franco (1892-1975). These Nationalists launched a three-year military offensive to take Spain region by region, town by town. The government ("Republicans") cobbled together an army of volunteers, local militias, and international fighters. The war pitted conservative Catholic priests against socialist factory workers, rich businessmen against radical students, sunburned farmers loyal to the old king against upwardly mobile small businessmen. People suffered. You'll notice that many elderly Spaniards are very short—a product of growing up during these hungry and very difficult civil war years.

Spain's civil war attracted international attention. Adolf Hitler and Benito Mussolini sent troops and supplies to their fellow fascist Franco. It was Hitler's Luftwaffe that helped Franco bomb the town of Guernica (April 1937), an event famously captured on canvas by Pablo Picasso (to read about the painting, see page 63). On the Republican side, hundreds of Americans (including Ernest Hemingway) steamed over to Spain, some to fight for democracy as part of the "Abraham Lincoln Brigade."

By 1938, only Barcelona and Madrid held out. But they were no match for Franco's army. On April 1, 1939, Madrid fell and the war ended, beginning 36 years of iron-fisted rule by Franco.

boys' choir, the "White Voices" (Spain's answer to the Vienna Boys' Choir).

VISITING THE VALLEY OF THE FALLEN

Approaching by car or bus, you enter the sprawling park through a granite gate. The best views of the cross are from the bridge (but note that it's illegal for drivers to stop anywhere along this road). To the right, tiny chapels along the ridge mark the Stations of the Cross, where pilgrims stop on their hike to this memorial.

In 1940, prison workers dug 220,000 tons of granite out of the hill beneath the cross to form an underground basilica, then used the stones to erect the cross (built like a chimney, from the inside). Since it's built directly over the dome of the subterranean basilica, a seismologist keeps a careful eye on things.

The stairs that lead to the imposing **monument** are grouped in sets of tens, meant to symbolize the Ten Commandments (including "Thou shalt not kill"—hmm). The emotional *pietà* draped over the basilica's entrance is huge—you could sit in the palm of Christ's hand. The statue was sculpted by Juan de Ávalos, the same artist who created the dramatic figures of the four Evangelists at the base of the cross. It must have had a powerful impact on mothers who came here to remember their fallen sons.

A solemn silence and a stony chill fill the **basilica.** At 300 yards long, it was built to be longer than St. Peter's...but the Vati-

can had the final say when it blessed only 262 of those yards. Many Spaniards pass under the huge, foreboding angels of fascism to visit the grave of General Franco—an unusual place of pilgrimage, to say the least.

After walking through the two long vestibules, stop at the iron gates of the actual basilica. The line of torch-like lamps adds to the shrine ambience. Franco's prisoners, the enemies of the right, dug this memorial out of solid rock from 1940 to 1950. (Though it looks like bare rock still shows on the ceiling, it's just a clever design.) The sides of the monument are lined with copies of 16th-century Brussels tapestries of the Apocalypse, and side chapels contain alabaster copies of Spain's most famous statues of the Virgin Mary.

Interred behind the high altar and side chapels (marked "RIP, 1936-1939, died for God and country") are the remains of approximately 34,000 people, both Franco's Nationalists and the anti-Franco Republicans (about 12,000), who lost their lives in the war. Regrettably, the urns are not visible, so it is Franco who takes center stage. His grave, strewn with flowers, lies behind the high altar. In front of the altar is the grave of José Antonio Primo de Rivera (1903-1936), the founder of Spanish fascism, who was killed by Republicans during the civil war. Between these fascists' graves, the statue of a crucified Christ is lashed to a timber Franco himself is said to have felled. The seeping stones seem to weep for the victims. Today, families of the buried Republicans remain upset that their kin are lying with Franco and his Nationalists.

As you leave, stare into the eyes of those angels with swords and two right wings and think about all the "heroes" who keep dying "for God and country," at the request of the latter. The expansive view from the monument's terrace includes the peaceful, forested valley and sometimes snow-streaked mountains.

While the **cross** is undergoing a lengthy restoration, access to it by funicular or by foot along the trail (marked *Sendero de la Cruz*) is closed.

SLEEPING AND EATING AT THE VALLEY OF THE FALLEN

Near the parking lot and bus stop are a café, WC, and some picnic tables. Basic overnight lodging is available at the **$$ Hospedería de la Santa Cruz,** a 100-room monastery behind the cross (Sb-€25-53, Db-€45-110, higher rates include meals, all include a pass to enter and leave the park after hours, tel. 918-905-511, www. valledeloscaidos.es/hospederia, info@hospederiasantacruz.com, no English spoken). A meditative night here is good mostly for monks.

Segovia

Fifty miles from Madrid, this town of 55,000 boasts a thrilling Roman aqueduct, a grand cathedral, and a historic castle. Since the city is more than 3,000 feet above sea level and just northwest of a mountain range, it is exposed to cool northern breezes, and people come here from Madrid for a break from the summer heat.

Day-Tripping from Madrid: Considering the easy train and bus connections (30 minutes one-way by AVE train, 1.5 hours by bus), Segovia makes a fine day trip from Madrid. The disadvantages of this plan are that you spend the coolest hours of the day (early and late) en route, you miss the charming evening scene in Segovia, and you'll pay more for a hotel in Madrid than in Segovia. If you have time, spend the night. But even if you just stay the day,

Segovia offers a rewarding and convenient break from the big-city intensity of Madrid.

Orientation to Segovia

Segovia is a medieval "ship" ready for your inspection. Start at the stern—the aqueduct—and stroll up Calle de Cervantes and Calle Juan Bravo to the prickly Gothic masts of the cathedral. Explore the tangle of narrow streets around playful Plaza Mayor and then descend to the Alcázar at the bow.

TOURIST INFORMATION

Segovia has four TIs. The TI on Plaza Mayor covers both Segovia and the surrounding region (at #10, daily July-mid-Sept 9:00-20:00, mid-Sept-June Mon-Sat 9:30-14:00 & 16:00-19:00, Sun 9:30-17:00, tel. 921-460-334, www.turismocastillayleon.com). The TI at Plaza del Azogüejo, at the base of the aqueduct, specializes in Segovia and has friendly staff, pay WCs, and a gift shop (daily 10:00-19:00, mid-Oct-Easter until 18:30, see wooden model of Segovia, tel. 921-466-720, www.turismodesegovia.com). Smaller TIs are at the bus station (behind a window, Wed-Sun 10:00-14:00, closed Mon-Tue, tel. 921-436-569) and the AVE train station (Mon-Fri 8:15-15:15, Sat-Sun 10:00-14:15 & 16:00-17:45, tel. 921-447-262).

ARRIVAL IN SEGOVIA

If day-tripping from Madrid, check the return schedule when you arrive here (or get one at the Segovia TI). You'll find luggage storage near the exit from the bus station (tokens sold daily 9:00-14:00 & 16:00-19:00, gives you access to locker until end of day). There's no luggage storage at the train station.

By Bus: It's a 10-minute walk from the bus station to the town center: Exit left out of the station, continue straight across the street, and follow Avenida Fernández Ladreda, passing San Millán church on the left, then San Clemente church on the right, before coming to the aqueduct.

By Train: From the AVE train station (called Guiomar), ride bus #11 for 20 minutes to the base of the aqueduct. To reach the center from the less-convenient *cercanías* train station, you can catch bus #6 or #8, take a taxi, or walk 30 minutes (start at Paseo del Conde de Sepulvedana—which becomes Paseo Ezequiel

González, head to the bus station, then turn right and head down Avenida Fernández Ladreda to the aqueduct).

HELPFUL HINTS

Free Churches: Segovia has plenty of little Romanesque churches that are free to enter shortly before or after Mass (see TI for a list of times), and many have architecturally interesting exteriors that are worth a look. On your way to the main sights, keep your eyes peeled for these hidden treasures: Coming from the bus station on Avenida Fernández Ladreda toward the center of town, you can see the San Millán church; on Plazas San Martín and San Esteban are two churches sharing their squares' names (though you can't go inside San Esteban); and on the way to the Alcázar on Plaza de la Merced is the San Andrés church.

Shopping: If you buy handicrafts such as tablecloths from street vendors, make sure the item you want is the one you actually get; some unscrupulous vendors substitute inferior goods at the last minute. A flea market is held on Plaza Mayor on Thursdays (roughly 8:00-15:00).

Local Guide: Elvira Valderrama Rascon, a hardworking young woman, is a good English-speaking guide (€115/3 hours, mobile 636-227-949, elvisvalrras@yahoo.es).

Sightseeing Bus: Bus Turístico is a weak version of a hop-on, hop-off bus, but it does give you a chance to take great panoramic photos of Segovia's boat-like shape, with the mountains as a backdrop. Pick it up at the aqueduct, and stay on for the full loop—it's not really worth using as a means of getting around town (€6.05, buy ticket on bus or at aqueduct TI; July-mid-Sept departs hourly 10:00-23:00, otherwise at 11:00, 12:00, 13:00, 16:00, and 17:00; tel. 921-466-721, www.urbanosdesegovia.com).

Segovia Walk

This 15-minute self-guided walk goes uphill from the Roman aqueduct to the city's main square along the pedestrian-only street. It's most enjoyable just before dinner, when it's cool and filled with strolling Segovians.

Start at Segovia's emblematic Roman aqueduct (described later, under "Sights in Segovia"). Walk about 100 yards up Calle de Cervantes, which becomes Calle Juan Bravo, until you reach the **"house**

NORTHWEST OF MADRID

of a thousand beaks" (Casa de los Picos) on your right. This building's original Moorish design is still easy to see, despite the wall just past the door that blocks your view from the street. This wall, the architectural equivalent of a veil, hid this home's fine courtyard—Moors didn't flaunt their wealth. You can step inside to see art students at work and perhaps an exhibit on display, but it's most interesting from the exterior. Notice its truncated tower, one of many fortified towers that marked the homes of feuding local noble families. In medieval Spain, clashing loyalties led to mini-civil wars. In the 15th century, as Ferdinand and Isabel centralized authority in Spain, nobles were required to lop their towers. You'll see the once-tall, now-stubby towers of 15th-century noble mansions all over Segovia. Another example of a similar once-fortified, now-softened house with a cropped tower is about 50 yards farther down the street, on the left, on tiny Plaza del Platero Oquendo.

Continue uphill until you come to the complicated **Plaza de San Martín,** a commotion of history surrounding a striking statue of Juan Bravo. When Charles V, a Habsburg who didn't even speak Spanish, took power, he imposed his rule over Castile. This threatened the local nobles, who, inspired and led by Juan Bravo, revolted in 1521. Although Juan Bravo lost the battle—and his head—he's still a symbol of Castilian pride. This statue was erected in 1921 on the 400th anniversary of his death.

In front of the Juan Bravo statue stands the bold and bulky **House of Siglo XV.** Its fortified *Isabelino* style was typical of 15th-century Segovian houses. Later, in a more peaceful age, the boldness of these houses was softened with the decorative stucco work—Arabic-style floral and geometrical patterns—that you see today (for example, in the big house across the street). The 14th-century Tower of Lozoya, behind the statue, is another example of the lopped-off towers.

On the same square, the 12th-century Church of St. Martín is Segovian Romanesque in style (a mix of Christian Romanesque and Moorish styles).

If you continue up the street another 100 yards, you'll see the **Corpus Christi Convent** on the left. For a donation, you can pop in to see the Franciscan church, which was once a synagogue, which was once a mosque. While sweet and peaceful, with lots of art featuring St. Francis, the church is skippable.

Keep going until you reach Segovia's inviting **Plaza Mayor**—once the scene of executions, religious theater, and bullfights with spectators jamming the balconies. The bullfights ended in the 19th century. When Segovians complained, they were given a more gentle form of entertainment—bands in the music kiosk. Today the very best entertainment here is simply enjoying a light meal,

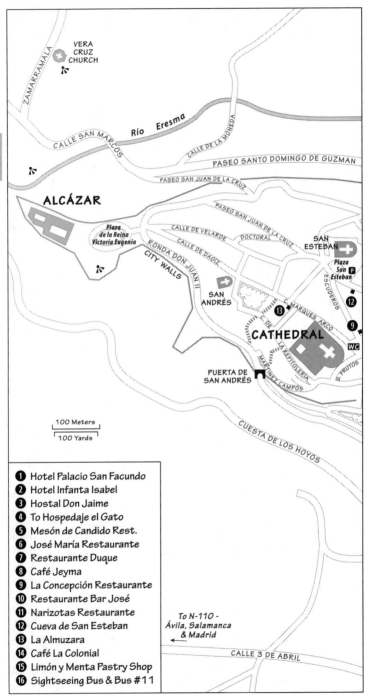

NORTHWEST OF MADRID

VERA CRUZ CHURCH

ZAMARRAMALA

CALLE SAN MARCOS

Río Eresma

CALLE DE LA MONEDA

PASEO SANTO DOMINGO DE GUZMAN

PASEO SAN JUAN DE LA CRUZ

ALCÁZAR

PASEO SAN JUAN DE LA CRUZ

Plaza de la Reina Victoria Eugenia

CALLE DE VELARDE

DOCTORAL

SAN ESTEBAN

CALLE DE DAOIZ

RONDA DON JUAN II

CITY WALLS

SAN ANDRÉS

Plaza San Esteban

ESCUDEROS

C. MARQUES ARCO

⓬

⓭

CATHEDRAL

⑨

C. DE LA REFITOLERIA

WC

S. FRUTOS

PUERTA DE SAN ANDRÉS

MARTINEZ CAMPOS

100 Meters
100 Yards

CUESTA DE LOS HOYOS

❶ Hotel Palacio San Facundo
❷ Hotel Infanta Isabel
❸ Hostal Don Jaime
❹ To Hospedaje el Gato
❺ Mesón de Candido Rest.
❻ José María Restaurante
❼ Restaurante Duque
❽ Café Jeyma
❾ La Concepción Restaurante
❿ Restaurante Bar José
⓫ Narizotas Restaurante
⓬ Cueva de San Esteban
⓭ La Almuzara
⓮ Café La Colonial
⓯ Limón y Menta Pastry Shop
⓰ Sightseeing Bus & Bus #11

To N-110 –
Ávila, Salamanca
& Madrid

CALLE 3 DE ABRIL

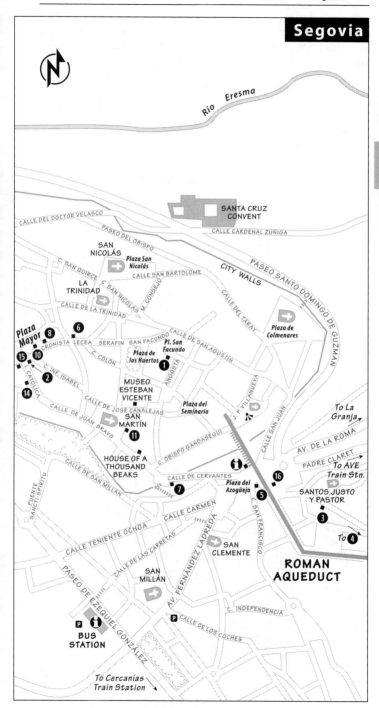

Segovia

NORTHWEST OF MADRID

Río Eresma

SANTA CRUZ CONVENT

CALLE DEL DOCTOR VELASCO

PASEO DEL OBISPO

CALLE CARDENAL ZÚÑIGA

SAN NICOLÁS

Plaza San Nicolás

C. SAN QUIRCE

C. SAN NICOLÁS

CALLE SAN BARTOLOMÉ

LA TRINIDAD

CALLE DE LA TRINIDAD

M. CONSEJO

PASEO SANTO DOMINGO DE GUZMÁN

CITY WALLS

CALLE DEL TARAY

Plaza de Colmenares

CALLE DE SAN AGUSTÍN

Plaza Mayor

8

6

CRONISTA LECEA

SERAFÍN

SAN FACUNDO

Pl. San Facundo

1

ANGOSTA

15

10

C. COLÓN

Plaza de los Huertos

C. INF. ISABEL

2

MUSEO ESTEBAN VICENTE

14

CATÓLICA

CALLE DE JOSÉ CANALEJAS

Plaza del Seminario

J. P. VILLANUEVA

To La Granja

CALLE DE JUAN BRAVO

SAN MARTÍN

11

AV. DE LA ROMA

CALLE SAN JUAN

PADRE CLARET

To AVE Train Stn.

HOUSE OF A THOUSAND BEAKS

C. OBISPO GANDÁSEGUI

CALLE DE SAN MILLÁN

PUENTE SANCTI-SPIRITU

CALLE DE CERVANTES

7

i

Plaza del Azoguejo

16

C. SAN FRANCISCO

5

SANTOS JUSTO Y PASTOR

3

CALLE CARMEN

To **4**

CALLE TENIENTE OCHOA

CALLE DE LAS CARRETAS

SAN CLEMENTE

AV. FERNÁNDEZ LADREDA

ROMAN AQUEDUCT

SAN MILLÁN

PASEO DE EZEQUIEL GONZÁLEZ

C. INDEPENDENCIA

P

i

BUS STATION

P

CALLE DE LOS COCHES

To Cercanías Train Station

snack, or drink in your choice of the many restaurants and cafés lining the square. The Renaissance church opposite the City Hall and behind the TI was built to replace the church where Isabel was proclaimed Queen of Castile in 1474. The symbol of Segovia is the aqueduct where you started—find it in the seals on the Theater Juan Bravo and atop the City Hall. Finally, treat yourself to the town's specialty pastry, *ponche segoviano* (marzipan cake), at the recommended Limón y Menta, the bakery on the corner where you entered Plaza Mayor.

Sights in Segovia

▲Roman Aqueduct

Segovia was a Roman military base and needed water. Emperor Trajan's engineers built a nine-mile aqueduct to channel water

from the Río Frío to the city, culminating at the Roman castle (which is the Alcázar today). The famous and exposed section of the 2,000-year-old *acueducto romano* is 2,500 feet long and 100 feet high, has 118 arches, was made from 20,000 granite blocks without any mortar, and can still carry a stream of water. It actually functioned until the late 19th century. On Plaza del Azoguejo, a grand stairway leads from the base of the aqueduct to the top—offering close-up looks at the imposing work. As you walk through the streets, keep an eye out for small plaques depicting the arches of the aqueduct, which tell you where the subterranean channel runs through the city.

▲Cathedral

Segovia's cathedral, built in Renaissance times (1525-1768, the third on this site), was Spain's last major Gothic building. Embellished to the hilt with pinnacles and flying buttresses, the exterior is a great example of the final, overripe stage of Gothic, called Flamboyant. Yet the Renaissance arrived before it was finished—as evidenced by the fact that the cathedral is crowned by a dome, not a spire.

Cost and Hours: €3, free Sun 9:30-13:15 (cathedral access only—no cloisters), open daily 9:30-

18:30, Oct-March until 17:30, last entry 30 minutes before closing, tel. 921-462-205.

Visiting the Cathedral: The spacious and elegantly simple interior provides a delightful contrast to the frilly exterior. The **choir** features finely carved wooden stalls from the previous church (1400s). The *cátedra* (bishop's chair) is in the center rear of the choir.

The many side chapels are mostly 16th-century, and come with big locking gates—a reminder that they were the private sacred domain of the rich families and guilds who "owned" them. They could enjoy private Masses here with their names actually spoken in the blessings and a fine burial spot close to the altar.

Find the **Capilla La Concepción** (a chapel in the rear that looks like a mini-art gallery). Its many 17th-century paintings

hang behind a mahogany wood gate imported from colonial America. The painting, *Tree of Life,* by Ignacio Ries (left of the altar), shows hedonistic mortals dancing atop the Tree of Life. As a skeletal Grim Reaper prepares to receive them into hell (by literally chopping down the tree...timberrrr), Jesus rings a bell imploring them to wake up before it's too late. The center statue is Mary of the Apocalypse (as described in Revelations, standing on a devil and half-moon, which looks like bull's horns). Mary's pregnant, and the devil licks his evil chops, waiting to devour the baby Messiah.

Opposite from where you entered, a fine door (which leads into the cloister) is crowned by a painted Flamboyant Gothic *pietà* in its tympanum (the statue of Jesus with a skirt, on the left, is a reminder of how prudishness from the past looks silly in the present).

The **cloisters** hold a nice little museum containing French tapestries, paintings, and silver reliquaries. The gilded chapter room is draped with precious Flemish tapestries. Notice the gilded wagon. The Holy Communion wafer is placed in the top of this temple-like cart and paraded through town each year during the Corpus Christi festival. Hanging just outside these rooms is a glass case displaying keys to the 17th-century private chapel gates. From the cloister courtyard, you can see the Renaissance dome rising above the otherwise Gothic rooftop.

▲Alcázar

In the Middle Ages, this fortified palace was one of the favorite residences of the monarchs of Castile, a key fortress for controlling the region. The Alcázar grew through the ages, and its function changed many times: After its stint as a palace, it was a prison for 200 years, and then a Royal Artillery School. It burned in 1862. Since the fire, it's basically been a museum.

Cost and Hours: Palace—€5, daily 10:00-19:00, Oct-March until 18:00, €3 audioguide describes each room (45 minutes); tower—€2, same hours as palace except closed third Tue of month; tel. 921-460-759, www.alcazardesegovia.com.

Getting In: Buy your tickets at Real Laboratorio de Chimia, facing the palace on your left. Pick up a free English leaflet at the desk across from the ticket counter. At the entrance, pass your ticket through the turnstiles on the right for the palace, or the turnstiles on the left for the tower.

Visiting the Alcázar: You'll enjoy a one-way route through 11 rooms, including a fine view terrace. Visit the tower afterward; its 152 steps up a tight spiral staircase reward you with the only 360-degree city view in town. What you see today in the Alcázar is rebuilt—a Disney-esque exaggeration of the original. Still, its fine Moorish decor and historic furnishings are fascinating. The sumptuous ceilings are accurately restored in Mudejar style, and the throne-room ceiling is the artistic highlight of the palace.

Look for a big mural of Queen Isabel the Catholic being proclaimed Queen of Castile and León in Segovia's main square in 1474. The **Hall of the Monarchs** is lined with the busts of the 52 rulers of Castile and León who presided during the long and ultimately successful Reconquista (711-1492): from Pelayo (the first), clockwise to Juana VII (the last). There were only seven queens during the period (the numbered ones). In this current age of Islamic extremists decapitating Christians, study the painting of St. James the Moor-Slayer—with Muslim heads literally rolling at his feet (poignantly...in the chapel). James is the patron saint of Spain. His name was the rallying cry in the centuries-long Christian crusade to push the Muslim Moors back into Africa.

Stepping onto the terrace (the site of the original Roman military camp, circa A.D. 100) with its vast views, marvel at the natural fortification provided by this promontory cut by the confluence of two rivers. The terrace is closed in the winter and sometimes on windy days. The Alcázar marks the end (and physical low point) of the gradual downhill course of the nine-mile-long Roman aqueduct. Can you find the mountain nicknamed *Mujer Muerta* ("dead woman")?

In the **armory** (just after the terrace), find the king's 16th-century ornately carved ivory crossbow, with the hunting scene shown in the adjacent painting. The final rooms are the Museum of Artillery, recalling the period (1764-1862) when this was the Royal Artillery School. It shows the evolution of explosive weaponry, with old photos and prints of the Alcázar.

Church of Santos Justo y Pastor

This simple yet stately old church has fascinating 12th- and 13th-century frescoes filled with Gothic symbolism, plus a stork's nest atop its tower. From the base of the aqueduct, it's a short climb uphill into the newer part of town. Kind old Rafael, the volunteer caretaker, welcomes you.

Cost and Hours: Free, Tue-Sat 11:00-14:00 & 17:00-19:00, Sun 11:00-14:00, closed Mon and when Rafael needs to run an errand; located a couple of blocks from Plaza del Azoguejo, tel. 921-422-413.

Museo de Arte Contemporáneo Esteban Vicente

A collection of local artist Esteban Vicente's abstract art is housed in two rooms of the remodeled remains of Henry IV's 1455 palace. Wilder than Rothko but more restrained than Pollock, Vicente's vibrant work influenced post-WWII American art. The temporary exhibits can be more interesting than the permanent collection.

Cost and Hours: €3, free on Thu; open Thu-Fri 11:00-14:00 & 16:00-19:00, Sat 11:00-20:00, Sun 11:00-15:00, closed Mon-Wed; tel. 921-426-010, www.museoestebanvicente.es.

NEAR SEGOVIA

Vera Cruz Church

This 12-sided, 13th-century Romanesque church, built by the Knights Templar, once housed a piece of the "true cross." You can enjoy a postcard view of the city from the church, and more views follow as you continue around Segovia on the small road below the castle, labeled *Ruta Turística Panorámica.*

Cost and Hours: €2, free Tue afternoon; open Tue 16:00-19:00, Wed-Sun 10:30-13:30 & 16:00-19:00, until 18:00 in winter, closed Mon and when caretaker takes his autumn holiday, sometime in Oct-Nov; outside town beyond the castle, 25-minute walk from main square; tel. 921-431-475.

▲La Granja de San Ildefonso Palace

This "little Versailles," six miles south of Segovia, is much smaller and happier than nearby El Escorial. The palace and gardens were built by the homesick French-born King Philip V, grandson of Louis XIV. Today it's restored to its original 18th-century

splendor, with its royal collection of tapestries, clocks, and crystal (actually made at the palace's royal crystal factory). Plumbers and gardeners imported from France and Italy made Philip a garden that rivaled Versailles'. The fanciful fountains feature mythological stories (explained in the palace audioguide). The Bourbon Philip chose to be buried here rather than with his Habsburg predecessors at El Escorial. His tomb is in the adjacent church, included with your ticket.

Cost and Hours: Palace—€9, open Tue-Sun 10:00-20:00, Oct-March until 18:00, closed Mon year-round, last entry one hour before closing, audioguide-€4, guided tour-€4 (ask for one in English—you might need to wait); park—free, daily 10:00-20:00, off-season until 19:00; tel. 921-470-019, www.patrimonionacional. es.

Getting There: La Sepulvedana buses make the 25-minute trip from Segovia (catch at the bus station) to San Ildefonso-La Granja (about 2/hour 7:30-21:30, fewer on weekends, tel. 902-119-699, www.lasepulvedana.es).

Sleeping in Segovia

The best places are on or near the central Plaza Mayor. This is where the city action is—the best bars, most tourist-friendly and *típico* eateries, and the TI. During busy times—on weekends and in July and August—arrive early or call ahead.

IN THE OLD CENTER, NEAR PLAZA MAYOR

$$$ Hotel Palacio San Facundo, on a quiet square a few blocks off Plaza Mayor, is luxuriously modern in its amenities but has preserved its Old World charm. This palace-turned-monastery has 29 uniquely decorated rooms surrounding a skylit central patio (Sb/Db-€100-170, superior Db-€160-220, Tb-€150-255, rates fluctuate significantly with season and demand, check online for best prices, includes breakfast, elevator, parking-€18/day, air-con, tel. 921-463-061, Plaza San Facundo 4, www.hotelpalaciosanfacundo. com, info@hotelpalaciosanfacundo.com, José Luis). From Plaza Mayor, take Cronista Lecea; it's a four-minute walk directly to Plaza San Facundo.

$$$ Hotel Infanta Isabel, right on Plaza Mayor, is the ritziest hotel in the old town, with 38 elegant rooms, some with plaza views (Sb-€60-90, Db-€60-110 depending on season, higher rates are for Fri-Sat, lower rates in winter, breakfast-€6-9, elevator, valet parking-€13/day, tel. 921-461-300, www.hotelinfantaisabel.com, admin@hotelinfantaisabel.com).

Sleep Code

Abbreviations   **(€1=about $1.10, country code: 34)**
S=Single, **D**=Double/Twin, **T**=Triple, **Q**=Quad, **b**=bathroom
Price Rankings
  $$$ **Higher Priced**—Most rooms €80 or more.
   $$ **Moderately Priced**—Most rooms €40-80.
    $ **Lower Priced**—Most rooms €40 or less.
Unless otherwise noted, credit cards are accepted, breakfast is not included, free Wi-Fi and/or a guest computer is generally available, and English is spoken. Some hotels include the 10 percent IVA tax in the room price; others tack it onto your bill. Prices change; verify current rates online or by email. For the best prices, always book directly with the hotel.

OUTSIDE THE OLD TOWN, NEAR THE AQUEDUCT

$$ Hostal Don Jaime, opposite the Church of San Justo, is a friendly family-run place with 38 basic, worn, yet well-maintained rooms. Seven more rooms are in an annex across the street (S-€25, D-€32, Db-€50, Tb-€60, Qb-€70; book directly with the hotel via email or by phone, show this book, and get a free breakfast in 2016—otherwise €3.50; parking-€8/day; Ochoa Ondategui 8—from TI at Plaza del Azogüejo, cross under the aqueduct, go right, angle left, then snake uphill for 2 blocks; tel. 921-444-787, hostaldonjaime@hotmail.com).

$ Hospedaje el Gato, a family-run place on a quiet nondescript square just outside the old town, has 10 modern, comfortable rooms (Sb-€30 Sun-Thu, Sb-€50 Fri-Sat, Db-€40-50, Tb-€65, air-con, bar serves breakfast and good tapas, uphill from Hostal Don Jaime and aqueduct at Plaza del Salvador 10, tel. 921-423-244, mobile 678-405-079, www.hostalsegovia.es, hbarelgato@yahoo.es).

Eating in Segovia

Look for Segovia's culinary claim to fame, roast suckling pig (*cochinillo asado:* 21 days of mother's milk, into the oven, and onto your plate—oh, Babe). It's worth a splurge here, or in Toledo or Salamanca.

For lighter fare, try *sopa castellana*—soup mixed with eggs, ham, garlic, and bread—or warm yourself up with the *judiones de La Granja,* a popular soup made with flat white beans from the region.

Ponche segoviano, a dessert made with an almond-and-honey *mazapán* base, is heavenly after an earthy dinner or with a coffee in the afternoon (at the recommended Limón y Menta).

PLACES TO EAT ROAST SUCKLING PIG

Mesón de Cándido, one of the top restaurants in Castile, is famous for its memorable dinners. Even though it's filled with tourists, it's a grand experience. Take time to wander around and survey the photos of celebs—from Juan Carlos I to Antonio Banderas and Melanie Griffith—who've suckled here. Try to get a table in a room with an aqueduct view (reservations recommended; €25-35 fixed-price *cochinillo* meal includes starter, dessert, and

wine; daily 13:00-16:30 & 20:00-23:00, Plaza del Azoguejo 5, air-con, under aqueduct, tel. 921-428-103, www.mesondecandido.es, candido@mesondecandido.es). Three gracious generations of the Cándido family still run the show.

José María is *the* place to pig out in the old town, a block off Plaza Mayor. And though it doesn't have the history or fanfare of Cándido, Segovians claim this high-energy place serves the best roast suckling pig in town. It thrives with a hungry mix of tourists and locals (reservations recommended, €40 à la carte dinner, €26 *cochinillo,* daily 13:00-16:00 & 20:00-23:30, air-con, Cronista Lecea 11, tel. 921-466-017, www.restaurantejosemaria.com, reservas@restaurantejosemaria.com).

Restaurante Duque claims to be the oldest eatery in Segovia, open since 1895. The venerable institution is currently run by fourth-generation Marisa, who is spearheading a modern menu of tapas alongside the rustic, traditional dishes of her ancestors. You'll find boisterous young people bellied up to the bar, while both locals and tourists enjoy the comfortable dining room (€33-39 three-course *cochinillo* dinners, daily 12:30-23:30, sometimes closes in afternoon, a few blocks from Plaza Mayor downhill from "house of a thousand beaks" at Calle de Cervantes 12, tel. 921-462-486).

MOSTLY PIG-FREE PLACES IN THE OLD CENTER

Plaza Mayor, the main square, provides a great backdrop for a light lunch, dinner, or drink. Prices at the cafés are generally reasonable, and many offer a good selection of tapas and *raciones.* Grab a table at the place of your choice and savor the scene. **Café Jeyma** has a fine setting and cathedral view. **La Concepción Restaurante** is also good (€35 meals, closer to the cathedral). For a filling lunch on the plaza, try **Restaurante Bar José,** which has a three-course fixed-price meal for €16 (includes wine, bread, and excellent cathedral views, tel. 921-460-919).

Narizotas serves more imaginative and non-Castilian alternatives to the gamey traditions. Dine outside on a delightful square or inside with modern art under medieval timbers. For a wonderful dining experience, try their chef's choice mystery samplers, either the "Right Hand" (€35, about nine courses) or the "Left Hand" (€30, about six courses); both include wine, water, dessert, and coffee. They offer a less elaborate three-course €13-17 fixed-priced meal, and their à la carte menu is also a treat (daily 13:00-16:00 & 20:30-24:00, midway down Calle Juan Bravo at Plaza de Medina del Campo 1, tel. 921-462-679, www.narizotas.net).

Cueva de San Esteban serves traditional home cooking with a stress-free photo menu at the door, hearty, big-enough-to-split plates, and—of course—*cochinillo* (daily 11:00-24:00, full meals served 13:00-16:00, 2 blocks past Plaza Mayor on a quiet back street, Calle Valdelaguila 15, tel. 921-460-982).

La Almuzara is a garden of veggie and organic delights: whole-wheat pizzas, tofu, seitan, and even a few dishes with meat (€10-13 plates, Tue 20:00-24:00, Wed-Sun 12:00-16:00 & 20:00-24:00, closed Mon, between cathedral and Alcázar at Marques del Arco 3, tel. 921-460-622).

Breakfast: In the morning, I like to eat on Plaza Mayor (many choices) while enjoying the cool air and the people scene. Or, 100 yards down the main drag toward the aqueduct, **Café La Colonial** serves good breakfasts (with seating on a tiny square or inside, Plaza del Corpus).

Nightlife: Inexpensive bars and eateries line Calle de Infanta Isabel, just off Plaza Mayor. For nightlife, the bars on Plaza Mayor, Calle de Infanta Isabel, and Calle de Isabel la Católica are packed. There are a number of late-night dance clubs along the aqueduct.

Dessert: **Limón y Menta** offers a good, rich *ponche segoviano* (marzipan) cake by the slice for €3—or try the lighter honey-and-almond *crocantinos* (daily 9:00-20:00 but hours can vary, seating inside, Calle de Isabel la Católica 2, tel. 921-462-141).

Market: An outdoor produce market thrives on Plaza Mayor on Thursday (roughly 8:00-15:00). Nearby, on Calle del Cronista Ildefonso Rodríguez, a few stalls are open daily except Sunday.

Segovia Connections

BY PUBLIC TRANSPORTATION

From Segovia to Madrid: You have three options: bus, fast train, or slow train. Even though the 30-minute AVE train takes less than half as long as the bus, you'll spend more time getting to the AVE stations in Segovia and Madrid than to the bus stations, so the total time spent in transit is about the same. *Cercanías* commuter trains also run to Madrid but take two hours and don't save you much money.

Buses run from Segovia to Madrid's Príncipe Pío Metro station;

NORTHWEST OF MADRID

many stop first at Madrid's Moncloa Metro station, where you can get off if convenient to your hotel (2/hour, departing on the half-hour, 1.5 hours; tel. 902-119-699, www.lasepulvedana.es). Consider busing from Segovia to Ávila for a visit, then continuing to Salamanca by bus or train.

If you're riding the bus from Madrid to Segovia, about 30 minutes after leaving Madrid you'll see—breaking the horizon on the left—the dramatic concrete cross of the Valley of the Fallen. Its grand facade marks the entry to the mammoth underground memorial.

The **AVE train** goes between Segovia's Guiomar Station and Madrid's Chamartín Station (8-10/day, 30 minutes). To get to Guiomar Station, take city bus #11 from the base of the aqueduct (20 minutes, buses usually timed to match arrivals). You can also take the *cercanías* **commuter train** to Madrid, though this option is slower (9/day, 2 hours, leaves from Segovia's inconvenient *cercanías* station, arrives in Madrid at both Chamartín and Atocha stations). To reach the sleepy, dead-end *cercanías* station, walk 20 minutes past the bus station along Paseo de Ezequiel González (which turns into Paseo del Conde de Sepulvedana); catch bus #6 (leaves from the bus station) or #8 (leaves from the aqueduct); or take a taxi. Train info: Tel. 902-320-320.

From Segovia by Bus to: La Granja Palace (about 2/hour, fewer on weekends, 25 minutes), **Ávila** (5/day weekdays, 2/day weekends, 1 hour), **Salamanca** (2/day, more with transfer in Labajos, 3-3.5 hours, Auto-Res bus, tel. 902-020-999, www.avanzabus.com).

ROUTE TIPS FOR DRIVERS

From Madrid to Segovia: Leave Madrid on A-6. Exit 39 gets you to Segovia via a slow, winding route over the scenic mountain. Exit at 60 (after a long toll tunnel—about €3 depending on time of day), or get there quicker by staying on the toll road all the way to Segovia (add roughly €2 weekdays or €3 on weekends). At the Segovia aqueduct, follow *casco histórico* signs to the old town (on the side where the aqueduct adjoins the crenellated fortress walls).

Parking in Segovia: Free parking is available in the Alcázar's lot, but you must move your car out by 19:00 (or by 18:00 Oct-March), when the gates close. Or try the lot northwest of the bus station by the statue of Cándido, along the street called Paseo de Ezequiel González. Outside the old city, there's an Acueducto Parking underground garage kitty-corner from the bus station. Although it can be a hard slog up the hill to the Alcázar on a hot day, it beats trying to maneuver uphill through tight bends. There's also the huge and convenient Padre Claret garage near the aqueduct (€1.55/hour).

The city center has lots of parking spaces, but they're not free. If you want to park in the old town, be legal or risk an expensive ticket. Buy a ticket from the nearby machine to park in areas marked by blue stripes, and place the ticket on your dashboard (€1.80/hour, pay meter every 2 hours 9:00-14:00 & 16:30-20:00; free parking 20:00-9:00, Sat afternoon, and all day Sun).

From Segovia to Salamanca (100 miles): Leave Segovia by driving around the town's circular road, which offers good views

from below the Alcázar. Then follow signs for *Ávila* (road N-110). Notice the fine Segovia view from the three crosses at the crest of the first hill. The Salamanca road leads around the famous Ávila walls to the right. The best wall view is from the signposted *Cuatro Postes,* a mile northwest of town. Salamanca (N-501) is clearly marked, about an hour's drive away.

About 20 miles before Salamanca, you might want to stop at the huge bull on the left side of the road. There's a little dirt lane leading right up to it. As you get closer, it becomes more and more obvious it isn't alive. Bad boys climb it for a goofy photo. For a great photo op of Salamanca, complete with river reflection, stop at the edge of the city (at the light before the first bridge).

Ávila

Yet another popular side-trip from Madrid, Ávila is famous for its perfectly preserved medieval walls, as the birthplace of St. Teresa, and for its yummy *yema* treats. For more than 300 years, Ávila was on the battlefront between the Muslims and Christians, changing hands several times. Today perfectly peaceful Ávila has a charming old town. With several fine churches and monasteries, it makes for an enjoyable quick stop between Segovia and Salamanca (each about an hour away by car).

Orientation to Ávila

On a quick stop, everything in Ávila that matters is within a few blocks of the cathedral (which actually forms part of the east end of the city wall).

TOURIST INFORMATION

The TI is just outside the wall gate near the cathedral (Mon-Sat 9:30-14:00 & 16:00-19:00, Sun 9:30-17:00, on Calle San Segundo, tel. 920-211-387). Another TI, with a friendlier staff, is located outside the wall, opposite the Basilica of San Vicente. They sell handy maps and mini-guidebooks in English, which provide details on the palaces and churches. If you want to see more than the highlights, consider the general *Descubre Ávila,* which outlines 10 walking-tour itineraries in the old town (daily April-Oct 9:00-20:00, Nov-March 9:00-18:00, public WCs, tel. 920-354-000 ext. 370, www.avilaturismo.com).

Sightseeing Pass: The **VisitÁvila** pass is €13 and valid for 48 hours. It includes the wall, cathedral, museum of St. Teresa, the Mysticism Interpretation Center, and a handful of other sights. If you plan on seeing them all you can save a few euros.

ARRIVAL IN ÁVILA

Approaching by bus, train, or car, you'll need to make your way through the nondescript modern part of town to find the walled old town.

By Bus or Train: There are lockers at Ávila's bus station (use the newer-looking locks), but not at the train station.

The cathedral and wall are 15 minutes by foot from the bus station and 20 minutes from the train station. City buses #4 and #1 run from the train station to the Basilica of San Vicente (to find the bus stop, exit the station, walk one block, and turn right at the first street). When you arrive at the basilica, check the posted return bus schedule to ensure you make your train connection.

By Car: Drivers can use the public parking east of Puerta del Alcázar, just south of the cathedral, or at Parking Dornier (€1.25/hour).

Sights in Ávila

▲Walking the Wall

Built from around 1100 on even more ancient remains, Ávila's fortified wall is the oldest, most complete, and best-preserved in

Spain. It has four gates and three entrances, allowing visitors the chance to walk almost three-quarters of the wall: One entrance is just off Plaza de Santa Teresa (Puerta del Alcázar). The best one, which leads to a longer walk, starts from inside the TI on Calle San Segundo, by the gate closest to the cathedral (Puerta del Peso

de la Harina) and takes you to the third and fourth gates: Puerta del Carmen (exit only) and Puerta Puente Adaja (on the end farthest from the cathedral—look for the door marked *subida a la muralla*).

An interesting paseo scene takes place along the wall each night—make your way along the southern wall (Paseo del Rastro) to Plaza de Santa Teresa for spectacular vistas across the plains.

Cost and Hours: €5; Tue-Sun 10:00-20:00, July-Aug until 21:00, Nov-March until 18:00, closed Mon except mid-June-mid-Oct; last entry 45 minutes before closing, ticket includes English audioguide.

Viewing the Wall: The best views of the wall itself are actually from street level. If you're wandering the city and see arched gates leading out of the old center, pop out to the other side and take in the impressive wall from the ground. Drivers can see the especially impressive north side as they circle to the right from Puerta de San Vicente to catch the highway to Salamanca.

Viewing Ávila from Cuatro Postes

The best overall view of the walled town of Ávila is about a mile away on the Salamanca road (N-501), at a clearly marked turnout for the Cuatro Postes (four posts). You can reach the Cuatro Postes by catching city bus #7 (€1) at the stop in front of the Basilica of San Vicente—it goes through the old town, then out to the Cuatro Postes viewpoint, back to San Vicente, and on to the RENFE train station. Bus #7 doesn't run on weekends; ask at the TI for walking directions (about 30 minutes each way), or take bus #1 to the stop nearest the Hermitage of San Segundo and walk five minutes to the viewpoint.

Cathedral

While it started as Romanesque, Ávila's cathedral, finished in the 16th century, is considered the first Gothic cathedral in Spain. Its position—with its granite apse actually part of the fortified wall—underlines the "medieval alliance between cross and sword." You can tour the cathedral, its sacristy, cloister, and museum—which includes an El Greco painting.

Cost and Hours: €4; Mon-Fri 10:00-17:30, Sat 10:00-19:00, Sun 12:00-15:00, generally closes one hour earlier off-season; last entry 45 minutes before closing, English audioguide-€2, Plaza de la Catedral.

Convent of St. Teresa

Built in the 17th century on the spot where the saint was born, this convent is a big hit with pilgrims (10-minute walk from cathedral). St. Teresa (1515-1582)—reforming nun, mystic, and writer—bought a house in Ávila and converted it into a convent with more stringent rules than the one she belonged to. She faced opposition

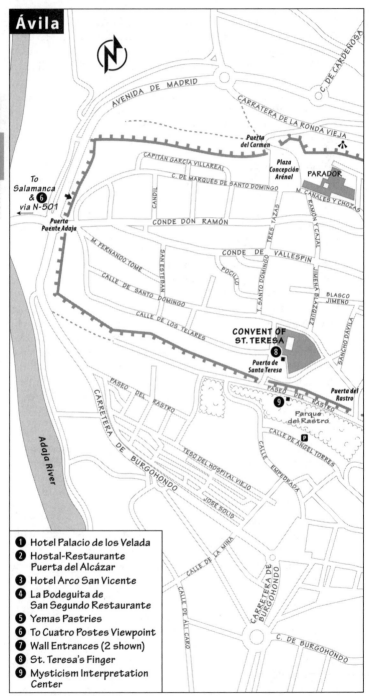

Ávila

To Salamanca & ❻ via N-501

Adaja River

AVENIDA DE MADRID

CARRATERA DE LA RONDA VIEJA

C. DE CARDENOSA

Puerta del Carmen

Plaza Concepción Arénal

PARADOR

CAPITÁN GARCÍA VILLAREAL

C. DE MARQUES DE SANTO DOMINGO

CANDIL

M. CANALES Y CHOZAS

RAMÓN Y CAJAL

Puerta Puente Adaja

CONDE DON RAMÓN

TRES TAZAS

M. FERNANDO TOME

SAN ESTEBAN

CONDE DE VALLESPIN

POCILLO

SANTO DOMINGO

JIMENA BLAZQUEZ

BLASCO JIMENO

CALLE DE SANTO DOMINGO

CALLE DE LOS TELARES

SANCHO DAVILA

CONVENT OF ST. TERESA ❽

Puerta de Santa Teresa

Puerta del Rastro

PASEO DEL RASTRO

PASEO DEL RASTRO ❾

Parque del Rastro

CALLE DE ANGEL TORRES P

CARRETERA DE BURGOHONDO

TESO DEL HOSPITAL VIEJO

CALLE EMPEDRADA

JOSE SOLIS

CALLE DE LA MINA

CALLE DE AJI CARO

CARRETERA DE BURGOHONDO

C. DE BURGOHONDO

❶ Hotel Palacio de los Velada
❷ Hostal-Restaurante Puerta del Alcázar
❸ Hotel Arco San Vicente
❹ La Bodeguita de San Segundo Restaurante
❺ Yemas Pastries
❻ To Cuatro Postes Viewpoint
❼ Wall Entrances (2 shown)
❽ St. Teresa's Finger
❾ Mysticism Interpretation Center

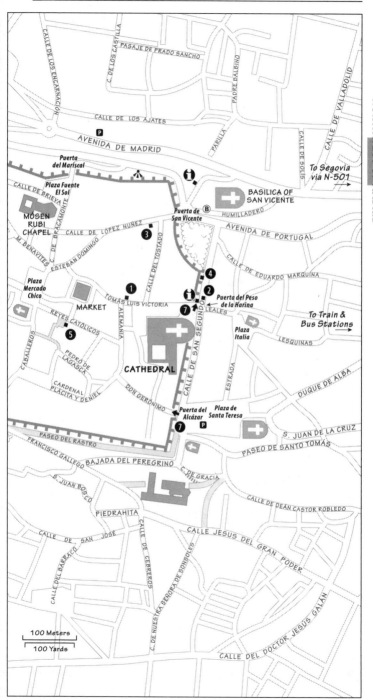

in her hometown from rival nuns and those convinced her visions of heaven were the work of the devil. However, with her mentor and fellow mystic St. John of the Cross, she established convents of Discalced (shoeless) Carmelites throughout Spain, and her visions and writings led her to sainthood (she was canonized in 1622).

A lavishly gilded side chapel marks the actual place of her birth (left of main altar, door may be closed). A separate room of relics (outside, facing the church on your right, Sala de Reliquias) houses a shop that shows off Teresa's finger, complete with a fancy emerald ring, along with one of her sandals and the bones of St. John of the Cross. A museum dedicated to the saint is in the crypt at the side entrance and is worth a visit for devotees.

Cost and Hours: Convent—free, daily 9:30-13:30 & 15:30-19:30, off-season until 19:00, no photos of finger allowed; museum—€2, April-Oct Tue-Sun 10:00-14:00 & 16:00-20:00, Nov-March Tue-Sun 10:00-13:30 & 15:30-17:30, closed Mon year-round, last entry 30 minutes before closing.

Mysticism Interpretation Center (Centro de Interpretación del Misticismo)

If St. Teresa were alive today, she'd love this place, which explores modern mysticism from a Catholic perspective. Pick up the English handout that explains the art and texts, then take the elevator down on a "journey to the inner realms of the Self."

Cost and Hours: €3, Tue-Sun 10:00-13:30 & 16:00-17:30, closed Mon, last entry 30 minutes before closing, Paseo del Rastro, tel. 920-212-154, www.avilamistica.es/interpretacion.

Yemas

These pastries, made by local nuns, are more or less soft-boiled egg yolks that have been cooled and sugared (*yema* means yolk). They're sold all over town. The shop **Las Delicias del Convento** is actually a retail outlet for the cooks of the convent (€4 for a small box, Tue-Sat 10:30-14:00 & 17:00-20:00, Sun 10:30-18:00, closed Mon, hours and closed day vary by season, between the TI and convent at Calle de los Reyes Católicos 12, tel. 920-220-293).

Sleeping in Ávila

Ávila is cold in fall, winter, and early spring, so you'll likely need to turn up the heat in these hotels.

$$$ Hotel Palacio de los Velada is antique and classy and faces the cathedral. Located in a five-centuries-old palace, it has 144 elegant rooms surrounding a huge and inviting arcaded courtyard (Sb-€92, Db-€132, third person-€30 extra on weekends, lower rates Mon-Thu and for 2-night weekend stays, higher on weekends and holidays, rates fluctuate wildly—check website for latest, air-con, elevator, Plaza de la Catedral 10, tel. 920-255-100, www.veladahoteles.com, reserves.avila@veladahoteles.com).

$$ Hostal Puerta del Alcázar has 27 basic yet spacious rooms right next to the Puerta del Peso de la Harina just outside the wall (Sb-€33-43, Db-€40-55, Tb-€77, Qb-€99, includes breakfast, air-con, San Segundo 38, tel. 920-211-074, www.puertadelalcazar. com, info@puertadelalcazar.com). It's home to a recommended restaurant.

$$ Hotel Arco San Vicente has a friendly staff and a great location two blocks from the cathedral and one block from the Basilica of San Vicente, with its handy stop for buses to the train station or the Cuatro Postes viewpoint (Sb-€40, Db-€45-65, breakfast-€5, restaurant, air-con on second floor, elevator, limited parking-€10/ day, Calle López Núñez 6, tel. 920-222-498, www.arcosanvicente. com, info@arcosanvicente.com).

Eating in Ávila

Ávila specialties include *chuletón,* a thick steak, and *judías del Barco de Ávila,* big white beans often cooked in a meaty stew. Around Plaza del Mercado Chico, the main square of the old center, are several good spots to try the stew or to have a reasonable fixed-price lunch (many of which include the *judías*).

La Bodeguita de San Segundo is good for a light lunch. Owned by a locally famous wine connoisseur, it serves fine wine by the glass with tapas such as smoked-cod salad and wild-mushroom scrambled eggs (Wed-Mon 11:00-24:00, sometimes closes in afternoon, closed Tue, €2 bread charge, along the outside of wall near cathedral at San Segundo 19, tel. 920-228-634).

Hostal-Restaurante Puerta del Alcázar, filled with more locals than hotel guests, serves elaborate salads, fixed-price meals (€13-21 Mon-Fri, €16-21 Sat-Sun), and more. You can sit indoors or, even better, outdoors with cathedral views (Mon-Sat 13:00-16:00 & 21:00-23:30—outside tables open for dinner at 20:00 in summer, Sun 13:00-16:00, San Segundo 38, tel. 920-211-074).

Picnics: The town's market house is a good spot to pick up fruit and water (Mon-Thu 9:00-14:00 & 17:00-20:00, Fri 9:00-20:00, Sat 9:00-14:00, closed Sun, between Plaza del Mercado Chico and the cathedral). On Friday mornings, there's a farmers' market on Plaza del Mercado Chico.

Café: For a pleasant break from sightseeing, pop in to the courtyard of the recommended **Hotel Palacio de los Velada** for a drink (€3 coffee and hot chocolate).

Ávila Connections

The bus terminal is closed on Sundays, but you can purchase tickets when boarding the bus.

From Ávila to: Segovia (5 buses/day weekdays, 2/day weekends, 1 hour), **Madrid** (trains run nearly hourly until 21:10, 1.5-2 hours, more frequent connections with Chamartín Station than Atocha; 9 buses/day weekdays, 6/day weekends, 1.5 hours; Estación Sur, tel. 914-684-200), **Salamanca** (8 trains/day, 1-1.5 hours; 4-5 buses/day, 1.5 hours). Train info: Toll tel. 902-320-320, www.renfe.com. Bus info: Tel. 902-020-052 or 902-020-999 (Avanza and Auto-Res), www.avanzabus.com.

TOLEDO

An hour south of Madrid by car, Toledo teems with tourists, souvenirs, and great art by day, and delicious dinners, echoes of El Greco, and medieval magic by night. Incredibly well-preserved and full of cultural wonder, the entire city has been declared a national monument.

Spain's former capital crowds 2,500 years of tangled history—Roman, Jewish, Visigothic, Moorish, and Christian—onto a high, rocky perch protected on three sides by the Tajo River. To keep the city's historic appearance intact, the Spanish government has forbidden any modern exteriors. The rich mix of Jewish, Moorish, and Christian heritages makes it one of Europe's cultural highlights.

Today, Toledo thrives as a provincial capital and a busy tourist attraction. The last decade has been an eventful one for Toledo. A high-speed AVE train connection has made Toledo a quick, 30-minute ride from Madrid. While locals worried that this link would turn their town into a bedroom community for wealthy Madrileños, the high real-estate prices minimized the impact.

Another civic boost was a convention center—the Palacio de Congresos Miradero. It was designed by Rafael Moneo—architect of the Los Angeles Cathedral, the Kursaal Conference Center in San Sebastián, and, in Madrid, the renovated Atocha Station and the Prado Museum's extension. While the center itself is of little interest to tourists, its huge underground parking garage and escalators into town make arrival by car efficient. The escalators make it easy to walk into town from the train station, too. The vision is to make the old city center essentially traffic-free (except for residents' cars, public transit, and service vehicles).

Despite its tremendously kitschy tourist vibe, this stony wonderland remains the historic, artistic, and spiritual center of Spain. Toledo sits enthroned on its history, much as it was when Europe's most powerful monarch, the Holy Roman Emperor Charles V (King Charles I in Spain), and its most famous resident artist, El Greco, called it home. Many of the town's sights were beautifully renovated in 2014, to mark the 400th anniversary of El Greco's death.

PLANNING YOUR TIME

To properly see Toledo's sights—including its museums (great El Greco) and cathedral (best in Spain)—and to experience its medieval atmosphere (wonderful after dark), you'll need two nights and a day.

Get an early start the day you're there and stay out late. If traveling to Toledo only for the day, keep in mind that the early and late trains tend to sell out to commuters and other day-trippers. Plan carefully for lunchtime closures and take a rest break during Toledo's notorious midday heat in summer. Day-tripping tourists can pack the city during midday, while those spending the night enjoy an entirely different (and better) Toledo experience.

Orientation to Toledo

Toledo sits atop a circular hill, with the cathedral roughly dead-center. Lassoed into a tight tangle of streets by the sharp bend of

the Tajo River (called the "Tejo" in Portugal, where it hits the Atlantic at Lisbon), Toledo has Spain's most confusing medieval street plan. But it's a small town within its walls, with only 10,000 inhabitants (84,000 live in greater Toledo, including its modern suburbs). The major sights are well-signposted, and most locals will politely point you in the right direction if you ask. (You are, after all, the town's bread and butter.)

The top sights stretch from the main square, Plaza de Zocodover (zoh-koh-doh-VEHR), southwest along Calle del Comercio (a.k.a. Calle Ancha, "Wide Street") to the cathedral, and beyond that to Santo Tomé and more. The visitor's city lies basically along this small but central street, and most tourists never stray from this axis. Make a point to get lost. The town is compact. When it's time to return to someplace familiar, pull out the map or ask, "¿Para Plaza de Zocodover?" From the far end of town, handy bus #12 circles back to Plaza de Zocodover.

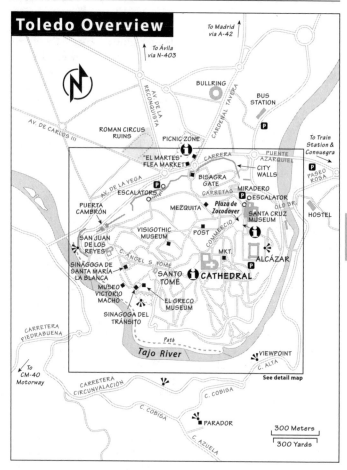

While the city is very hilly (in Toledo, they say everything's uphill—it certainly feels that way), nothing is more than a short hike away.

TOURIST INFORMATION

Toledo has four TIs. There's one at the train station (daily 9:30-15:00, tel. 925-239-121); one at Bisagra Gate, in a freestanding building in the park just outside the gate (Mon-Sat 10:00-18:00, Sun 9:00-14:00, tel. 925-211-005); another on Plaza del Ayuntamiento near the cathedral (daily 10:00-18:00, WC, tel. 925-254-030); and a regional TI on Plaza de Zocodover (Mon-Sat 10:00-18:00, Sun 10:00-14:00). At any TI, you can pick up the town map and a copy of the *Toledo Tourist and Cultural Guide*. The TIs share a website: www.toledo-turismo.com.

Sightseeing Passes: Skip Toledo's sightseeing passes. You'd pay more for any of the **Toledo Pass** or **Toledo Card** options than you would buying individual tickets, making either only worth buying if you want the included guided tours to a handful of sights.

The **Pulsera Turística** wristband makes sense only if you have ample time and interest in its covered monuments and churches (Santo Tomé, Sinagoga de Santa María la Blanca, San Juan de los Reyes Monasterio, Mezquita del Cristo de la Luz, Church of El Salvador, and Church of San Ildefonso/Jesuitas; sold at participating sights). If you saw all six, you'd save around €7, but it could take all day to visit just these monuments. Note that the wristband doesn't cover the city's top three sights.

ARRIVAL IN TOLEDO

"Arriving" in Toledo means getting uphill to Plaza de Zocodover. As the bus and train stations are outside the town center and parking can be a challenge, this involves a taxi, a city bus, or a walk plus a ride up a series of escalators.

By Train: Toledo's early-20th-century train station is Neo-Moorish and a national monument itself for its architecture and art, which both celebrate the three cultures that coexisted here.

Remember that early and late trains can sell out; reserve ahead. If you haven't yet bought a ticket for your departure from Toledo (even if it's for the next day), get it before you leave the Toledo station and choose a specific time rather than leave it open-ended. (If you prefer more flexibility, take the bus instead—see "By Bus" later.)

From the train station to Plaza de Zocodover, it's a €4.50 **taxi** ride (to hotels, the ride is metered), a 25-minute walk with the help of escalators, or an easy ride on various buses. You can take **city bus** #5, #11, #61, or #62; leaving the station, you'll see the bus stop 30 yards to the right (€1.40, pay on bus, confirm by asking, *"¿Para Plaza de Zocodover?"*). The red **Toledo City Tour bus**, which circles the city, also picks up outside the station, and stops briefly at the famous El Greco viewpoint before heading up to Plaza de Zocodover (€5.50; €9 for hop-on, hop-off version).

To **walk** into town, turn right as you leave the station and follow the fuchsia line on the sidewalk labeled *Up Toledo, Follow the Line*. Track this line (and periodic escalator symbols) past a bus stop, over the bridge, around the roundabout to the left, and into a bus parking area. From here, go up a series of escalators that take you to the center of town: You'll emerge about a block from the Plaza de Zocodover.

By Bus: At the bus station, buses park downstairs. Luggage lockers and a small bus-information office—where you can buy locker tokens—are upstairs opposite the cafeteria. From the bus

Toledo's History

Perched strategically in the center of Iberia, for centuries Toledo was a Roman transportation hub with a thriving Jewish population. After Rome fell, the city became a Visigothic capital (A.D. 554). In 711 the Moors (Muslims) made it a regional center. In 1085 the city was reconquered by Christians, but many Moors remained in Toledo, tolerated and respected as scholars and craftsmen.

Whereas Jews were commonly persecuted elsewhere in Europe, Toledo's Jewish community—educated, wealthy, and cosmopolitan—thrived from the city's earliest times. Jews of Spanish origin are called Sephardic Jews. The American expression "Holy Toledo" likely originated from the Sephardic Jews who eventually immigrated to America. To them, Toledo was the holiest Jewish city in Europe...Holy Toledo!

During its medieval heyday (c. 1350), Toledo was a city of the humanities, where God was known by many names. In this haven of cultural diversity, people of different faiths lived together in harmony.

Toledo remained Spain's political capital until 1561, when Philip II moved to more-spacious Madrid. Historians fail to agree on the reason for the move; some say that Madrid was the logical place for a capital in the geographic center of newly formed *España*, while others say that Philip wanted to separate politics from religion. (Toledo remained Spain's religious capital.) Whatever the reason, when the king moved out, Toledo was mothballed, only to be rediscovered by 19th-century Romantic travelers. They wrote of it as a mystical place, which it remains today.

TOLEDO

station, Plaza de Zocodover is a 15-minute **hike**, a €4.50 **taxi** ride, or a short **bus** ride (catch #5 or #12 downstairs; €1.40, pay on bus).

Before leaving the station, confirm your departure time (around 2/hour to Madrid). Unlike the faster trains, buses don't tend to get booked up. You can put off buying a return ticket for the bus until just minutes before you leave Toledo. Specify you'd like a *directo* bus (the *ruta* trip takes longer—1 hour versus 1.5 hours). But if you miss the *directo* bus (or if it's sold out), the *ruta* option offers a peek of off-the-beaten-path Madrid suburbia; you'll arrive at the same time as taking the next *directo* bus.

By Car: If you're arriving by car, enjoy a scenic big-picture orientation by following the *Ronda de Toledo* signs on a big circular

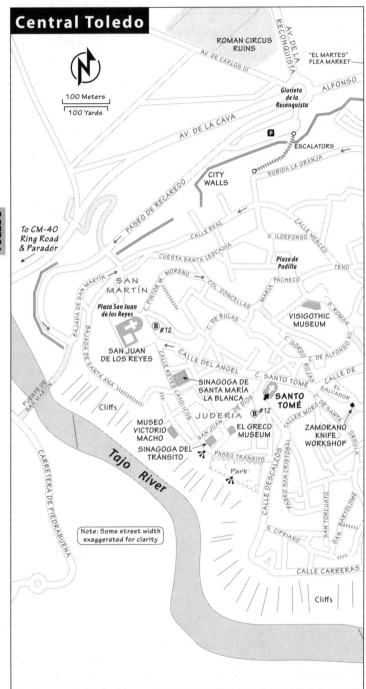

Central Toledo

ROMAN CIRCUS RUINS

"EL MARTES" FLEA MARKET

AV. DE LA RECONQUISTA

AV. DE CARLOS III

ALFONSO

Glorieta de la Reconquista

AV. DE LA CAVA

100 Meters
100 Yards

P

ESCALATORS

SUBIDA LA GRANJA

CITY WALLS

PASEO DE RECAREDO

CALLE REAL

CALLE MERCED

S. ILDEFONSO

To CM-40 Ring Road & Parador

CUESTA SANTA LEOCADIA

Plaza de Padilla

TEND

SAN MARTÍN

C. PINTOR M. MORENO

COL. DONCELLAS

PACHECO

MARÍA

S. ROMAN

VISIGOTHIC MUSEUM

BAJADA DE SAN MARTÍN

Plaza San Juan de los Reyes

C. DE BULAS

B #12

C. GORDO

C. DE ALFONSO XII

CALLE DEL ÁNGEL

C. SANTO TOMÉ

CALLE DE

SAN JUAN DE LOS REYES

BAJADA DE SANTA ANA

CALLE REYES CATÓLICOS

SINAGOGA DE SANTA MARÍA LA BLANCA

EL SALVADOR

SANTO TOMÉ

PUENTE DE SAN MARTÍN

Cliffs

JUDERÍA

SAN JUAN DE DIOS

B #12

EL GRECO MUSEUM

TALLER MORO

C. DE SANTA URSULA

ZAMORANO KNIFE WORKSHOP

MUSEO VICTORIO MACHO

SINAGOGA DEL TRÁNSITO

PASEO TRÁNSITO

Park

CARRETERA DE PIEDRABUENA

Tajo River

PASEO SAN CRISTÓBAL

CALLE DESCALZOS

SAN BARTOLOMÉ

SAN TORCUATO

Note: Some street width exaggerated for clarity

S. CIPRIANO

CALLE CARRERAS

Cliffs

TOLEDO

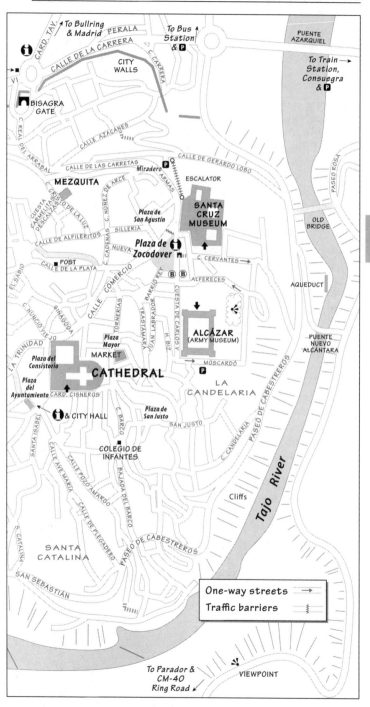

CARD. TAV.
To Bullring
& Madrid
PERALA
To Bus
Station
& P
PUENTE
AZARQUIEL

CALLE DE LA CARRERA
CITY
WALLS
C. CARRERA
To Train →
Station,
Consuegra
& P

VI

BISAGRA
GATE
C. REAL DEL ARRABAL

CALLE AZACANES

CALLE DE LAS CARRETAS
CALLE DE GERARDO LOBO

Miradero
P
CALLE DE
ARMAS
ESCALATOR

MEZQUITA
C. NÚÑEZ DE ARCE
SANTA
CRUZ
MUSEUM

CUESTA CARMELITA DESCALZA
CRISTO DE LA LUZ
Plaza de
San Agustín
OLD
BRIDGE

CALLE DE ALFILERITOS
SILLERIA
CADENAS

POST
EL SABIO
CALLE DE LA PLATA
NUEVA
Plaza de
Zocodover
C. CERVANTES
AQUEDUCT

CALLE COMERCIO
BARRIO REY
B B
ALFERECES

C. NUNCIO VIEJO
SINAGOGA
TORNERIAS
TRASTAMARA
CUESTA DE CARLOS V
ALCÁZAR
(ARMY MUSEUM)
PUENTE
NUEVO
ALCÁNTARA

LA TRINIDAD
JUAN LABRADOR
H. BIZ
MOSCARDÓ
P

Plaza
Mayor
MARKET

Plaza del
Consistorio
CATHEDRAL
LA
CANDELARIA

Plaza
del
Ayuntamiento
CARD. CISNEROS
& CITY HALL

SANTA ISABEL
C. BARCO
Plaza de
San Justo
SAN JUSTO

CALLE AVE MARIA
CALLE POZO AMARGO
COLEGIO DE
INFANTES
C. CANDELARIA
PASEO DE CABESTREROS

S. CATALINA
CALLE DE PLEGADERO
BAJADA DEL BARCO
Cliffs
Tajo River

SANTA
CATALINA
PASEO DE CABESTREROS

SAN SEBASTIÁN

One-way streets →
Traffic barriers

To Parador &
CM-40
Ring Road
VIEWPOINT

PASEO ROSA

TOLEDO

drive around the city. You'll view the city from many angles along the Circunvalación road across the Tajo Gorge. Stop at a viewpoint or drive to Parador de Toledo, just south of town, for the view (from the balcony) that El Greco made famous in his portrait of Toledo. The best time for this trip is the magic hour before sunset, when the top viewpoints are busy with tired old folks and frisky young lovers.

If you're willing to pay, the most convenient place to park is in the big Miradero Garage at the convention center (€16/day; drive through Bisagra Gate, go uphill half a mile, look for sign on the left directing you to *Plaza del Miradero*). There's also parking farther into town at the Alcázar Garage (just past the Alcázar—€1.80/hour, €20/day). There are also two big, free, uncovered parking lots: the one between the river and the bus station is best if you want to use the escalators to get up to the center; the other lot is between the river and the train station. North of the city walls, you'll find parking and another set of escalators going up near the Glorieta de la Reconquista roundabout, but at the top you'll still be far from Plaza de Zocodover.

Many hotels offer discounted parking rates at nearby garages; ask when making your reservation.

A car is useless within Toledo's city walls, where the narrow, twisting streets are no fun to navigate. Ideally, see the old town outside of car-rental time.

HELPFUL HINTS

Useful App: Toledo Be Your Guide is a simple but useful free travel app. Ignore the sections on restaurants, shopping, and nightlife; instead select "Attractions" for information on different sights around town. The app can be used offline and has some handy navigation links.

Taxis: There are three taxi stands in the old center: Plaza de Zocodover, Bisagra Gate, and Santo Tomé. Taxis routinely give visitors scenic circles around town with photo stops for around €15.

Local Guidebook: Consider the readable *Toledo: Its Art and Its History* (€5-6 big version, €4 small version, same text and photos in both, sold all over town). It explains all of the sights (which generally provide no on-site information) and gives you a photo to point at and say, *"¿Dónde está...?"*

Tours in Toledo

▲Tourist Bus

Toledo City Tour offers three tourist bus options for day-trippers. For transportation with a view to the city center, meet the bus at the train station, ride along the river to the famous "El Greco" lookout point, where you can get off for a five-minute photo stop. Then the bus continues around the city and up to Plaza de Zocodover, where you can get off and visit Toledo. Pay a little more, and you get a hop-on, hop-off version that allows you to stop at the photo viewpoint, Bisagra Gate, and the San Martín medieval bridge (but be prepared to wait an hour for the next bus). Skip the *lanzadera* bus, which offers the same ride up to Plaza de Zocodover as the city bus described earlier (under "Arrival in Toledo—By Train"), but costs about €1 more (€2.50 *lanzadera*, €5.50 with one stop, €9 for hop-on, hop-off option, pay at stand in train station; departures timed to train arrivals—first bus leaves train station at 9:50, then almost hourly until about 20:00 in summer, shorter hours off-season; longer rides include recorded English commentary on headphones; tel. 925-950-000, www.toledocitytour.es, infotoledo@toledocitytour.es).

Tourist Train

For a pleasant city overview, hop on the cheesy TrainVision Tourist Train. Crass as it feels, you get a 45-minute putt-putt through Toledo and around the Tajo River Gorge. It's a fine way for non-drivers to enjoy views of the city from across the Tajo Gorge (€5.50, buy ticket from kiosk on Plaza de Zocodover, leaves Plaza de Zocodover daily 1-2/hour 10:00-18:30, later in summer, recorded English/Spanish commentary, tel. 625-301-890, www.busvision.net). For the best views of Toledo across the gorge, sit on the right side, not behind the driver. There's a five-minute photo stop at the viewpoint.

Public Buses

For the cheapest tour, use public transportation. Take the "Bus #12 Self-Guided Tour" through town. Or, for a "gorge-ous" loop trip, try bus #71, which leaves from opposite the entrance of the Alcázar (hourly 7:45-21:45) and offers the same classic view across the gorge as the tourist train; its route circles around to El Greco's famous viewpoint, where you can hop off and snap some photos, then wait about an hour at the same stop for the next bus to take you back.

Local Guide

For a good guide who enjoys sharing his hometown in English, try **Juan José Espadas** (a.k.a. Juanjo, who gracefully brings meaning to the complex mix of Toledo's history, art, and culture; 3-hour tour-€150, tel. 667-780-475, juanjo@guiadetoledo.es).

Sights in Toledo

▲▲▲CATHEDRAL

Holy Toledo! Spain's leading Catholic city has a magnificent cathedral. Shoehorned into the old center, its exterior is hard to appreciate. (As is so typical of religious sites in hard-fought Iberia, it was built after the Reconquista on the spot where a mosque once stood.) But the interior is so lofty, rich, and vast that it'll have you wandering around like a Pez dispenser stuck open, whispering "Wow." The sacristy has a collection of paintings that would put any museum on the map.

Cost and Hours: €8 includes audioguide; €11 also includes trip up bell tower at assigned times; €12 combo-ticket including cathedral, bell tower, and cathedral tapestry collection in Colegio de Infantes; tickets sold in shop opposite church entrance on Calle Cardenal Cisneros; Mon-Sat 10:00-18:30, Sun 14:00-18:30, open earlier for prayer only, last entry 30 minutes before closing; photos allowed without flash, tel. 925-222-241. A WC is in the ticket center.

❂ Self-Guided Tour

Wander among the pillars, thick and sturdy as a redwood forest. Sit under one and imagine a time when the light bulbs were candles and the tourists were pilgrims—when every window provided spiritual as well as physical light. The cathedral is primarily Gothic. But since it took more than 250 years to build (1226-1495)—with continuous embellishments after that (every archbishop wanted to leave his imprint)—it's a mix of styles, including Gothic, Renaissance, Baroque, and Neoclassical. Enjoy the elaborate wrought-iron work, lavish wood carvings, and window after colorful window of 500-year-old stained glass. Circling the interior are ornate chapels, purchased by the town's most noble families, and the sacristy, with its world-class collection of El Grecos and works by other famous painters.

This confusing collage of great Spanish art deserves a close look. Hire a private guide, discreetly freeload on a tour (they come by every few minutes during peak season), listen to the audioguide, or follow this quick tour.

• *First, walk to the high altar.*

High Altar: Climb two steps and grip the iron grille as you marvel at one of the most stunning altars in Spain. Real gold on wood, by Flemish, French, and local artists, it's one of the country's

Toledo at a Glance

▲▲▲Cathedral One of Europe's best, with a marvelously vast interior and great art. **Hours:** Mon-Sat 10:00-18:30, Sun 14:00-18:30. See page 150.

▲▲Santa Cruz Museum Renaissance building housing wonderful artwork, including 15 El Grecos, but sections may be closed during your visit. **Hours:** Mon-Sat 10:00-19:00, Sun 10:00-14:30. See page 158.

▲▲Army Museum Covers all things military located in the imposing fortress, the Alcázar. **Hours:** Thu-Tue 11:00-17:00, closed Wed. See page 159.

▲Santo Tomé Simple chapel with El Greco's masterpiece, *The Burial of the Count of Orgaz*. **Hours:** Daily 10:00-18:45, until 17:45 mid-Oct-Feb. See page 162.

▲El Greco Museum Small collection of paintings, including the *View and Plan of Toledo*, El Greco's panoramic map of the city. **Hours:** Tue-Sat 9:30-20:00, until 18:30 Oct-March, Sun 10:00-15:00, closed Mon. See page 163.

▲Museo Victorio Macho Collection of 20th-century Toledo sculptor's works, with expansive river-gorge view. **Hours:** Mon-Sat 10:00-19:00, Sun 10:00-15:00. See page 165.

▲San Juan de los Reyes Monasterio Church/monastery intended as final resting place of Isabel and Ferdinand. **Hours:** Daily 10:00-18:45, until 18:00 mid-Oct-March. See page 166.

Visigothic Museum Romanesque church housing the only Visigothic artifacts in town. **Hours:** Tue-Sat 10:00-14:30 & 16:00-19:00, Sun 10:00-14:30, closed Mon. See page 161.

Sinagoga del Tránsito Museum of Toledo's Jewish past. **Hours:** Tue-Sat 9:30-20:00, Sun 10:00-15:00, shorter hours off-season, closed Mon year-round. See page 163.

Sinagoga de Santa María la Blanca Synagogue that harmoniously combines Toledo's three religious influences: Jewish, Christian, and Moorish. **Hours:** Daily 10:00-18:45, until 17:45 in winter. See page 166.

Toledo's Cathedral

To Plaza de Zocodover →

SAN BLAS CHAPEL

PUERTA DEL RELOJ

ARCO DE PALACIO

CLOISTER

SACRISTY

NEW KINGS CHAPEL

← TREASURY

TRANSPARENTE

PUERTA PERDÓN

CHOIR

HIGH ALTAR

GRILLE

Plaza del Ayuntamiento

MOZARABIC CHAPEL

CHAPTER HOUSE

PUERTA LLANA
MAIN ENTRANCE

PUERTA LEONES

To City Hall & 🛈

CALLE   CARDENAL   CISNEROS

WC ■ BUY TICKETS HERE AT SHOP

20 Meters
20 Yards

best pieces of Gothic art. Study the wall of scenes from the life of Christ, frame by frame. All of the images seem to celebrate the colorful Assumption of Mary in the center, with Mary escorted by six upwardly mobile angels. The crucified Christ on top is nine feet tall—taller than the lower statues—to keep this towering

altar approachable. Don't miss the finely worked gold-plated iron grille itself—considered to be the best from the 16th century in Spain.

• *About-face to the...*

Choir: Facing the high altar, the choir is famous for its fine and richly symbolic carving. It all seems to lead to the archbishop's throne in the rear center. First, look carefully at the fine alabaster relief in the center (about where the bishop would rest his head on his throne): It shows a seventh-century Visigothic miracle, when

Mary came down to give the local bishop the holy robe, legitimizing Toledo as the spiritual capital (and therefore political capital) of Spain.

Because of its primacy in Iberia, Toledo was the first city in the crosshairs of the Reconquista Christian forces. They recaptured the city in 1085 (over 400 years before they retook Granada). The fall of Toledo marked the beginning of the end of the Muslim domination of Iberia. A local saying goes, "A carpet frays from the edges, but the carpet of Al-Andalus (Muslim Spain) frayed from the very center" (meaning Toledo).

The lower wooden stalls are decorated with scenes showing the steady one-city-at-a-time finale of the Christian Reconquista, when Muslims were slowly pushed back into Africa. Set in the last decade of the Reconquista, these images celebrate the retaking of the towns around Granada: Each idealized castle has the reconquered town's name on it, culminating in the final victory at Granada in 1492 (these two reliefs flank the archbishop's throne). Although the castles are romanticized, the carvings of the clothing, armor, and weaponry are so detailed and accurate that historians have studied them to learn the evolution of weaponry.

The upper stalls feature Old Testament figures—an alabaster genealogy of the church—starting with Adam and Eve and working counterclockwise to Joseph and "S. M. Virgo Mater" (St. Mary the Virgin Mother). Notice how the statues on the Adam and Eve side (left) are more lifelike; they were done by Alonso Berruguete, nicknamed "the Michelangelo of Spain" for his realistic figures. All this imagery is designed to remind viewers of the legitimacy of the bishop's claims to religious power. Check out the seat backs, made of carved walnut and featuring New Testament figures—with Peter (key) and Paul (sword)—alongside the archbishop himself.

And, as is typical of choir decoration, the carvings on the misericords (the tiny seats that allowed tired worshippers to lean while they "stand") represent various sins and feature the frisky, folksy, sexy, profane art of the day. Apparently, since you sat on it, it could never be sacred anyway.

Take a moment to absorb the marvelous complexity, harmony, and cohesiveness of the art around you. Look up. There are two fine pipe organs: one early 18th-century Baroque and the other late 18th-century Neoclassical. As you leave the choir, note the serene beauty of the 13th-century Madonna and child at the front (Virgin Blanca), thought to be a gift from the French king to Spain. Its naturalism and intimacy was proto-Renaissance—radical in its day.

The iron grille of the choir is notable for the dedication of the man who built it. Domingo de Céspedes, a Toledo ironworker, accepted the commission to build the grille for 6,000 ducats. The project, which took from 1541 to 1548, was far more costly than he anticipated. The medieval Church didn't accept cost overruns, so to finish it he sold everything he owned and went into debt. He died a poor—but honorable—man. (That's a charming story, but the artistic iron gate before the high altar—described earlier—is the true treasure.)

• *Face the altar, and go around it to your right to the...*

Chapter House (Sala Capitular): Under its lavish ceiling, a fresco celebrates the humanism of the Italian Renaissance. There's a Deposition (taking crucified Jesus off the cross), a *pietà*, and a Resurrection on the front wall; they face a fascinating Last Judgment, where the seven sins are actually spelled out in the gang going to hell: arrogance (the guy striking a pose), avarice (holding his bag of coins), lust (the easy woman with the lovely hair and fiery crotch), anger (shouting at lust), gluttony (the fat guy), envy, and laziness. Think about how instructive this was in 1600.

Below the fresco, a pictorial review of 1,900 years of Toledo archbishops circles the room. The upper row of portraits dates from the 16th century. Except for the last two, these were not painted from life (the same face seems to be recycled over and over). The lower portraits were added one at a time from 1515 on and are of more historic than artistic interest. Imagine sitting down to church business surrounded by all this tradition and theology.

The current cardinal—whose portrait will someday grace the next empty panel—is the top religious official in Spain. He's conservative on issues unpopular with Spain's young: divorce, abortion, and contraception. When he speaks, it makes news all over Spain.

As you leave, notice the iron-pumping cupids carved into the pear-tree panels lining the walls.

• *Go behind the high altar to find the...*

Transparente: The Transparente is a unique feature of the cathedral. In the 1700s, a hole was cut into the ceiling to let a sunbeam brighten Mass. The opening faces east, and each morning the rising sun reminds all that God is light. Melding this big hole with the Gothic church presented a challenge: The result was a Baroque masterpiece. Gape up at this riot of angels doing flip-flops, babies breathing thin air, bottoms of feet, and gilded sunbursts. Carved out of marble from Italy, it's bursting with motion and full of energy. Appreciate those tough little cherubs who are supporting the whole thing—they've been waiting for help for about 300 years now.

Step back to study the altar, which

looks chaotic, but is actually structured thoughtfully: The good news of salvation springs from Baby Jesus, up past the archangels (including one in the middle who knows how to hold a big fish correctly) to the Last Supper high above, and beyond into the light-filled dome. I like it, as did (I guess) the two long-dead cardinals whose faded red hats hang from the edge of the hole. (A perk that only a cardinal enjoys is to choose a burial place in the cathedral, and hang his hat over that spot until the hat rots.)

• *Before entering the sacristy (to your right), peek into the...*

Chapel of the New Kings (Capilla de Reyes Nuevos): In the 16th century, Emperor Charles V moved the tombs of eight kings who reigned before Ferdinand and Isabel to this spot.

• *Leaving this chapel, the next door on your right takes you into the...*

Sacristy: The cathedral's sacristy is a mini-Prado, with 19 El Grecos and masterpieces by Francisco de Goya, Titian, Diego Velázquez, Caravaggio, and Giovanni Bellini. First, notice the fine perspective work on the ceiling. It was painted by Neapolitan artist Lucca Giordano around 1690. (You can see the artist himself—with his circa-1690 spectacles—painted onto the door high above on the left; look for it at the base of the ceiling.) Then walk to the end of the room for the most important painting in the collection, El Greco's *The Spoliation* (a.k.a. *Christ Being Stripped of His Garments*).

Spain's original great painter was Greek, and this is his first masterpiece after arriving in Toledo. El Greco's painting from 1579 hangs exactly where he intended it to—in the room where priests prepared themselves for Mass. It shows Jesus surrounded by a sinister mob and suffering the humiliation of being stripped in public before his execution.

The scarlet robe is about to be yanked off, and the women (lower left) avert their eyes, turning to watch a carpenter at work (lower right) who bores the holes for nailing Jesus to the cross. While the carpenter bears down, Jesus—the other carpenter—looks up to heaven. The contrast between the motley crowd gambling for his clothes and Jesus' noble face underscores the quiet dignity with which he endures this ignoble treatment. Jesus' delicate white hand stands out from the flaming red tunic with an odd gesture that's common in El Greco's paintings. Some say this was the way Christians of the day swore they were true believers, not merely Christians-in-name-only, such as former Muslims or Jews who converted to survive.

On the right is a religious painting by Goya, the *Betrayal of Christ*, which shows Judas preparing to kiss Jesus, thus identifying him to the Roman soldiers. Across the room is a scene rarely painted: a touching El Greco portrait called *St. Joseph and the Christ Child*. Joseph is walking with Jesus, just as El Greco enjoyed walk-

TOLEDO

ing around the Toledo countryside with his sons. Notice Joseph's gentle expression—and the Toledo views in the background.

Enjoy the many other El Grecos here. Before exiting the sacristy, look for a glass case to the left of the door containing a small-but-lifelike 17th-century carving of St. Francis by Pedro de Mena (1628-1688).

• *As you step out of the sacristy, look high up to your right at the oldest stained glass in the church (from the 14th century). Then, passing a chapel reserved for worship, just before the treasury, you come to...*

The Cloister: The cloister is worth a stroll for its finely carved colonnade. Take a peaceful detour to the funerary San Blas Chapel. The ceiling over the marble tomb of a bishop is a fresco by a student of Giotto (a 14th-century Italian Renaissance master).

Treasury: The *tesoro* is tiny, but radiant with riches. The highlight is the 10-foot-high, 430-pound monstrance—the tower designed to hold the Holy Communion wafer (the host) during the festival of Corpus Christi ("body of Christ") as it's paraded through the city. Built in 1517 by Enrique de Arfe, it's made of 5,000 individual pieces held together by 12,500 screws. There are diamonds, emeralds, rubies, and 400 pounds of gold-plated silver. The inner part (which is a century older) is 35 pounds of solid gold. Yeow. The base is a later addition from the Baroque period.

To the right of the monstrance is a beautiful red-coral cross given by the Philippines. Below the cross is a facsimile of a 700-year-old Bible hand-copied and beautifully illustrated by French monks; it was a gift from St. Louis, the 13th-century king of France. Imagine looking on these lavish illustrations with medieval eyes—an exquisite experience. (The precious and fragile lamb-skin original is preserved out of public view.) The finely painted small crucifix on the opposite side in the corner (with the mirror behind it) is by the great Gothic Florentine painter Fra Angelico. It depicts Jesus alive on the back and dead on the front, and was a gift from Mussolini to Franco. Underneath, near the floor, you'll find Franco's rather plain sword. Hmmm. To the right of Fra Angelico's crucifix, find the gift (humble amid all this splendor) from Toledo's sister city: Toledo, Ohio.

Mozarabic Chapel: Before 10:00, the cathedral is open only for prayer (from north entrance). If you're here to worship at the 9:00 Mass (daily except Sunday), you can peek into the otherwise-locked Mozarabic Chapel (Capilla Mozárabe). This Visigothic Mass (in Latin) is the oldest surviving Christian ritual in Western Europe. You're welcome to partake in this stirring example of peaceful coexistence of faiths. Toledo's proud Mozarabic community of 1,500 people traces its roots to Visigothic times.

Bell Tower: If you paid for the bell tower, meet just to the left of the San Blas Chapel at your assigned time. You'll climb up several sections of tight spiral staircases to reach panoramic views of Toledo and the largest (though cracked) bell in Spain.

CENTRAL TOLEDO

In addition to the cathedral, the city's historic core contains these sights:

Plaza de Zocodover

The main square is Toledo's center and your gateway to the old town. The word "Zocodover" derives from the Arabic for "livestock market."

Because Toledo is the state capital of Castile-La Mancha, the regional government administration building overlooks Plaza de

Zocodover. Look for the three flags: one for Europe, one for Spain, and one for Castile-La Mancha. And speaking of universal symbols—find the low-key McDonald's. A source of controversy, it was finally allowed... with only one small golden arch. Next came the bigger Burger King, which no one blinked at twice.

The square is a big local hangout and city hub. Once the scene of Inquisition judgments and bull-fights, today it's a lot more peaceful. Old people arrive in the morning, and young people come in the evening. The goofy tourist train leaves from here, as well as the Tourist Bus and city buses #5, #11, #61, and #62, which lumber to the train station. Just uphill, near the taxi stand, is the stop for bus #12, which travels around the old town to Santo Tomé (and works as a good self-guided tour) and for bus #71, which heads out to the panoramic viewpoint made famous by El Greco.

Colegio de Infantes

The cathedral displays its fine collection of tapestries and vestments at the nearby Colegio de Infantes. Many of the 17th-century tapestries here are still used to decorate the cathedral during the one of the city's biggest events, the festival of Corpus Christi. You'll also find the lavish-but-faded *Astrolabe Tapestry* (c. 1480, Belgian). It shows a new view of the cosmos at the dawn of the Age of Discovery: God (far left) oversees all, as Atlas (with the help of two women and a crank handle) spins the universe, containing the circular Earth. The wisdom gang (far right) heralds the wonders of the coming era. Rather than a map of Earth, this is a chart showing the cosmic order of things as the constellations spin around the stationary North Star (center).

Cost and Hours: €2, €12 combo-ticket includes cathedral and bell tower, daily 10:00-18:00, from the cathedral go down Calle Barco to Plaza Colegio Infantes, tel. 925-258-723.

▲▲Santa Cruz Museum (Museo de Santa Cruz)

This stately Renaissance building was formerly an orphanage and hospital, funded by money left by the humanist and diplomat

Cardinal Mendoza when he died in 1495. The cardinal, confirmed as Chancellor of Castile by Queen Isabel, was so influential that he was called "the third royal."

In 2014, the museum hosted an impressive gathering of paintings by El Greco to commemorate the 400th anniversary of his death. Since then, some of the museum has been closed while curators reorganize its collection—so some parts of the museum may not be on view when you visit.

Cost and Hours: Likely €6, Mon-Sat 10:00-19:00, Sun 10:00-14:30; from Plaza de Zocodover, go through arch to Calle Miguel de Cervantes 3; tel. 925-221-036, www.patrimoniohistoricoclm.es. A WC is in the far corner of the lower cloister.

Visiting the Museum: The building's facade still wears bullet scars from the Spanish Civil War. The exterior, cloister arches, and stairway leading to the upper cloister are fine examples of the Plateresque style. This ornate strain of Spanish Renaissance is named for the fancy work of silversmiths of the 16th century. During this time (c. 1500-1550), the royal court moved from Toledo to Madrid—when Madrid was a village and Toledo was a world power. (You'll see no Plateresque work in Madrid.) Note the Renaissance-era mathematics, ideal proportions, round arches, square squares, and classic columns.

While the interior is being reorganized, look for the following artworks and exhibits:

The museum has 15 **El Greco** paintings. A highlight is the impressive *Assumption of Mary,* a spiritual poem on canvas. This altarpiece, finished one year before El Greco's death in 1614, is the culmination of his unique style, combining all of his techniques to express an otherworldly event.

Study the *Assumption* (which some believe is misnamed, and actually shows the Immaculate Conception—the plaque describing the work entitles it *Inmaculada Concepción*). Bound to earth, the city of Toledo sleeps, but a vision is taking place overhead. An angel in

Toledo's Muslim Legacy

You can see the Moorish influence in these sights:

- Mezquita del Cristo de la Luz, the last of the town's mosques
- Sinagoga del Tránsito's Mudejar plasterwork
- Sinagoga de Santa María la Blanca's mosque-like horseshoe arches and pinecone capitals
- Puerta del Sol (Gate of the Sun) and other surviving gates (with horseshoe arches) along the medieval wall
- The city's labyrinthine, medina-like streets

a billowing robe, as if doing the breaststroke with his wings, flies up, supporting Mary, the mother of Christ. She floats up through warped space, to be serenaded by angels and wrapped in the radiant light of the Holy Spirit. Mary flickers and ripples, charged from within by her spiritual ecstasy, caught up in a vision that takes her breath away. No painter before or since has captured the supernatural world better than El Greco.

A beautiful private collection of **tiles and ceramics,** which the Carranza family has loaned to the museum for the last 20 years, dates from the end of the Reconquista (1492). Each piece is categorized by the Spanish region where it was made. This may be the only place in Spain where you can compare regional differences in tile work and pottery.

The museum's collection also includes **prehistoric** pieces, some **Roman** artifacts, and a marble well bearing an **Arabic** inscription. If the well is on view, note the grooves in the sides made by generations of Muslims pulling their buckets up by rope. This well was once located in the courtyard of an 11th-century mosque, which stood where the cathedral does today.

▲▲Army Museum (Museo del Ejército)

This museum features endless rooms of Spanish military collections of armor, uniforms, cannons, guns, paintings, and models. It tells the military history of Spain from 1492 to the 20th century. The displays are wonderfully explained in English, and the audioguide is excellent. If you like military history, allow at least three hours for this, one of Europe's top military museums. The museum has one major flaw: its skimpy coverage of the Spanish Civil War (1936-1939).

Cost and Hours: €5, €8 ticket

includes excellent 2-hour audioguide, free on Sun; open Thu-Tue 11:00-17:00, closed Wed; last entry 30 minutes before closing, café/restaurant where you can bump elbows with Spanish military, tel. 925-238-800, www.museo.ejercito.es.

Visiting the Museum: The museum is located in the Alcázar, the huge former imperial residence that dominates Toledo's skyline. It's built on the site of Roman, Visigothic, Moorish, and early Renaissance fortresses, the ruins of which (displayed just past the turnstile) are a poignant reminder of the city's strategic importance through the centuries.

Today's structure (originally built in the 16th century, then destroyed in the civil war and rebuilt) became a kind of right-wing Alamo. During the civil war, Franco's Nationalists (and hundreds of hostages) were besieged here by Republican troops for two months in 1936. The Republicans took the son of the Alcázar's commander—Colonel José Moscardó—hostage and called Colonel Moscardó, threatening to execute his son if he didn't surrender in 10 minutes. Moscardó asked for his son to be put on the line, and told him that he would have to be a hero and die for Spain. Moscardó then informed the Republican leader that he didn't need 10 minutes: the choice was made—he would never give up the Alcázar. (While the Nationalists believed the son was shot immediately, he was actually executed with other prisoners weeks later in a reprisal for an air raid.)

Finally, after many fierce but futile Republican attacks that destroyed much of the Alcázar, Franco sent in an army that took Toledo, a major victory for the Nationalists. After the war, the place was rebuilt and glorified under Franco. Only one room on the sixth floor (labeled as *CM-Despacho del Coronel Moscardó* on the museum map) has been left in a tattered ruin since the siege: the office of Colonel Moscardó.

It's a confusing floor plan, but if you start at the top floor and follow the "historical round" arrows, you'll enjoy a roughly chronological sweep. Since so much of this country's history is military, this museum tells much of the story of Spain.

Look for special theme rooms (e.g., the use of photography in the army, and the evolution of Spain's flag). The main courtyard—Italian-inspired Renaissance in style—comes with a proud statue of Holy Roman Emperor Charles V (a.k.a. King Charles I of Spain), the ultimate military king and Europe's most powerful 16th-century leader. While in the courtyard, consider the restoration of this massive-yet-elegant fortress.

The 20th-century section comes with some fascinating videos, but has just three small rooms of civil-war artifacts, including uniforms from both sides, Franco's cloak and cane, and posters. In addition there are photographs of the conflict and a small audiovisual slide show. As the museum was preparing to open, controversy broke out on how to handle the civil war. The curators dodged the issue by going light on *the* major event of 20th-century Spanish history; it's not even marked on the museum's map (look for *El Siglo XX*).

Mezquita del Cristo de la Luz

Of Muslim Toledo's 10 mosques, this barren little building (dating from about 1000) is the best survivor. Looking up, you'll notice

the Moorish fascination with geometry—each dome is a unique design. The lovely keyhole arch faces Mecca. In 1187, after the Reconquista, the mosque was changed to a church, the Christian apse (with its crude Romanesque art) was added, and the former mosque got its current name. The small garden with its fountains is a reminder of the Quranic image of heaven. From the outside of the building, you can see a Roman road, leading to the city wall, that was discovered and excavated when the mosque was undergoing restoration.

Cost and Hours: €2.50, Mon-Fri 10:00-14:00 & 15:30-18:40, until 17:45 in winter, Sat-Sun 10:00-17:45, Cuesta de las Carmelitas Descalzas 10, tel. 925-254-191.

Visigothic Museum in the Church of San Román (Museo de los Concilios y de la Cultura Visigoda)

This 13th-century Mudejar church (with its rare, strangely modernist 13th-century Romanesque frescoes) provides an exquisite space for a small but interesting collection of Visigothic artifacts. The Visigoths were the Christian barbarian tribe who ruled Spain between the fall of Rome and the rise of the Moors. The only things Visigothic about the actual building are the few capitals topping its columns, recycled from a seventh-century Visigothic church. Though the elaborate crowns are copies (the originals are in Madrid), other glass cases show off metal and stone artifacts from the age when Toledo was the capital of the Visigoths. The items, while featuring almost no human figures, are rich in symbolism. Their portability fits that society's nomadic heritage. Archaeologists have found almost no Visigothic artifacts within Toledo's fortified hill location. They lived in humble settlements along the river—apparently needing no defense system...until the Moors swept through in 711, ending two centuries of Visigothic rule in Iberia. Climb the steep stairs for a view of Toledo's rooftops from the church tower.

Cost and Hours: Likely €3, Tue-Sat 10:00-14:30 & 16:00-

TOLEDO

19:00, Sun 10:00-14:30, closed Mon, no English information, Plaza San Román, tel. 925-227-872.

SOUTHWEST TOLEDO

These sights cluster at the southwest end of town. For efficient sightseeing, visit them in this order, then zip back home on bus #12 (listed at the end of this section).

▲Santo Tomé

A simple chapel on the Plaza del Conde holds El Greco's most beloved painting. *The Burial of the Count of Orgaz* couples heaven and

earth in a way only The Greek could. It feels so right to see a painting in the same church where the artist placed it 400 years ago. It originally filled the space immediately to the right of where it is now, but as the popularity of this masterpiece was disturbing the main church, it was moved. Church officials even created a special entryway for viewing it.

Cost and Hours: €2.50, daily 10:00-18:45, until 17:45 mid-Oct-Feb, audioguide-€1, tel. 925-256-098. This sight often has a line; try going early or late to avoid tour groups.

Visiting Santo Tomé: Take this slow. Stay a while—let it perform. The year is 1323. Count Don Gonzalo Ruiz has died. You're at his burial right here in this chapel. The good count was so holy, even saints Augustine and Stephen have come down from heaven to lower his body into the grave. (The painting's subtitle is "Such is the reward for those who serve God and his saints.")

More than 250 years later, in 1586, a local priest (depicted on the far right, reading the Bible) hired El Greco to make a painting of the burial to hang over the count's tomb. The funeral is attended by Toledo's most distinguished citizens. (El Greco used local nobles as models.) The painting is divided in two by a serene line of noble faces—heaven above and earth below. Above the faces, the count's soul, symbolized by a little baby, rises up through a mystical birth canal to be reborn in heaven, where he's greeted by Jesus, Mary, and all the saints. A spiritual wind blows through as colors change and shapes stretch. This is Counter-Reformation propaganda—notice Jesus pointing to St. Peter, the symbol of the pope in Rome, who controls the keys to the pearly gates. Each face is a detailed portrait. It's clear that these portraits inspired the next great Spanish painter, Velázquez, a century later. El Greco himself (eyeballing you, seventh figure in from the left) is the only one not involved in the burial. The boy in the foreground—pointing to the two saints as if to say, "One's from the first century, the other's from the fourth...it's a miracle!"—is El Greco's son. On the handkerchief in the boy's pocket is El Greco's signature, written in Greek.

Don Gonzalo Ruiz's actual granite tombstone is at your feet. The count's two wishes upon his death were to be buried here and for his village to make an annual charity donation to feed Toledo's poor. Finally, more than two centuries later, the people of Orgaz said, "Enough!" and stopped the payments. The last of the money was spent to pay El Greco for this painting.

▲El Greco Museum (Museo del Greco)

This small museum, built near the site of El Greco's house, gives a look at the genius of his art and Toledo in his day. Its small collection of paintings is accompanied by interactive touch screens and videos.

A comfy little theater shows a fine 10-minute video on both the life of the artist and the story of this museum. You then proceed through halls that show the evolution of El Greco's art. While there aren't many great El Grecos here, you'll see a hall lined with his *Twelve Apostles, San Bernardino of Siena* (in a chapel), and the highlight of the museum—the *View and Plan of Toledo*. El Greco's panoramic map shows the city in 1614. Study the actual map and list of sights. It was commissioned to promote the city (suddenly a former capital) after the king moved to Madrid.

Cost and Hours: €3, €5 combo-ticket with Sinagoga del Tránsito, free Sat afternoon from 14:00 and all day Sun; open Tue-Sat 9:30-20:00, until 18:30 Oct-March, Sun 10:00-15:00, closed Mon; next to Sinagoga del Tránsito on Calle Samuel Leví, tel. 925-223-665.

Sinagoga del Tránsito (Museo Sefardí)

Built in 1361, this is the best surviving slice of Toledo's Jewish past. Serving as Spain's national Jewish museum, it displays Jewish artifacts, including costumes, menorahs, and books. Your visit comes with three parts: the nave, a ground floor exhibition space with a history of Spain's Jews, and the women's gallery upstairs, which shows lifestyles and holy rituals among Sephardic Jews. While English sheets in each room explain the collection, to get the most out of the exhibits, rent the audioguide.

Cost and Hours: €3, €5 combo-ticket with El Greco Museum, free Sat afternoon from 14:00 and all day Sun; open Tue-Sat 9:30-20:00, Sun 10:00-15:00, shorter hours off-season, closed Mon year-round; near El Greco Museum on Calle de los Reyes Católicos, tel. 925-223-665.

Tours: You can rent an audioguide for €2, or connect to the synagogue's Wi-Fi with your mobile device for a free audioguide

TOLEDO

TOLEDO

El Greco (1541-1614)

Born on Crete and trained in Venice, Doménikos Theotokópoulos (tongue-tied friends just called him "The Greek") came to Spain to get a job decorating El Escorial. He failed there, but succeeded in Toledo, where he spent the last 37 years of his life. He mixed all three regional influences into his palette. From his Greek homeland, he absorbed the solemn, abstract style of icons. In Italy, he learned the bold use of color, elongated figures, twisting poses, and dramatic style of the later Renaissance. These elements were then fused in the fires of fanatic Spanish-Catholic devotion.

Not bound by the realism so important to his fellow artists, El Greco painted dramatic visions of striking colors and figures—bodies unnatural and lengthened as though stretched between heaven and earth. He painted souls, not faces. His work is on display at nearly every sight in Toledo. Thoroughly modern in his disregard for realism, he didn't impress the austere Philip II. But his art still seems as fresh as contemporary art does today. El Greco was essentially forgotten through the 18th and most of the 19th centuries. Then, with the Romantic movement (and the discovery of Toledo by Romantic-era travelers, artists, and poets), the paintings of El Greco became the hits they are today.

(starts automatically). You can also download the audioguide from www.audioviator.com (search for "Museo Sefardi").

Visiting the Synagogue: This 14th-century synagogue was built at the peak of Toledo's enlightened tolerance—constructed for Jews with Christian approval by Muslim craftsmen. Nowhere else in the city does Toledo's three-culture legacy shine brighter than at this place of worship. But in 1391, just a few decades after it was built, the Church and the Spanish kings began a violent campaign to unite Spain as a Christian nation, forcing Jews and Muslims to convert or leave. In 1492 Ferdinand and Isabel exiled Spain's remaining Jews. It's estimated that in the 15th century, while some of Spain's Jews were expelled, many others survived by converting to Christianity. A third left the country.

Surveying the synagogue from the back, its interior decor looks more Muslim than Jewish. After Christians reconquered the city in 1085, many Moorish workmen stayed on, beautifying the city with their unique style called Mudejar. The synagogue's intricate, geometrical carving in stucco—nearly all original, from 1360—features leaves, vines, and flowers; there are no human shapes, which are forbidden by the Torah—like the Quran—as being "graven images." In the frieze (running along the upper wall, just below the ceiling), the Arabic-looking script is actually Hebrew, quoting psalms (respected by all "people of the book"—Muslims, Jews, and Christians alike). The balcony was the traditional separate worship area for women.

Move up to the front. Stand close to the holy wall and study the exquisite workmanship (with reminders of all three religions: the coat of arms of the Christian king, Hebrew script, and Muslim decor). Look down. The small rectangular patch of the original floor only survived because the Christian altar table sat there. In the side room and upstairs, scale models of the development of the Jewish quarter and video displays give a picture of Jewish life in medieval Toledo.

▲Museo Victorio Macho

Overlooking the gorge and Tajo River, this small, attractive museum—once the home and workshop of the early-20th-century sculptor Victorio Macho—offers a delightful collection of his bold Art Deco-inspired work. If you skip the museum, you can still enjoy the terrace view from its gate. The museum's theater hosts a gimmicky multimedia show called the Toledo Time Capsule, which isn't worth the extra fee even if it's pouring down rain.

Cost and Hours: €3, Mon-Sat 10:00-19:00, Sun 10:00-15:00, between the two *sinagogas* at Plaza de Victorio Macho 2, tel. 925-284-225. A free audioguide is available for those with mobile devices (connect to museum Wi-Fi—audioguide starts automatically; or download from www.audioviator.com—search for "Victorio Macho").

Visiting the Museum: The house itself is a cool oasis of calm in the city. Your visit comes in four stages: ticket room with theater, courtyard with view, crypt, and museum.

The small theater in the ticket room shows a good nine-minute video about the history of Toledo (nothing about Macho, but it's well worth the time—request the English-language version). Macho was Spain's first great modern sculptor. When his left-wing Republican (say that three times) politics made it dangerous for him to stay in Franco's Spain, he fled to the USSR, then Mexico and Peru, where he met his wife, Zoila. They later returned to Toledo, where they lived and worked until he died in 1966. Zoila eventually gave the house and Macho's art to the city.

Enjoy the peaceful and expansive view from the terrace. From here it's clear how the Tajo River served as a formidable moat protecting the city. Imagine trying to attack. The 14th-century bridge (on the right) connected the town with the region's *cigarrales*—

mansions of wealthy families, whose orchards of figs and apricots dot the hillside even today. To the left (in the river), look for the stubs of 15th-century watermills; directly below is a riverside trail that's delightful for a stroll or jog.

The door marked *Crypta* leads to *My Brother Marcelo*—the touching tomb Macho made for his brother. Eventually he featured his entire family in his art.

A dozen steps above the terrace, you'll find a single room marked *Museo* filled with Macho's art. A *pietà* is carved expressively in granite. Next to the *pietà*, several self-portrait sketches show the artist's genius. The bronze statue is a self-portrait at age 17. In the next section, exquisite pencil-on-paper studies illustrate how a sculptor must understand the body (in this case, Zoila's body). The sketch of Zoila from behind is entitled *Guitar* (Spaniards traditionally think of a woman's body as a guitar). Other statues show the strength of the peoples' spirit as leftist Republicans stood up to Franco's fascist forces, and Spain endured its 20th-century bloodbath. The highlight is *La Madre* (from 1935), Macho's life-size sculpture of his mother sitting in a chair. It illustrates the sadness and simple wisdom of Spanish mothers who witnessed so much suffering. Upon a granite backdrop, her white marble hands and face speak volumes.

Sinagoga de Santa María la Blanca

This synagogue-turned-church has Moorish horseshoe arches and wall carvings. It's a vivid reminder of the religious cultures that shared (and then didn't share) this city.

While it looks like a mosque, it never was one. Built as a Jewish synagogue by Muslim workers around 1200, it became a church in 1492 when Toledo's Jews were required to convert or leave—hence the mix-and-match name. After being used as horse stables by Napoleonic troops, it was further ruined in the 19th century. Today, it's an evocative space, beautiful in its simplicity.

Cost and Hours: €2.50, daily 10:00-18:45, until 17:45 in winter, Calle de los Reyes Católicos 4, tel. 925-227-257. Note the thirst-quenching bottled-water machine in the courtyard.

▲San Juan de los Reyes Monasterio

"St. John of the Monarchs" is a grand Franciscan monastery, impressive church, and delightful "Isabeline" cloistered courtyard. The style is late Gothic, contemporaneous with Portugal's Manueline (c. 1500) and Flamboyant Gothic elsewhere in Europe. It was the intended burial site of the Catholic Monarchs, Isabel and Ferdinand. But after the Moors were expelled in 1492 from Granada, their royal bodies were planted there to show Spain's commitment to maintaining a Moor-free peninsula.

Cost and Hours: €2.50, daily 10:00-18:45, until 18:00 mid-Oct-March, last entry 30 minutes before closing, San Juan de los Reyes 2, tel. 925-223-802. After buying your ticket, look up. A skinny monk welcomes you (and reminds us of our mortality).

Visiting the Sight: Before entering and getting your ticket, take in the **facade.** It is famously festooned with 500-year-old chains. Moors used these to shackle Christians in Granada until 1492. It's said that the freed Christians brought these chains to the church, making them a symbol of their Catholic faith and a sign of victory. Enter the monastery at the side door.

Even without the royal tombs that would have dominated the space, the glorious **chapel** gives you a sense of Spain when it was Europe's superpower. The monastery was built to celebrate the 1476 Battle of Toro, which made Isabel the queen of Castile. Since her husband, Ferdinand, was king of Aragon, this effectively created the Spain we know today. (You could say 1476 is to Spain what 1776 is to the US.) Now united, Spain was able to quickly finish the Reconquista, ridding Iberia of its Moors within the next decade and a half.

Sitting in the chapel, you're surrounded by propaganda proclaiming Spain's greatness. The coat of arms is repeated obsessively. The eagle with the halo disk represents St. John, protector of the royal family. The yoke and arrows are the symbols of Ferdinand and Isabel. The lions remind people of the power of the kingdoms joined together under Ferdinand and Isabel. The coat of arms is complex because of Iberia's many kingdoms (e.g., a lion for León, and a castle for Castile).

As you leave, look up over the door to see the Franciscan coat of arms—with the five wounds of the crucifixion (the stigmata—which St. Francis earned through his great faith) flanked by angels with dramatic wings.

Enjoy a walk around the **cloister.** Notice details of the fine carvings. Everything had meaning in the 15th century. In the corner (opposite the entry), just above eye level, find a small monkey—an insulting symbol of Franciscans—on a toilet reading the Bible upside-down. Perhaps a stone carver snuck in a not-too-subtle comment on Franciscan pseudo-intellectualism, with their big libraries and small brains.

Napoleon's troops are mostly to blame for the destruction of the church, a result of Napoleon's view that monastic power in Europe was a menace. While Napoleon's biggest error was to invade Russia, his second dumbest move was to alienate the Catholic faithful by destroying monasteries such as this one. This strategic mistake eroded popular support from people who might have seen Napoleon as a welcome alternative to the tyranny of kings and the Church.

If you're tired, skip going upstairs—if not, you can take a simple walk around the top level of the courtyard under a finely renovated Moorish-style ceiling.

▲Bus #12 Self-Guided Tour (A Sweat-Free Return Trip from Santo Tomé to Plaza de Zocodover)

When you're finished with the sights at the Santo Tomé end of town, you can hike all the way back (not fun)—or simply catch bus #12 (fun!) back to Plaza de Zocodover. The ride offers tired sightseers a quick, interesting 15-minute look at the town walls. You can catch the bus from Plaza del Conde in front of Santo Tomé. This is the end of the line, so buses wait to depart from here twice hourly (at :25 and :55, until 21:25, pay driver €1.40). You can also catch the same bus across the street from the San Juan de los Reyes ticket entrance (at :28 and :58). Here's what you'll see on your way if you catch it from Santo Tomé:

Leaving Santo Tomé, you'll first ride through Toledo's Jewish section. On the right, you'll pass the El Greco Museum, Sinagoga del Tránsito, and Sinagoga de Santa María la Blanca, followed by—on your left—the ornate Flamboyant Gothic facade of San Juan de los Reyes Monasterio. After squeezing through the 16th-century city gate, the bus follows along the outside of the mighty 10th-century wall. (Toledo was never conquered by force...only by siege.)

Just past the big escalator (which brings people from parking lots up into the city) and the Hotel Cardinal, the wall gets fancier, as demonstrated by the little old Bisagra Gate. Soon after, you see the big new Bisagra Gate, the main entry into the old town. While the city walls date from the 10th century, this gate was built as an arch of triumph in the 16th century. The massive coat of arms of Emperor Charles V, with the double eagle, reminded people that he ruled a unified Habsburg empire (succes-

sor of ancient Rome), and they were entering the capital of an empire that, in the 1500s, included most of Western Europe and much of America. (We'll enter the town through this gate in a couple minutes after a stop at the bus station.)

Just outside the big gate is a well-maintained and shaded park—a picnic-perfect spot and one of Toledo's few green areas. After a detour to the bus station basement to pick up people coming from Madrid, you swing back around Bisagra Gate. As an example of how things have changed in the last generation, as recently as 1960, all traffic into the city at this point had to pass through this gate's tiny original entrance.

As you climb back into the old town, you'll pass the fine, 14th-century Moorish Puerta del Sol (Gate of the Sun) on your right. Then comes the modern Palacio de Congresos Miradero convention center on your left, which is artfully incorporated into the more historic cityscape. Within moments you pull into the main square, Plaza de Zocodover. You can do this tour in reverse by riding bus #12 from Plaza de Zocodover to Plaza del Conde (departing at :25 and :55, same price and hours).

Shopping in Toledo

Toledo probably sells more souvenirs than any city in Spain. This is *the* place to buy medieval-looking swords, armor, maces, three-legged stools, lethal-looking letter-openers, and other nouveau antiques. It's also Spain's damascene center, where, for centuries, craftspeople have inlaid black steel with gold, silver, and copper wire. Spain's top bullfighters wouldn't have their swords made anywhere else.

Knives: At the workshop of English-speaking **Mariano Zamorano,** you can see swords and knives being made. His family has been putting its seal on handcrafted knives since 1890. Judging by what's left of Mariano's hand, his knives are among the sharpest (Mon-Fri 10:00-14:00 & 16:00-19:00, Sat-Sun 10:00-14:00—although you may not see work done on weekends, 10 percent discount with this book, behind Ayuntamiento/City Hall at Calle Ciudad 19, tel. 925-222-634, www.marianozamorano.com).

Damascene: You can find artisans all over town pounding gold and silver threads into a steel base to create shiny inlaid plates, decorative wares, and jewelry. The damascene is a real tourist racket, but it's fun to pop into a shop and see the intricate handiwork in action.

Nun-Baked Sweet Treats: Signs posted on convent doors all over town invite you in to buy *Dulces Artesanos* (sweets) including *mazapán*. Try the Santa Rita Convent—go in the main door to the left, press the buzzer, and a nun will appear in five minutes or so behind a turnstile window to take your order (small box-€6, Mon-Fri 9:00-13:00 & 15:00-16:15, Sat until 18:00, closed Sun, hours sometimes vary, Calle Santa Ursula 3).

El Martes: Toledo's colorful outdoor market is a lively scene on Tuesdays at Paseo de Merchan, better known to locals as "La Vega" (9:00-14:00, outside Bisagra Gate near TI).

Sleeping in Toledo

Madrid day-trippers darken the sunlit cobbles, but few stay to see Toledo's medieval moonrise. Spend the night. Hotels often have a two-tiered price system, with prices 20 percent higher on Friday and Saturday. Spring and fall are high season; November through March and July and August are less busy. Similar to other places in Spain, Toledo's big and small hotels are making deals to confront the hard economic times. Fish around for deals and discounts. Most places have an arrangement with parking lots in town that can save you a few euros; ask when you reserve.

NEAR PLAZA DE ZOCODOVER

$$ Hotel Toledo Imperial sits efficiently above Plaza de Zocodover, and rents 29 business-class rooms that are a solid value (Db-€50 Sun-Thu, Db-€85-100 Fri-Sat, higher rates with increased demand, breakfast-about €5, air-con, elevator, Calle Horno de los Bizcochos 5, tel. 925-280-034, www.hoteltoledoimperial.com, reservas@hoteltoledoimperial.com).

$ Hotel La Conquista de Toledo, a three-star hotel with 33 rooms, gleams with marble. It's so sleek and slick it almost feels more like a hospital than a hotel (Sb-€35, Db-€45-60, book directly by email and ask for their best Rick Steves price, skimpy breakfast-€8, air-con, elevator, near the Alcázar at Juan Labrador 8, tel. 925-210-760, www.hotelconquistadetoledo.com, conquistadetoeldo@githoteles.com, Yuki).

$ Hostal Centro rents 28 spacious rooms with sparse, well-worn furniture and a ramshackle feel. It's wonderfully central, with a third of its rooms overlooking the main square. Request a quiet room on the back side to minimize night noise (Sb-€30-35, Db-

Sleep Code

Abbreviations (€1=about $1.10, country code: 34)
S=Single, **D**=Double/Twin, **T**=Triple, **Q**=Quad, **b**=bathroom
Price Rankings
  $$$ **Higher Priced**—Most rooms €100 or more.
   $$ **Moderately Priced**—Most rooms €60-100.
    $ **Lower Priced**—Most rooms €60 or less.
Unless otherwise noted, credit cards are accepted, breakfast
is not included, free Wi-Fi and/or a guest computer is generally available, and English is spoken. Some hotels include the
10 percent IVA tax in the room price; others tack it onto your
bill. Prices change; verify current rates online or by email. For
the best prices, always book directly with the hotel.

€45-50, Tb-€60-65, book directly via email with hotel for a 10
percent weekday discount with this book, 50 yards off Plaza de Zocodover—take the first right off Calle del Comercio to Calle Nueva
13, tel. 925-257-091, www.hostalcentrotoledo.com, hostalcentro@
telefonica.net, warmly run by Asun and David).

NEAR BISAGRA GATE

$$$ Hacienda del Cardenal, a 17th-century cardinal's palace
built into Toledo's wall, is quiet and elegant, with a cool garden,
a less-than-helpful staff, and a stuffy restaurant. This poor man's
parador, at the dusty old gate of Toledo, is close to the station,
but below all the old-town action (Sb-€59-91, Db-€75-118, Fri-
Sat-€20-40 more, breakfast-€9, enter through town wall 100 yards
below Bisagra Gate, Paseo de Recaredo 24, tel. 925-224-900,
www.haciendadelcardenal.com, hotel@haciendadelcardenal.com).

$$ Hospedería de los Reyes has 15 colorful and thoughtfully
appointed rooms in an attractive, quiet, yellow building 100 yards
downhill from Bisagra Gate, outside the wall. They also offer 11
apartments near the gate, with kitchens and living rooms (Sb-€40-
59, Db-€49-80, apartments for up to 6 people-€65-180, break-
fast-€4-6, air-con, street parking nearby, Calle Perala 37, tel. 925-
283-667, www.hospederiadelosreyes.com, hospederiadelosreyes@
hospederiadelosreyes.com, Alicia and Carolina).

$$ Hotel Abad sits at the bottom of the old town's hill just
a block inside the Bisagra Gate and offers 22 clean, rustic rooms
with stone walls, wooden rafters, and contemporary furnishings
(Db-€64-84 Sun-Thu, Db-€90-125 Fri-Sat, extra bed-€20, break-
fast-€8, air-con, elevator, Real del Arrabal 1, tel. 925-283-500,
www.hotelabadtoledo.com, reservas@hotelabad.com).

$ El Hostal Puerta Bisagra is in a sprawling old building that
is fresh and modern inside. Located just across from Bisagra Gate,

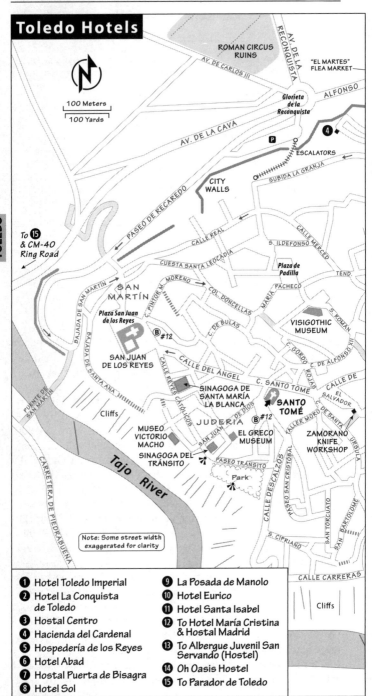

Toledo Hotels

TOLEDO

100 Meters
100 Yards

ROMAN CIRCUS RUINS

AV. DE CARLOS III

AV. DE LA RECONQUISTA

"EL MARTES" FLEA MARKET

ALFONSO

Glorieta de la Reconquista

AV. DE LA CAVA

❹

ESCALATORS

CITY WALLS

SUBIDA LA GRANJA

PASEO DE RECAREDO

CALLE REAL

S. ILDEFONSO MERCED

To ❶⑤ & CM-40 Ring Road

CUESTA SANTA LEOCADIA

Plaza de Padilla

TEND.

C. PINTOR M. MORENO

COL. DONCELLAS

MARÍA

PACHECO

SAN MARTÍN

BAJADA DE SAN MARTÍN

Plaza San Juan de los Reyes

ⓑ#12

C. DE BULAS

VISIGOTHIC MUSEUM

S. ROMÁN

BAJADA DE SANTA ANA

SAN JUAN DE LOS REYES

CALLE DEL ÁNGEL

C. GORDO

C. DE ALFONSO XII

CALLE REYES CATÓLICOS

C. SANTO TOMÉ

CALLE DE EL SALVADOR

PUENTE DE SAN MARTÍN

Cliffs

SINAGOGA DE SANTA MARÍA LA BLANCA

SANTO TOMÉ

JUDERÍA

ⓑ#12

DE SANTA URSULA

CARRETERA DE PIEDRABUENA

MUSEO VICTORIO MACHO

SINAGOGA DEL TRÁNSITO

SAN JUAN DE DIOS

EL GRECO MUSEUM

KALER MORO

ZAMORANO KNIFE WORKSHOP

PASEO TRÁNSITO

Park

Tajo River

Note: Some street width exaggerated for clarity

PASEO DESCALZOS

CALLE DESCALZOS

PASEO SAN CRISTÓBAL

S. CIPRIANO

SAN TORCUATO

SAN BARTOLOMÉ

CALLE CARRERAS

Cliffs

❶ Hotel Toledo Imperial
❷ Hotel La Conquista de Toledo
❸ Hostal Centro
❹ Hacienda del Cardenal
❺ Hospedería de los Reyes
❻ Hotel Abad
❼ Hostal Puerta de Bisagra
❽ Hotel Sol

❾ La Posada de Manolo
❿ Hotel Eurico
⓫ Hotel Santa Isabel
⓬ To Hotel María Cristina & Hostal Madrid
⓭ To Albergue Juvenil San Servando (Hostel)
⓮ Oh Oasis Hostel
⓯ To Parador de Toledo

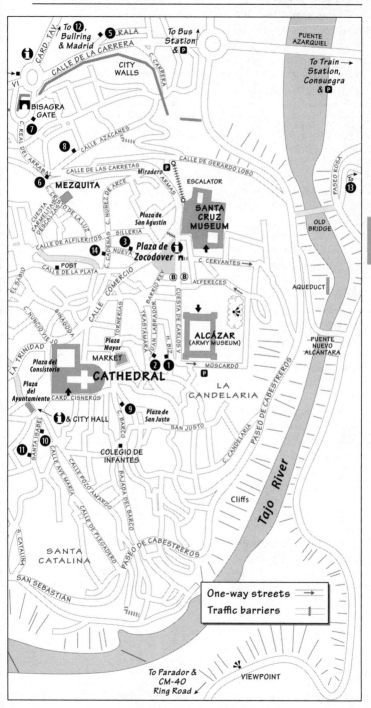

TOLEDO

One-way streets →
Traffic barriers ⫲

it's convenient for arrivals, but a long hike uphill to the action (hop on any bus). Its 38 comfortable rooms are rented at some of the best prices in town (Sb-€40-50, Db-€50-70, lower rates Sun-Thu; breakfast-€6, air-con, Calle del Potro 5, tel. 925-285-277, www. puertabisagra.com, elhostal@puertabisagra.com).

$ Hotel Sol, with 15 nicely decorated pastel rooms, is a good value. It's on a quiet, ugly side street between Bisagra Gate and Plaza de Zocodover (Sb-€32-48, Db-€43-58, Tb-€61-72, higher rates for Fri-Sat, slightly cheaper Nov-March, 10 percent discount with this book, breakfast-€4, air-con, private parking-€10/day; leave the busy main drag at Hotel Imperial and head 50 yards down the lane to Azacanes 8; tel. 925-213-650, www.hotelyhostalsol. com, info@hotelyhostalsol.com, José Carlos). Their 11-room **$ Hostal Sol** annex across the street is just as comfortable, smoke-free, and a bit cheaper (Sb-€30-39, Db-€39-48, Tb-€57-62, higher rates for Fri-Sat, slightly cheaper Nov-March, 10 percent discount with this book, breakfast-€4).

DEEP IN TOLEDO

$$ La Posada de Manolo rents 14 furnished rooms across from the downhill corner of the cathedral. Manolo Junior opened this *hostal* according to his father's vision: a place with each of its three floors themed differently—Moorish, Jewish, and Christian. Listed in several US and European guidebooks, they tend to fill up (Sb-€39, Db-€50 Sun-Thu, Db-€61 Fri, Db-€72 Sat, more for rooms with bigger beds, 10 percent discount with this book when you reserve directly with hotel, breakfast-€3, air-con, no elevator, two nice view terraces, Calle Sixto Ramón Parro 8, tel. 925-282-250, www.laposadademanolo.com, toledo@laposadademanolo.com).

$$ Hotel Eurico cleverly fits 23 sleek rooms into a medieval building buried deep in the old town. The staff is friendly, and the hotel offers a good value (Sb-€55-60, Db-€60-90, Tb-€70-120, higher rates for Fri-Sat, breakfast-€5-8, air-con, Calle Santa Isabel 3, tel. 925-284-178, www.hoteleurico.com, reservas@hoteleurico. com).

$ Hotel Santa Isabel, in a 15th-century building two blocks from the cathedral, has 41 clean, modern, and comfortable rooms and squeaky tile hallways (Sb-€30-42, small old Db-€45-55, big new Db-€55-65, Db with view-€70-85, higher rates for Fri-Sat, extra bed-€10, 5 percent discount with this book, breakfast-€5, elevator, scenic roof terrace, parking-€12/day, buried deep in old town—take a taxi instead of the bus, drivers enter from Calle Pozo Amargo, Calle Santa Isabel 24, tel. 925-253-120, www. hotelsantaisabel.net, info@hotelsantaisabel.net).

OUTSIDE OF TOWN, NEAR THE BULLRING

These places are on a modern street next to the bullring (Plaza de Toros, bullfights only on holidays), just beyond Bisagra Gate. They have none of Toledo's charm or character but are inexpensive and can be practical options. In this area, parking is free on the street. The bus station is a five-minute walk away, and city bus #5 lumbers by and goes directly to Plaza de Zocodover. There are many other similarly nondescript, comfy, and cheap places in this neighborhood.

$$ Hotel María Cristina, a sprawling 69-room hotel, has all the comforts under a layer of prefab tradition. Rates vary greatly—ask them for any special pricing or check website (Sb-€50-80, Db-€50-120, Tb-€148-160, suites-€100-170, breakfast-€8, aircon, elevator, restaurant, parking-€10/day, Marqués de Mendigorría 1, tel. 925-213-202, www.hotelesmayoral.com, informacion@ hotelmariacristina.com).

$ Hostal Madrid has two locations on the same street with 29 rooms and a café next door (Sb-€30, Db-€36, Tb-€50, breakfast-€3, air-con, parking-€8/day, Marqués de Mendigorría 7 and 14, reception at #7, tel. 925-221-114, www.hostal-madrid.net, info@hostal-madrid.net).

HOSTELS

$ Albergue Juvenil San Servando youth hostel is lavish but fairly cheap, with 96 beds and small rooms for two or four people (€17/ bed plus €13 obligatory *alberguista* membership, extra €3.50/day for the first six days of membership, swimming pool, views, cafeteria, good management, located in 10th-century Arab castle of San Servando, 10-minute walk from train station, 15-minute hike from town center, over Puente Viejo outside town, tel. 925-224-554, reservations tel. 925-221-676, alberguesclm@jccm.es, no English spoken).

$ Oh Oasis Hostel is a fresh, 21-room hostel right around the corner from Plaza de Zocodover, with a pleasant rooftop terrace. Weekends may be noisy because there is no curfew (€14-18/ bed, Db-€34-60, includes towel and sheets, elevator, air-con, Calle Cadenas 5, tel. 925-227-650, www.hosteloasis.com, toledo@ hostelsoasis.com).

OUTSIDE OF TOWN WITH
THE GRAND TOLEDO VIEW

$$$ Parador de Toledo, with 79 rooms, is one of Spain's best-known inns. Its guests enjoy the same Toledo view that El Greco made famous from across the Tajo Gorge (Sb-€120-128, Db-€120-180, superior Db with view-€145-200, extra bed-€61, higher rates for March-Oct, call or check online for deals, breakfast-€18, €29 fixed-price meals sans drinks in their fine restaurant overlooking Toledo, 2 windy miles from town at Cerro del Emperador—it may come up as Carretera de Cobisa on GPS systems, tel. 925-221-850, www.parador.es, toledo@parador.es).

Eating in Toledo

DINING IN TRADITIONAL ELEGANCE

A day full of El Greco and the romance of Toledo after dark puts me in the mood for game and other traditional cuisine. Typical Toledo dishes include partridge *(perdiz)*, venison *(venado)*, wild boar *(jabalí)*, roast suckling pig *(cochinillo asado)*, or baby lamb (*cordero*—similarly roasted after a few weeks of mother's milk). After dinner, find a *mazapán* place for dessert. Restaurants generally serve lunch from 13:00 to 16:00 and dinner from 20:00 until very late (Spaniards don't start dinner until about 21:00).

Los Cuatro Tiempos Restaurante ("The Four Seasons") specializes in local game and roasts, proficiently served in a tasteful and elegant setting. They offer spacious dining with an extensive and inviting Spanish wine list. It's a good choice for a quiet, romantic dinner, and a good value for a midday meal (€19 weekend three-course lunches and dinners—drinks not included, €35 à la carte dinners, Mon-Sat 13:00-16:00 & 20:30-23:00, Sun 13:00-16:00 only, at downhill corner of cathedral, Calle Sixto Ramón Parro 5, tel. 925-223-782, www.restauranteloscuatrotiempos.es).

Colección Catedral is the wine bar of the highly respected local chef Adolfo, who runs a famous gourmet restaurant nearby plus several eateries in Madrid. His hope is to introduce the younger generation to the culture of fine food and wine. The bar offers up a somewhat pricey but always top-notch list of gourmet plates, including some traditional local dishes like *carcamusas*—pork and vegetable stew (€7-19 each) and fine local wines (about €3/glass), as well as a €15 three-course meal, wine included.

I like to sit next to the kitchen to be near the creative action. If the Starship *Enterprise* had a Spanish wine-and-tapas bar on its holodeck, this would be it. Wine is sold to take home or drink there for €3-8 more than the shop price (daily 12:00-23:30, across from cathedral at Calle Nuncio Viejo 1, tel. 925-224-244, Michael Angel takes good care of diners).

El Botero Taberna is a delightful little hideaway. The barman downstairs, who looks like a young Pavarotti, serves mojitos, fine wine, and exquisite tapas. Upstairs, there's an intimate, seven-table restaurant with romantic, white-tablecloth ambience and modern Mediterranean dishes (€29-€48 fixed-price meals, €15 starters, €20 main courses, lunch only Sun-Tue, lunch and dinner Wed-Sat, a block below cathedral at Calle de la Ciudad 5, tel. 925-229-088, www.tabernaelbotero.com).

SIMPLE RESTAURANTS WITH CHARACTER

These places are listed in geographical order from Plaza de Zocodover to Santo Tomé. Plaza de Zocodover is busy with eateries serving edible food at affordable prices, and its people-watching scene is great. But my recommended eateries are just a bit off the main drag on side streets. It's worth a few extra minutes—and the navigating challenge—to find places where you'll be eating with locals as well as tourists. There is a lively midday tapas scene in Toledo, and almost every bar you pop into for a stand-up drink will come with a small plate of something to nibble.

To dine with younger Spaniards, drop into **El Trébol,** tucked peacefully away just a short block off Plaza de Zocodover. Their €10 mixed grill can feed two. Locals enjoy their *pulgas* (€2.50 sandwiches). The seating inside is basic, but the outdoor tables are nice (daily 9:00-24:00, Calle de Santa Fe 1, tel. 925-281-297).

Restaurante Ludeña is a classic eatery with a bar, a well-worn dining room in back, and a handful of tables on a sunny courtyard. It's very central; locals duck in here to pretend there's no tourism in Toledo (Plaza de la Magdalena 10, tel. 925-223-384).

Madre Tierra Restaurante Vegetariano is Toledo's answer to a vegetarian's prayer. Bright, spacious, classy, air-conditioned, and tuned in to the healthy eater's needs, its appetizing dishes are based on both international and traditional Spanish cuisine (€8-13 main courses, €13.50 fixed-price weekday meal, good tea selection, great veggie pizzas, closed Mon night and all day Tue, 20 yards below La Posada de Manolo just before reaching Plaza de San Justo, Bajada de le Tripería 2, tel. 925-223-571).

Taberna La Flor de la Esquina is a local bar with a simple basement dining room and wonderful seating on a leafy square under a towering Jesuit church facade. Rustic and part of a fun neighborhood scene, this place is best when you want to eat outside on a square (€10 lunch specials, basic *raciones,* open daily, Plaza Juan de Mariana 2, tel. 925-253-801).

Restaurante Placido, run by high-energy Anna and Abuela (grandma) Sagradio, serves traditional family-style cuisine on a

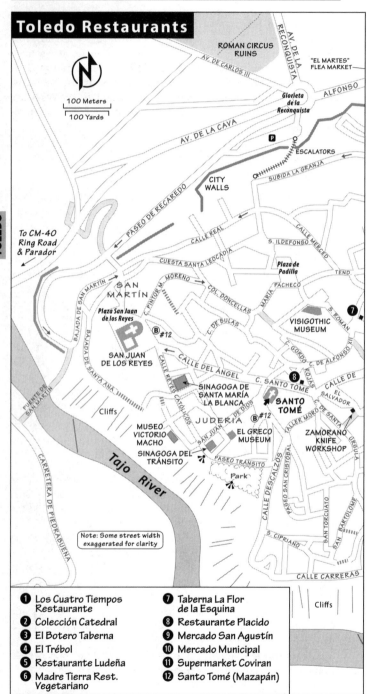

Toledo Restaurants

TOLEDO

1. Los Cuatro Tiempos Restaurante
2. Colección Catedral
3. El Botero Taberna
4. El Trébol
5. Restaurante Ludeña
6. Madre Tierra Rest. Vegetariano
7. Taberna La Flor de la Esquina
8. Restaurante Placido
9. Mercado San Agustín
10. Mercado Municipal
11. Supermarket Coviran
12. Santo Tomé (Mazapán)

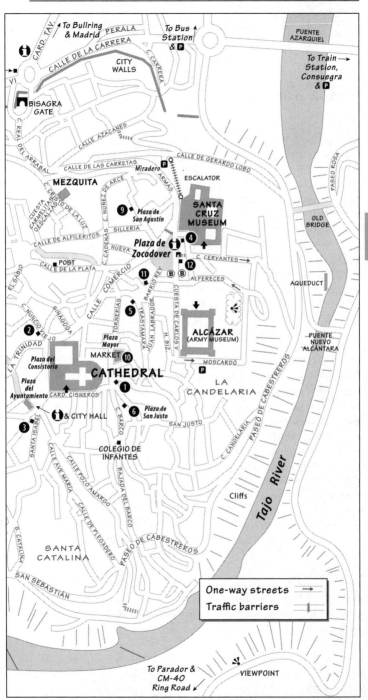

TOLEDO

leafy terrace or in a wonderful Franciscan monastery courtyard (€13, €15, and €22 fun fixed-price meals—more expensive option comes with partridge; open daily for lunch and dinner in summer, lunch only in winter, about a block uphill from Santo Tomé at Calle Santo Tomé 2, tel. 925-222-603).

Mercado San Agustín is part of a trend to create a space for several different eateries in a fancy food court. You can taste gourmet cheeses, wines, hamburgers, Spanish delicacies, Japanese cuisine, fusion foods, and sweet delights. Explore the five levels before deciding, then find a table on any of the levels to dig in, or go to the top-floor terrace for a cocktail (Tue-Sun 10:00-24:00, closed Mon, at Calle Cuesta de Águila 1 right off of Plaza San Agustín, tel. 925-215-898, www.mercadodesanagustin.com).

Picnics: Picnics are best assembled at the city market, **Mercado Municipal,** on Plaza Mayor (on the Alcázar side of cathedral, with a supermarket inside open Mon-Sat 9:00-15:00 & 17:00-20:00 and stalls open mostly in the mornings until 14:00, closed Sun). **Supermarket Coviran,** on Plaza de la Magdalena, has groceries and lots of other stuff at good prices (Mon-Sat 9:50-15:00 & 16:00-22:00, shorter hours on Sun, just below Plaza de Zocodover). For a picnic with people-watching on an atmospheric square, consider Plaza de Zocodover or Plaza del Ayuntamiento.

AND FOR DESSERT: *MAZAPÁN*

Toledo's famous almond-fruity-sweet *mazapán* is sold all over town. As you wander, keep a lookout for convents advertising their version, *Dulces Artesanos.* The big *mazapán* producer is **Santo Tomé** (several outlets, including a handy one on Plaza de Zocodover, daily 9:00-22:00). Browse their tempting window displays. They sell *mazapán* goodies individually (two for about €1.50, *sin relleno*—without filling—is for purists, *de piñon* has pine nuts, *imperiales* is with almonds, others have fruit fillings). Boxes are good for gifts, but sampling is much cheaper when buying just a few pieces. Their *Toledana* is a nutty, crumbly, not-too-sweet cookie with a subtle thread of squash filling (€1.40 each).

For a sweet and romantic evening moment, pick up a few pastries and head down to the cathedral. Sit on the Plaza del Ayuntamiento's benches (or stretch out on the stone wall to the right of the TI). The fountain is on your right, Spain's best-looking City Hall is behind you, and there before you is her top cathedral—built back when Toledo was Spain's capital—shining brightly against the black night sky.

Toledo Connections

FROM TOLEDO TO MADRID

While the AVE bullet train makes the trip to Madrid in half the time, buses depart twice as frequently. Three or four people traveling together can share a taxi economically. Whichever way you travel, Madrid and Toledo are very easily connected.

By Bus: 2/hour, 1-1.5 hours, *directo* is faster than *ruta,* bus drops you at Madrid's Plaza Elíptica Metro stop, Alsa bus company, tel. 902-422-242, www.alsa.es; you can almost always just drop in and buy a ticket minutes before departure.

By Train: Nearly hourly, 30 minutes by AVE or Avant to Madrid's Atocha Station, tel. 902-240-202, www.renfe.com; early and late trains can sell out—reserve ahead.

By Taxi: While it may seem extravagant, if you have limited time, lots of luggage, and a small group, simply taking a taxi from your Toledo hotel to your Madrid hotel is breathtakingly efficient (€90, one hour door-to-door, tel. 925-255-050 or 925-227-070). You can ask several cabbies for their best "off the meter" rate. A taxi to the Madrid airport costs €110 (find one who will go "off the meter") and takes an hour.

FROM TOLEDO TO OTHER POINTS

To get to Granada, Sevilla, and elsewhere in Spain from Toledo, assume you'll have to transfer in Madrid. See "Madrid Connections" at the end of that chapter for information on reaching various destinations.

ROUTE TIPS FOR DRIVERS

Granada to Toledo (250 miles, 3.5 hours): The Granada-Toledo drive is long, hot, and boring. Start early to minimize the heat and make the best time you can. Follow signs for *Madrid/ Jaén/A-44* into what some call "the Spanish Nebraska"—La Mancha (see next section). After Puerto Lapice, you'll see the Toledo exit.

Toledo to Madrid (40 miles, 1 hour): It's a speedy *autovía* north, past one last billboard to Madrid (on A-42). The highways converge into M-30, which encircles Madrid. Follow it to the left (*Nor* or *Oeste*) and take the Plaza de España exit to get back to Gran Vía. If you're airport-bound, keep heading into Madrid until you see the airplane symbol (N-II).

To drive to Atocha Station in Madrid, take the exit off M-30 for Plaza de Legazpi, then take Delicias (second on your right off the square). Parking for rental-car return is on the north side of the train station.

La Mancha

La Mancha, which is worth a visit if you're driving between Toledo and Granada, shows a side of Spain that you'll see nowhere else—vast and flat. Named for the Arabic word for "parched earth," it makes you feel small—lost in rough seas of olive-green polka dots. Random buildings look like houses and hotels hurled off some heavenly Monopoly board.

This is the setting of Miguel de Cervantes' *Don Quixote,* published in the early 17th century, after England sank the Armada and the Spanish Empire began its decline. Cervantes' star character fights doggedly for good, for justice, and against the fall of Spain and its traditional old-regime ideals. Ignoring reality, Don Quixote is a hero fighting a hopeless battle. Stark La Mancha is the perfect stage.

The epitome of *Don Quixote* country, the town of **Consuegra** (TI tel. 925-475-731, www.aytoconsuegra.es) must be the La Mancha Cervantes had in mind. Drive up to the ruined 12th-century castle and joust with a windmill. It's hot and buggy here,

but the powerful view overlooking the village, with its sun-bleached light-red roofs, modern concrete reality, and harsh, windy silence, makes for a profound picnic (a one-hour drive south of Toledo). The castle belonged to the Knights of St. John (12th and 13th centuries) and is associated with their trip to Jerusalem during the Crusades. Originally built from the ruins of a nearby Roman circus, it has been recently restored (€4, includes windmill and archaeological museum in town). Sorry, the windmills are post-Cervantes, only 200 to 300 years old—but you can go inside the Molino de Bolero to see how it works (€1.50, included with €4 castle entry, daily 10:00-13:30 & 16:30-18:30—except opens at 10:30 Sat-Sun, shorter hours in winter). If your heart is set on fighting the windmills like Don Quixote—and you don't have a car—you can hire a taxi to drive you here from Toledo for about €95 (includes round-trip travel and an hour stop).

The next castle north (above Almonacid, 8 miles from Toledo) is free. Follow the ruined lane past the ruined church up to the ruined castle. The jovial locals hike up with kids and kites.

PRACTICALITIES

This section covers just the basics on traveling in Spain (for much more information, see *Rick Steves Spain*). You'll find free advice on specific topics at www.ricksteves.com/tips.

MONEY

Spain uses the euro currency: 1 euro (€) = about $1.10. To convert prices in euros to dollars, add about 10 percent: €20 = about $22, €50 = about $55. (Check www.oanda.com for the latest exchange rates.)

The standard way for travelers to get euros is to withdraw money from ATMs (which locals call a *cajero automático*) using a debit or credit card, ideally with a Visa or MasterCard logo. Before departing, call your bank or credit-card company: Confirm that your card(s) will work overseas, ask about international transaction fees, and alert them that you'll be making withdrawals in Europe. Also ask for the PIN number for your credit card in case it'll help you use Europe's "chip-and-PIN" payment machines (see below); allow time for your bank to mail your PIN to you. To keep your valuables safe, wear a money belt.

Chip and PIN: Much of Europe (including Spain) is adopting a "chip-and-PIN" system for credit cards, and some merchants rely on it exclusively. European chip-and-PIN cards are embedded with an electronic chip, in addition to the magnetic stripe used on American-style cards. This means that your credit (and debit) card might not work at payment machines, such as those at train and subway stations, toll roads, parking garages, luggage lockers, and unattended gas pumps. Major US banks are beginning to offer credit cards with chips, but many of these are not true chip-and-PIN cards. Instead, they are chip-and-signature cards, for which your signature verifies your identity. In Europe, these cards should work for live transactions and at most payment machines, but won't work for offline transactions such as at unattended gas pumps. If a payment machine won't take your card, look for a machine that takes cash or a cashier who can manually process your transaction. Often the easiest solution is to pay for your purchases with cash you've withdrawn from an ATM using your debit card (Europe's ATMs still accept magnetic-stripe cards).

Dynamic Currency Conversion: If merchants or hoteliers offer to convert your purchase price into dollars (called dynamic currency conversion, or DCC), refuse this "service." You'll pay more in fees for the expensive convenience of seeing your charge in dollars. If an ATM offers to "lock in" or "guarantee" your conversion rate, choose "proceed without conversion." Other prompts might state, "You can be charged in dollars: Press YES for dollars, NO for euros." Always choose the local currency.

STAYING CONNECTED

Smart travelers call ahead or go online to double-check tourist information, learn the latest on sights (special events, tour schedules, and so on), book tickets and tours, make reservations, reconfirm hotels, and research transportation connections.

To call Spain from the US or Canada: Dial 011-34 and then the nine-digit number. (The 011 is our international access code, and 34 is Spain's country code.)

To call Spain from a European country: Dial 00-34 followed by the nine-digit number. (The 00 is Europe's international access code.)

To call within Spain: Just dial the local nine-digit number.

To call from Spain to another country: Dial 00 followed by the country code (for example, 1 for the US or Canada), then the area code and number. If calling European countries whose phone numbers begin with 0, you'll usually have to omit that 0 when you dial.

Tips: Traveling with a mobile phone—whether an American one that works in Spain, or a European one you buy when you arrive—is handy, but can be pricey. Consider getting an international plan; most providers offer a global calling plan that cuts the per-minute cost of phone calls and texts, and a flat-fee data plan.

Use Wi-Fi (pronounced *wee-fee* in Spanish), whenever possible. Most hotels and many cafés offer free Wi-Fi, and you'll likely also find it at tourist information offices, major museums, and public-transit hubs. With Wi-Fi you can use your smartphone to make free or inexpensive domestic and international calls by taking advantage of a calling app such as Skype, FaceTime, or Google+ Hangouts. When you can't find Wi-Fi, you can use your cellular

From:	rick@ricksteves.com
Sent:	Today
To:	info@hotelcentral.com
Subject:	Reservation request for 19-22 July

Dear Hotel Central,

I would like to reserve a room for 2 people for 3 nights, arriving 19 July and departing 22 July. If possible, I would like a quiet room with a double bed and private bathroom inside the room.

Please let me know if you have a room available and the price.

Thank you!
Rick Steves

network to connect to the Internet, text, or make voice calls. When you're done, avoid further charges by manually switching off "data roaming" or "cellular data."

It's possible to stay connected without a mobile phone. To make cheap international calls from any phone (even your hotel-room phone), you can buy an international phone card in Spain (called a *tarjeta telefónica con código*). These work with a scratch-to-reveal PIN code, allow you to call home to the US for pennies a minute, and also work for domestic calls. Calling from your hotel-room phone without using an international phone card is usually expensive. Though they are disappearing in Spain, you can still find public pay phones in post offices and train stations. For more on phoning, see www.ricksteves.com/phoning.

MAKING HOTEL RESERVATIONS

I recommend reserving rooms in advance, particularly during peak season. For the best rates, book directly with the hotel using their official website (not a booking agency's site). If there's no secure reservation form, or for complicated requests, send an email with the following information: number and type of rooms; number of nights; arrival date; departure date; and any special needs. (For a sample email, see the sidebar.) Use the European style for writing dates: day/month/year. Hoteliers typically ask for your credit-card number as a deposit.

Some hotels are willing to deal to attract guests—try emailing several to ask their best price. In general, hotel prices can soften if you do any of the following: offer to pay cash, stay at least three nights, or travel off-season. You can also try asking for a cheaper room or a discount.

Some hotels include Spain's 10 percent IVA tax in the room price; others tack it onto your bill. When asking about prices, it's smart to check about the room tax.

PRACTICALITIES

EATING

By our standards, Spaniards eat late, having lunch—their biggest meal of the day—around 13:00-16:00, and dinner starting about 21:00. At restaurants, you can dine with tourists at 20:00, or with Spaniards if you wait until later.

For a fun early dinner at a bar, build a light meal out of tapas—small appetizer-sized portions of seafood, salads, meat-filled pastries, deep-fried tasties, and so on. Many of these are displayed behind glass, and you can point to what you want. Tapas typically cost about €2 apiece, but can run up to €10 for seafood. While the smaller "tapa" size (which comes on a saucer-size plate) is handiest for maximum tasting opportunities, many bars sell only larger sizes: the *ración* (full portion, on a dinner plate) and *media-ración* (half-size portion). *Jamón* (hah-MOHN), an air-dried ham similar to prosciutto, is a Spanish staple. Other key terms include *bocadillo* (baguette sandwich), *frito* (fried), *a la plancha* (grilled), *queso* (cheese), *tortilla* (omelet), and *surtido* (assortment).

Many bars have three price tiers, which should be clearly posted: It's cheapest to eat or drink while standing at the bar (*barra),* slightly more to sit at a table inside (*mesa* or *salón*), and most expensive to sit outside *(terraza).* Wherever you are, be assertive or you'll never be served. *Por favor* (please) grabs the attention of the server or bartender. If you're having tapas, don't worry about paying as you go (the bartender keeps track). When you're ready to leave, ask for the bill: *"¿La cuenta?"* To tip for a few tapas, round up to the nearest euro; for a full meal, tip about 5 to 10 percent for good service.

TRANSPORTATION

By Train and Bus: For train schedules, check www.renfe.com. Since trains can sell out, it's smart to buy your tickets in advance at a travel agency (easiest), at the train station (can be crowded; be sure you're in the right line), or online (at www.renfe.com; when asked for your Spanish national ID number, enter your passport number). Be aware that the website rejects nearly every attempt to use a US credit card—use PayPal; or from the US try www.ricksteves.com/rail. Futuristic, high-speed trains (such as AVE) can be priced differently according to their time of departure. To see if a railpass could save you money, check www.ricksteves.com/rail.

Buses pick up where the trains don't go, reaching even small villages. But because routes are operated by various competing companies, it can be tricky to pin down schedules (check with local bus stations, tourist info offices, or www.movelia.es).

By Plane: Consider covering long distances on a budget flight, which can be cheaper than a train or bus ride. For flights within Spain, check out www.vueling.com, www.iberia.com, or www.

aireuropa.com; to other European cites, try www.easyjet.com and www.ryanair.com.

By Car: It's cheaper to arrange most car rentals from the US. For tips on your insurance options, see www.ricksteves.com/cdw, and for route planning, consult www.viamichelin.com. Bring your driver's license. You're also technically required to have an International Driving Permit—a translation of your driver's license (sold at your local AAA office for $15 plus the cost of two passport-type photos; see www.aaa.com).

Superhighways come with tolls, but save lots of time. Each toll road *(autopista de peaje)* has its own pricing structure, so tolls vary. Spaniards love to tailgate; otherwise, local road etiquette is similar to that in the US. Ask your car-rental company for details, or check the US State Department website (www.travel.state.gov, click on "International Travel," then specify your country of choice and click "Traffic Safety and Road Conditions").

A car is a worthless headache in cities—park it safely (get tips from your hotelier). As break-ins are common, be sure all of your valuables are out of sight and locked in the trunk, or even better, with you or in your hotel room.

HELPFUL HINTS

Emergency Help: For police help, dial 091. To summon an ambulance, call 112. For passport problems, call the US Embassy (in Madrid, tel. 915-872-240, after-hours emergency tel. 915-872-200) or the Canadian Embassy (in Madrid, tel. 913-828-400). If you have a minor illness, do as the locals do and go to a pharmacist for advice. Or ask at your hotel for help—they'll know of the nearest medical and emergency services. For other concerns, get advice from your hotelier.

Theft or Loss: Spain has particularly hardworking pickpockets—wear a money belt. Assume beggars are pickpockets and any scuffle is simply a distraction by a team of thieves. If you stop for any commotion or show, put your hands in your pockets before someone else does.

To replace a passport, you'll need to go in person to an embassy (see above). Cancel and replace your credit and debit cards by calling these 24-hour US numbers collect: Visa—tel. 303/967-1096, MasterCard—tel. 636/722-7111, American Express—tel. 336/393-1111. In Spain, to make a collect call to the US, dial 900-99-0011; press zero or stay on the line for an operator. File a police report either on the spot or within a day or two; you'll need it to submit an insurance claim for lost or stolen railpasses or electronics, and it can help with replacing your passport or credit and debit cards. Precautionary measures can minimize the effects of loss—back up your digital photos and other files frequently. For more information, see www.ricksteves.com/help.

PRACTICALITIES

Time: Spain uses the 24-hour clock. It's the same through 12:00 noon, then keep going: 13:00, 14:00, and so on. Spain, like most of continental Europe, is six/nine hours ahead of the East/West Coasts of the US.

Siesta and Paseo: Many Spaniards (especially in rural areas) still follow the traditional siesta schedule: From around 13:00 to 16:00, many businesses close as people go home for a big lunch with their family. Then they head back to work (and shops reopen) from about 16:00 to 20:00. (Many bigger stores stay open all day long, especially in cities.) Then, after a late dinner, whole families pour out of their apartments to enjoy the cool of the evening, stroll through the streets, and greet their neighbors—a custom called the paseo.

Sights: Major attractions can be swamped with visitors; carefully read and follow this book's crowd-beating tips (visit at quieter times of day, or—where possible—reserve ahead). Opening and closing hours of sights can change unexpectedly; confirm the latest times on their websites or at the local tourist information office. At many churches, a modest dress code is encouraged and sometimes required (no bare shoulders or shorts).

Holidays and Festivals: Spain celebrates many holidays, which can close sights and attract crowds (book hotel rooms ahead). For more on holidays and festivals, check Spain's website: www.spain.info. For a simple list showing major—though not all—events, see www.ricksteves.com/festivals.

Numbers and Stumblers: What Americans call the second floor of a building is the first floor in Europe. Europeans write dates as day/month/year, so Christmas 2016 is 25/12/16. Commas are decimal points and vice versa—a dollar and a half is 1,50, and there are 5.280 feet in a mile. Spain uses the metric system: A kilogram is 2.2 pounds; a liter is about a quart; and a kilometer is six-tenths of a mile.

RESOURCES FROM RICK STEVES

This Snapshot guide is excerpted from my latest edition of *Rick Steves Spain*, which is one of more than 30 titles in my series of guidebooks on European travel. I also produce a public television series, *Rick Steves' Europe*, and a public radio show, *Travel with Rick Steves*. My website, www.ricksteves.com, offers free travel information, a forum for travelers' comments, guidebook updates, my travel blog, an online travel store, and information on European railpasses and our tours of Europe. If you're bringing a mobile device on your trip, you can download my free Rick Steves Audio Europe app, featuring podcasts of my radio shows, audio tours of major sights in Europe, and travel interviews about Spain. You can get Rick Steves Audio Europe via Apple's App Store, Google

Play, or the Amazon Appstore. For more information, see www.ricksteves.com/audioeurope. You can also follow me on Facebook and Twitter.

ADDITIONAL RESOURCES
Tourist Information: www.spain.info
Passports and Red Tape: www.travel.state.gov
Packing List: www.ricksteves.com/packing
Travel Insurance: www.ricksteves.com/insurance
Cheap Flights: www.kayak.com
Airplane Carry-on Restrictions: www.tsa.gov
Updates for This Book: www.ricksteves.com/update

HOW WAS YOUR TRIP?
If you'd like to share your tips, concerns, and discoveries after using this book, please fill out the survey at www.ricksteves.com/feedback. Thanks in advance.

PRACTICALITIES

Spanish Survival Phrases

Spanish has a guttural sound similar to the J in Baja California.
In the phonetics, the symbol for this clearing-your-throat sound
is the italicized *h*.

English	Spanish	Pronunciation
Good day.	*Buenos días.*	**bway**-nohs **dee**-ahs
Do you speak English?	*¿Habla Usted inglés?*	**ah**-blah oo-**stehd** een-**glays**
Yes. / No.	*Sí. / No.*	see / noh
I (don't) understand.	*(No) comprendo.*	(noh) kohm-**prehn**-doh
Please.	*Por favor.*	por fah-**bor**
Thank you.	*Gracias.*	**grah**-thee-ahs
I'm sorry.	*Lo siento.*	loh see-**ehn**-toh
Excuse me.	*Perdóneme.*	pehr-**doh**-nay-may
(No) problem.	*(No) problema.*	(noh) proh-**blay**-mah
Good.	*Bueno.*	**bway**-noh
Goodbye.	*Adiós.*	ah-dee-**ohs**
one / two	*uno / dos*	**oo**-noh / dohs
three / four	*tres / cuatro*	trays / **kwah**-troh
five / six	*cinco / seis*	**theen**-koh / says
seven / eight	*siete / ocho*	see-**eh**-tay / **oh**-choh
nine / ten	*nueve / diez*	**nway**-bay / dee-**ayth**
How much is it?	*¿Cuánto cuesta?*	**kwahn**-toh **kway**-stah
Write it?	*¿Me lo escribe?*	may loh ay-**skree**-bay
Is it free?	*¿Es gratis?*	ays **grah**-tees
Is it included?	*¿Está incluido?*	ay-**stah** een-kloo-**ee**-doh
Where can I buy / find...?	*¿Dónde puedo comprar / encontrar...?*	**dohn**-day **pway**-doh kohm-**prar** / ayn-kohn-**trar**
I'd like / We'd like...	*Quiero / Queremos...*	kee-**ehr**-oh / kehr-**ay**-mohs
...a room.	*...una habitación.*	**oo**-nah ah-bee-tah-thee-**ohn**
...a ticket to ___.	*...un billete para ___.*	oon bee-**yeh**-tay **pah**-rah ___
Is it possible?	*¿Es posible?*	ays poh-**see**-blay
Where is...?	*¿Dónde está...?*	**dohn**-day ay-**stah**
...the train station	*...la estación de trenes*	lah ay-stah-thee-**ohn** day **tray**-nays
...the bus station	*...la estación de autobuses*	lah ay-stah-thee-**ohn** day ow-toh-**boo**-says
...the tourist information office	*...la oficina de turismo*	lah oh-fee-**thee**-nah day too-**rees**-moh
Where are the toilets?	*¿Dónde están los servicios?*	**dohn**-day ay-**stahn** lohs sehr-**bee**-thee-ohs
men	*hombres, caballeros*	**ohm**-brays, kah-bah-**yay**-rohs
women	*mujeres, damas*	moo-**heh**-rays, **dah**-mahs
left / right	*izquierda / derecha*	eeth-kee-**ehr**-dah / day-**ray**-chah
straight	*derecho*	day-**ray**-choh
When do you open / close?	*¿A qué hora abren / cierran?*	ah kay **oh**-rah **ah**-brehn / thee-**ay**-rahn
At what time?	*¿A qué hora?*	ah kay **oh**-rah
Just a moment.	*Un momento.*	oon moh-**mehn**-toh
now / soon / later	*ahora / pronto / más tarde*	ah-**oh**-rah / **prohn**-toh / mahs **tar**-day
today / tomorrow	*hoy / mañana*	oy / mahn-**yah**-nah

In a Spanish Restaurant

English	Spanish	Pronunciation
I'd like / We'd like...	Quiero / Queremos...	kee-**ehr**-oh / kehr-**ay**-mohs
...to reserve...	...reservar...	ray-sehr-**bar**
...a table for one / two.	...una mesa para uno / dos.	**oo**-nah **may**-sah **pah**-rah **oo**-noh / dohs
Non-smoking.	No fumador.	noh foo-mah-**dohr**
Is this table free?	¿Está esta mesa libre?	ay-**stah** ay-stah **may**-sah **lee**-bray
The menu (in English), please.	La carta (en inglés), por favor.	lah **kar**-tah (ayn een-**glays**) por fah-**bor**
service (not) included	servicio (no) incluido	sehr-**bee**-thee-oh (noh) een-kloo-**ee**-doh
cover charge	precio de entrada	**pray**-thee-oh day ayn-**trah**-dah
to go	para llevar	**pah**-rah yay-**bar**
with / without	con / sin	kohn / seen
and / or	y / o	ee / oh
menu (of the day)	menú (del día)	may-**noo** (dayl **dee**-ah)
specialty of the house	especialidad de la casa	ay-spay-thee-ah-lee-**dahd** day lah **kah**-sah
tourist menu	menú turístico	meh-**noo** too-**ree**-stee-koh
combination plate	plato combinado	**plah**-toh kohm-bee-**nah**-doh
appetizers	tapas	**tah**-pahs
bread	pan	pahn
cheese	queso	**kay**-soh
sandwich	bocadillo	boh-kah-**dee**-yoh
soup	sopa	**soh**-pah
salad	ensalada	ayn-sah-**lah**-dah
meat	carne	**kar**-nay
poultry	aves	**ah**-bays
fish	pescado	pay-**skah**-doh
seafood	marisco	mah-**ree**-skoh
fruit	fruta	**froo**-tah
vegetables	verduras	behr-**doo**-rahs
dessert	postres	**poh**-strays
tap water	agua del grifo	**ah**-gwah dayl **gree**-foh
mineral water	agua mineral	**ah**-gwah mee-nay-**rahl**
milk	leche	**lay**-chay
(orange) juice	zumo (de naranja)	**thoo**-moh (day nah-**rahn**-hah)
coffee	café	kah-**feh**
tea	té	tay
wine	vino	**bee**-noh
red / white	tinto / blanco	**teen**-toh / **blahn**-koh
glass / bottle	vaso / botella	**bah**-soh / boh-**tay**-yah
beer	cerveza	thehr-**bay**-thah
Cheers!	¡Salud!	sah-**lood**
More. / Another.	Más. / Otro.	mahs / **oh**-troh
The same.	El mismo.	ehl **mees**-moh
The bill, please.	La cuenta, por favor.	lah **kwayn**-tah por fah-**bor**
tip	propina	proh-**pee**-nah
Delicious!	¡Delicioso!	day-lee-thee-**oh**-soh

For hundreds more pages of survival phrases for your trip to Spain, check out *Rick Steves' Spanish Phrase Book*.

INDEX

A

Accommodations: *See* Sleeping
Airport, in Madrid: 8, 102–103
Air travel: 188–189, 191
Alcázar: Segovia, 125–127; Toledo, 160
Almonacid: 183
Almudena Cathedral (Madrid): 28
Ambulance: 189
American Express: 189
Archaeological museum, in Madrid: 16, 68
Architecture, Museum of (El Escorial): 110
Armory: Madrid, 43–44; Segovia, 126–127
Army Museum (Toledo): 151, 159–161
Arrival: in Madrid, 6, 8; in Segovia, 119–120; in Toledo, 144–145, 148
Art museums: CaixaForum (Madrid), 67; Centro de Arte Reina Sofía (Madrid), 16, 60–66; El Greco Museum (Toledo), 151, 163; Museo de Arte Contemporáneo Esteban Vicente (Segovia), 127; Museo Sorolla (Madrid), 70; Museo Victorio Macho (Toledo), 151, 165–166; Museum of Paintings (El Escorial), 110–111; Palacio de Cibeles (Madrid), 3, 67, 87; Santa Cruz Museum (Toledo), 151, 158–159; Thyssen-Bornemisza Museum (Madrid), 16, 59–60. *See also* Prado Museum
Assassination Attempt Memorial (Madrid): 27
Astrolabe Tapestry: 157
ATMs: 185–186
Atocha Station (Madrid): 6, 8, 99–100
Audio Europe, Rick Steves: 190–191
AVE trains: 99, 100, 119–120, 132, 181

Ávila: 133–140; eating, 139; map, 136–137; sights, 134–135, 138; sleeping, 138–139; tourist information, 134; transportation, 134, 140
Ávila Cathedral: 135
Ávila Wall: 134–135

B

Baggage storage: *See* Luggage storage
Barajas Airport (Madrid): 102–103
Bernabéu Stadium (Madrid): 74
Bisagra Gate (Toledo): 148, 168–169; sleeping near, 171, 174
Bocadillos de calamares: 25, 96
Bookstores, in Madrid: 13
Bosch, Hieronymus: 51–52, 109, 114
Bravo, Juan, statue of: 121
Breakfast: Madrid, 95; Segovia, 131
Bruegel, Pieter: 52
Bullfighting bar, in Madrid: 24–25, 96
Bullfighting Museum (Madrid): 74
Bullfights: Madrid, 16, 73; Segovia, 121, 124
Buñuel, Luis: 62
Burial of the Count of Orgaz (El Greco): 151, 162–163
Buses: 188; Ávila, 134, 140; El Escorial, 107; Madrid, 8, 15, 101–102; tours, 18–19, 70–71; Segovia, 119, 131–132; Toledo, 144–145, 181; tours, 149, 168–169; Valley of the Fallen, 115

C

Cabs: *See* Taxis
CaixaForum (Madrid): 67
Calle Cava Baja (Madrid), tapas: 92–93
Calle Comercio (Toledo): 142
Calle de Jesús (Madrid), tapas: 91–92
Calle de la Montera (Madrid): 22, 85
Calle del Arenal (Madrid): 29–32

Calle de Postas (Madrid): 23

Calle Mayor (Madrid): 23, 27–28

Capilla La Concepción (Segovia): 125

Car rentals: 189; Madrid, 104

Car travel (driving): 189; Ávila, 134; El Escorial, 108; Madrid, 104; Segovia, 132–133; Toledo, 144, 148, 181

Casa de los Picos (Segovia): 120–121

Casa Rúa (Madrid): 96

Casa Yustas (Madrid): 24

Casita Museo de Ratón Pérez (Madrid): 32

Catedral de Nuestra Señora de la Almudena (Madrid): 28

Centro de Arte Reina Sofía (Madrid): 16, 60–66

Centro de Interpretación del Misticismo (Ávila): 138

Centro Dramático Nacional (Madrid): 72

Cervantes, Miguel de: 182–183

Chamartín Station (Madrid): 6, 8, 98

Chapel of St.Anthony of La Florida (Madrid): 17, 69

Chapel of the New Kings (Toledo): 155

Chapter House (Toledo): 154

Charles III Bedroom (Madrid's Royal Palace): 40–41

Churches and cathedrals: Almudena Cathedral (Madrid), 28; Ávila Cathedral, 135; Corpus Christi Church (Madrid), 26; St. Ginès Church (Madrid), 29–30; San Román Church (Toledo), 151, 161–162; Santos Justo y Pastor Church (Segovia), 127; Santo Tomé (Toledo), 151, 162–163; Segovia Cathedral, 124–125; Toledo Cathedral, 150, 151, 152–157; Valley of the Fallen Basilica, 117–118; Vera Cruz Church, 127

Churros con chocolate: 97–98

Cibeles CentroCentro of Culture and Citizenship (Madrid): 67, 87

Circulo de Bellas Artes (Madrid): 33–34

Classical guitars, shopping for, in Madrid: 76

Clothing Museum (Madrid): 17, 69

Coin market, in Madrid: 24, 75

Colegio de Infantes (Toledo): 157–158

Consuegra: 182

Convent of St. Teresa (Ávila): 135, 138

Corpus Christi Church and Convent (Madrid): 26

Corpus Christi Convent (Segovia): 121

Credit cards: 185–186, 189

Cuatro Postes (Ávila): 135

Currency and exchange: 185–186

D

Dalí, Salvador: 62

Damascene: 170

Debit cards: 185–186, 189

Descalzas Royal Monastery (Madrid): 45

Discounts: *See* Money-saving tips

Don Quixote (Cervantes): 182

Driving: *See* Car travel

Dürer, Albrecht: 50

E

Eating: 188; Ávila, 139; El Escorial, 109; Madrid, 86–98; Segovia, 129–131; Spanish restaurant phrases, 194; Toledo, 176–180; Valley of the Fallen, 118. *See also* Tapas

El Corte Inglés (Madrid): 12, 74; books, 13; cafeterias, 97; travel agency, 13

El Escorial: 107–115; eating, 109; maps, 108, 110; planning tips, 105–106; sights, 109–115; transportation, 107–108

El Escorial Monastery: 107, 109–115; history of, 112; map, 110

El Greco: 135; biographical sketch, 164; El Escorial, 109, 114; Museum (Toledo), 151, 163; Parador de Toledo, 175–176; Prado Museum (Madrid), 54–55; Santa Cruz Museum (Toledo), 151, 158–159; Santo Tomé (Toledo), 151, 162–163; Toledo Cathedral, 150, 155–156

El Martes (Toledo): 170

El Rastro (Madrid): 17, 74–75

E-mail, in Madrid: 12–13, 102

Embassies: 189

Emergencies: 189; Madrid, 8

Entertainment: Madrid, 76–79; current schedule, 7; Segovia, 131

Ermita de San Antonio de la Florida (Madrid): 17, 69

Euro currency: 185–186

F

Fans, shopping for, in Madrid: 76

Ferpal (Madrid): 31–32

Festivals: 190

Flamenco, in Madrid: 16, 77–78

Flea market, in Madrid: 17, 74–75

Food: *See Churros con chocolate;* Eating; Markets; *Mazapán;* Roast suckling pig; Tapas

"Football," in Madrid: 31, 74

G

Garden of Earthly Delights, The (Bosch): 51

Gasparini Room (Madrid's Royal Palace): 39–40

Giordano, Lucca: 155

Goya, Francisco de: 22, 38–39, 61, 155; Prado Museum (Madrid), 56–59; Tomb (Madrid), 17, 69

Granada: 181

Gran Vía (Madrid): 3, 33–34; map, 32–33; nightlife, 76; sleeping, 79, 82–83

Guernica (Picasso): 63–65

Guía del Ocio: 6, 79

Guidebooks: Rick Steves, 190–191; updates, 13; Toledo, 148

Guided tours: *See* Tours

Guitars, shopping for, in Madrid: 76

H

Ham, Museum of (Madrid): 93–94

Helpful hints: 189–190; Madrid, 8, 12–13; Segovia, 120; Toledo, 148

Hemingway, Ernest: 18, 87, 116

Hermitage of San Antonio de la Florida (Madrid): 17, 69

History Museum (Madrid): 70

Holidays: 190

Hostels: Madrid, 86; Toledo, 175

Hotels: *See* Sleeping

House of Siglo XV (Segovia): 121

I

Ice cream, in Madrid: 93

Information: *See* Tourist information

Internet access, in Madrid: 12–13, 102

Itineraries: Madrid, 2–3; Toledo, 142

J

Jazz bars, in Madrid: 78

Jewish museum, in Toledo: 151, 163–165

K

"Kilometer zero" (Madrid): 22

Knives, shopping for, in Toledo: 169

L

La Granja de San Ildefonso Palace: 127–128

La Mallorquina (Madrid): 22–23

La Mancha: 182–183

Las Meninas (Velázquez): 52–53

La Torre del Oro Bar Andalú (Madrid): 24–25, 96

Laundry, in Madrid: 13

Lavapiés (Madrid): 71–73

Luggage storage: Madrid, 102; Segovia, 119; Toledo, 144–145

M

Macho (Victorio) Museum (Toledo): 151, 165–166

Madrid: 1–104; at a glance, 16–17; arrival in, 6, 8; daily reminder, 9;

eating, 86–98; experiences, 70–74; helpful hints, 8, 12–13; maps, 4–5, 7, 10–11, 20–21, 32–33, 47, 88–89; sleeping, 80–81; nightlife, 76–79; orientation, 3; planning tips, 2–3; shopping, 12, 74–76; sights, 34–70; sleeping, 79–86; tourist information, 3, 6; tours, 15–19; transportation, 6, 8, 13–15, 98–104; walking tour, 19–34

Madrid Card: 6

Madrid History Museum: 70

Madrid Royal Palace: *See* Royal Palace

Madrid Tower: 29

Madrid Town Hall: 27

Maids of Honor (Velázquez): 52–53

Mantegna, Andrea: 49–50

Maps: Ávila, 136–137; El Escorial, 108, 110; Madrid, 4–5, 20–21; Central, 10–11; eating, 88–89; Gran Vía, 32–33; Greater, 7; Metro, 14; museum neighborhood, 47; sleeping, 80–81; northwest of Madrid, 106; Segovia, 122–123; Toledo, 143, 146–147; eating, 178–179; sleeping, 172–173

Markets: Ávila, 139; El Escorial, 109; Madrid, 17, 24, 25–26, 74–75, 96; Segovia, 120, 131; Toledo, 170, 180

Mazapán: 170, 180

Medical help: 189

Mercado de San Miguel (Madrid): 25–26, 96

Mesón de Cándido (Segovia): 130

Mesones: 25–26, 78

Metric system: 190

Metro (Madrid): 13–15, 103; map, 14

Mezquita del Cristo de la Luz (Toledo): 161

Modern District (Madrid): 71

Monasterio de las Descalzas Reales (Madrid): 45

Monasterio de San Juan de los Reyes (Toledo): 151, 166–168

Monasterio de San Lorenzo de El Escorial: 107, 109–115; map, 110

Moncloa Station (Madrid): 102

Money: 185–186

Money belts: 8, 185, 189

Money-saving tips: Madrid, 3, 6, 45; Segovia, 120; Toledo, 143–144

Movie theaters, in Madrid: 78–79

Mozarabic Chapel (Toledo): 156

Murillo, Bartolomé: 53–54

Museo Arqueológico Nacional (Madrid): 16, 68

Museo de América (Madrid): 17, 68–69

Museo de Arte Contemporáneo Esteban Vicente (Segovia): 127

Museo de Historia de Madrid: 70

Museo del Arte Thyssen-Bornemisza (Madrid): 16, 59–60

Museo del Ejército (Toledo): 151, 159–161

Museo del Greco (Toledo): 151, 163

Museo del Jamón (Madrid): 93–94

Museo de los Concilios y de la Cultura Visigoda (Toledo): 151, 161–162

Museo del Traje (Madrid): 17, 69

Museo de Santa Cruz (Toledo): 151, 158–159

Museo Nacional del Prado (Madrid): *See* Prado Museum

Museo Naval (Madrid): 17, 67

Museo Sefardí (Toledo): 151, 163–165

Museo Sorolla (Madrid): 70

Museo Taurino (Madrid): 74

Museo Victorio Macho (Toledo): 151, 165–166

Museum of Architecture (El Escorial): 110

Museum of Paintings (El Escorial): 110–111

Museum of Tapestries (El Escorial): 109

Museum of the Americas (Madrid): 17, 68–69

Music, in Madrid: 76–78
Mysticism Interpretation Center (Ávila): 138

N
National Archaeological Museum (Madrid): 16, 68
Naval Museum (Madrid): 17, 67
Nightlife: Madrid, 76–79; Segovia, 131

O
Organized tours: *See* Tours

P
Packing list: 191
Palacio de Cibeles (Madrid): 3, 67, 87
Palacio de Congresos Miradero (Toledo): 141, 169
Palacio Real (Madrid): *See* Royal Palace
Parador de Toledo: 175–176
Parque del Buen Retiro (Madrid): 17, 66
Paseo de la Castellana (Madrid): 70–71
Paseo del Arte (Madrid): 3, 45
Passports: 189, 191
Phones: 186–187
Picasso, Pablo: 62–65
Planning tips: Madrid, 2–3; Toledo, 142
Plaza de Castilla (Madrid): 71
Plaza de Colón (Madrid): 3
Plaza de España (Madrid): 34
Plaza de Isabel II (Madrid): 29
Plaza de la Villa (Madrid): 27
Plaza del Carmen (Madrid), sleeping near: 84
Plaza de Oriente (Madrid): 28–29
Plaza de San Martín (Segovia): 121
Plaza de Toros (Madrid): 73
Plaza de Zocodover (Toledo): 142, 157; eating, 177, 180; map, 172–173; sleeping near, 170–171
Plaza Mayor (Madrid): 17, 23–25;
eating, 92–93, 96; information, 3; maps, 20–21, 88–89; market, 24, 75; sleeping near, 83–84
Plaza Mayor (Segovia): 121, 124; eating, 130–131; market, 120, 131; sleeping, 128
Plaza Santa Ana (Madrid): 72, 95
Police: 189
Porcelain Room (Madrid's Royal Palace): 41
Prado Museum (Madrid): 16, 45–59; eating, 48; free evenings, 9; guided tours, 18, 46; information, 6, 46; map, 48; self-guided tour, 49–59; sleeping near, 84, 85–86
Príncipe Pío Station (Madrid): 101–102
Pronovias (Madrid): 32
Prostitution: 12
Puerta de Europa (Madrid): 33–34, 70, 71
Puerta del Sol (Madrid): 3, 16, 19–23; eating near, 96–97; map, 20–21; sleeping near, 79, 82–83, 84–85

R
Reader feedback: 191
Real Fábrica de Tapices (Madrid): 68
Real Jardín Botánico (Madrid): 17, 66–67
Real Madrid: 31, 74
Reina Sofía (Madrid): 16, 60–66
Resources from Rick Steves: 190–191
Restaurants: *See* Eating
Retiro Park (Madrid): 17, 66
Ribera, José: 114
Roast suckling pig: 87, 130
Roman Aqueduct (Segovia): 124
Royal Botanical Garden (Madrid): 17, 66–67
Royal Chapel (Madrid's Royal Palace): 42
Royal Chapel of St. Anthony of La Florida (Madrid): 17, 69

Royal families of Spain: 30–31
Royal Palace (Madrid): 16, 28, 34–44; eating near, 36–37; maps, 20–21, 36; self-guided tour, 37–44; tours, 35
Royal Palace of La Granja de San Ildefonso: 127–128
Royal Pantheon (El Escorial): 113
Royal Tapestry Factory (Madrid): 68
Royal Theater (Madrid): 29
Rubens, Peter Paul: 45, 54

S
Sacristy (Toledo): 155–156
St. Ginès Church (Madrid): 29–30
St. Teresa Convent (Ávila): 135, 138
Salamanca: 133
San Antonio de la Florida Hermitage (Madrid): 17, 69
San Juan de los Reyes Monasterio (Toledo): 151, 166–168
San Lorenzo de El Escorial Monastery: 107, 109–115; map, 110
San Miguel market (Madrid): 25–26, 96
San Román Church (Toledo): 151, 161–162
Santa Cruz Museum (Toledo): 151, 158–159
Santa María la Blanca Synagogue (Toledo): 151, 166
Santos Justo y Pastor Church (Segovia): 127
Santo Tomé (Toledo): 151, 162–163, 180
SATE: 8, 12
Segovia: 118–133; arrival in, 119–120; eating, 129–131; helpful hints, 120; map, 122–123; orientation, 119; planning tips, 105–106; shopping, 120; sights, 124–128; sleeping, 128–129; tourist information, 119; transportation, 119–120, 131–133; walking tour, 120–124
Segovia Cathedral: 124–125

Shopping: Madrid, 12, 74–76; Segovia, 120; Toledo, 169–170. *See also* Markets
Siesta: 190
Sights: general tips, 190; Ávila, 134–135, 138; El Escorial, 109–115; Madrid, 34–70; at a glance, 16–17; daily reminder, 9; free, 9; Segovia, 124–128; Toledo, 150–169. *See also specific sights*
Sightseeing passes: Madrid, 6; Segovia, 120; Toledo, 143–144
Silla de Felipe: 108
Sinagoga del Tránsito (Toledo): 151, 163–165
Sinagoga de Santa María la Blanca (Toledo): 151, 166
Sleeping: Ávila, 138–139; Madrid, 79–86; reservations, 187; Segovia, 128–129; Toledo, 170–176; Valley of the Fallen, 118
Sobrino del Botín (Madrid): 87
Soccer, in Madrid: 31, 74
Sorolla (Joaquín) Museum (Madrid): 70
Spanish Civil War: about, 116
Spanish restaurant phrases: 194
Spanish survival phrases: 193
Stamp market, in Madrid: 24, 75
Stradivarius Room (Madrid's Royal Palace): 42
Subway: *See* Metro

T
Tapas: 188; Ávila, 139; Madrid, 90–95; Segovia, 130–131; Toledo, 176–177
Taxis: Madrid, 15, 103; Toledo, 144, 148, 181; Valley of the Fallen, 115
Teatro Real (Madrid): 29
Telephones: 186–187
Temple of Debod (Madrid): 69–70
Teresa, Saint: 133, 135, 138
Terrorism Memorial (Madrid): 100
Theft alerts: 189; Madrid, 8
Third of May, 1808 (Goya): 22, 57

Throne Room (Madrid's Royal Palace): 43

Thyssen-Bornemisza Museum (Madrid): 16, 59–60

Tiepolo, Giambattista: 38, 39, 40, 43

Time zone: 190

Titian: 55, 114, 155

Toledo: 141–181; at a glance, 151; arrival in, 144–145, 148; eating, 176–180; helpful hints, 148; history of, 145; layout of, 142–143; maps, 143, 146–147, 172–173, 178–179; orientation, 142–143; planning tips, 142; shopping, 169–170; sights, 150–169; sleeping, 170–176; tourist information, 143–144; tours, 149; transportation, 144–145, 148, 181

Toledo: Its Art and Its History: 148

Toledo Card: 144

Toledo Cathedral: 150, 151, 152–157; map, 152; self-guided tour, 150, 152–157

Torre del Oro Bar Andalú (Madrid): 24–25, 96

Tour guides: Madrid, 18; Segovia, 120; Toledo, 149

Tourist information: 191; Ávila, 134; El Escorial, 109; Madrid, 3, 6; Segovia, 119; Toledo, 143–144

Tours: El Escorial, 109; Madrid, 15–19; Royal Palace, 35; Toledo, 149

Train stations, in Madrid: 6, 8, 98–100

Train travel: 188; Ávila, 134; El Escorial, 107–108; Madrid, 6, 8, 98–101; Segovia, 119–120, 132; Toledo, 144, 149, 181

Transportation: 188–189; Ávila, 134, 140; El Escorial, 107–108; Madrid, 6, 8, 13–15, 98–104; Segovia, 119–120, 131–133; Toledo, 144–145, 148, 181; Valley of the Fallen, 115. *See also* Buses; Car travel; Metro; Taxis; Train travel

Travel agencies, in Madrid: 13

Travel insurance: 191

Treasury (Toledo): 156

V

Valley of the Fallen: 115–118

Valley of the Fallen Basilica: 117–118

Van der Weyden, Roger: 50, 110–111

Velázquez, Diego: 52–53, 114, 155

Vera Cruz Church: 127

Vicente (Esteban) Museum (Segovia): 127

Visigothic Museum (Toledo): 151, 161–162

Visitor information: *See* Tourist information

W

Walking tours, guided, in Madrid: 15–18

Walking tours, self-guided: Madrid, 19–34; Segovia, 120–124

Y

Yemas, in Ávila: 138

Youth hostels: Madrid, 86; Toledo, 175

Z

Zarzuela, in Madrid: 17, 76–77

INDEX